Cyl

Cyber Security

Threats and Responses for Government and Business

JACK CARAVELLI AND NIGEL JONES

Praeger Security International

BLOOMSBURY ACADEMIC
NEW YORK • LONDON • OXFORD • NEW DELHI • SYDNEY

BLOOMSBURY ACADEMIC
Bloomsbury Publishing Inc
1385 Broadway, New York, NY 10018, USA
50 Bedford Square, London, WC1B 3DP, UK
29 Earlsfort Terrace, Dublin 2, Ireland

BLOOMSBURY, BLOOMSBURY ACADEMIC and the Diana logo
are trademarks of Bloomsbury Publishing Plc

First published in the United States of America by ABC-CLIO 2019
Paperback edition published by Bloomsbury Academic 2024

Library of Congress Cataloging-in-Publication Data
Names: Caravelli, Jack, 1952-author. | Jones, Nigel, 1965-author.
Title: Cyber security: threats and responses for government and business /
Jack Caravelli and Nigel Jones.
Description: Santa Barbara, CA: Praeger, an Imprint of ABC-CLIO, LLC, [2019] |
Series: Praeger Security International |
Includes bibliographical references and index.
Identifiers: LCCN 2018046740 | ISBN 9781440861734 (print) |
ISBN 9781440861741 (ebook)
Subjects: LCSH: Computer networks—Security measures—Government policy. |
Computer crimes—Prevention. | Security, International.
Classification: LCC TK5105.59.C364 2019 | DDC 658.4/78—dc23
LC record available at https://lccn.loc.gov/2018046740

ISBN: HB: 978-1-4408-6173-4
PB: 979-8-7651-1528-2
ePDF: 978-1-4408-6174-1
eBook: 979-8-2160-7050-4

Series: Praeger Security International

To find out more about our authors and books visit www.bloomsbury.com
and sign up for our newsletters.

*To an extraordinary group of family and
friends who made dark days a bit brighter.*
—Jack Caravelli

To Susan
—Nigel Jones

Contents

Introduction		*ix*
1.	Cyber Terrorism and Covert Action	1
2.	Cyber Crime	23
3.	The Geopolitics of Cyber and Cyber Espionage	43
4.	The Internet of Things: Systemically Vulnerable	73
5.	Disruption: Big Data, Artificial Intelligence, and Quantum Computing	109
6.	Can We Find Solutions to the Challenges of Cyber Security?	133
7.	Innovation as a Driver of Cyber Security	157
8.	International Policy: Pitfalls and Possibilities	181
9.	Global Strategies: The United Kingdom as a Case Study	213
Index		*239*

Introduction

From the outset, our goal as coauthors has been to broadly and comprehensively address the salient current and future of cyber and cyber security issues. The results are in your hands. Along with Padraic (Pat) Carlin, our highly supportive editor, we hope you will share our view that this is a particularly relevant topic that is ripe for broad discussion of a number of issues that have been ripped from today's headlines with a myriad of political, economic, and social overtones.

Recognizing these dynamics is important, but even more important is the extent to which this book captures and presents the significant, fascinating, and sometimes troubling elements of today's cyber world and the challenges of enhancing cyber security in it. We have endeavored to present these dynamics with all the skill and insight our collective expertise provides. At the same time, we are humbled in acknowledging, that the cyber domain continues to evolve rapidly, perhaps even more than at the project start, and that there are almost endless more cyber stories to be told.

Perhaps there was no better microcosm that ties these themes together than the spectacle that unfolded on national television in early April as we were completing the draft. For two days, Facebook CEO, Mark Zuckerberg, endured often hostile grilling from Senate and Congressional members over the policies and performance of the company he founded, one of the world's most famous and popular. Facebook also has turned Zuckerberg into one of the richest men on earth while carrying out its stated mission of "connecting the world."

Facebook reflects one of the overarching themes of this book, that the application of clever, sophisticated, and even laudable technology can be distorted and lead to highly undesirable outcomes. In Facebook's case, the problems Zuckerberg confronted centered on the admission that his company had failed to protect the personal data of tens of millions of customers. Instead, that data had been used by a British-based firm, Cambridge Analytica, to carry out political research on behalf of its clients. Zuckerberg also was taken to task for Facebook's frequent practice of making its own value judgments, such as censoring conservative political and religious thought.

Under the glare of congressional scrutiny, Zuckerberg was contrite, admitting serious mistakes were made, that he was ultimately responsible for them, and that Facebook would devote sizable resources to becoming a more responsible global citizen in protecting data and also ferreting out fake news and incendiary postings. Whether that happens or not remains to be seen; various American politicians, relishing their time in front of the cameras, were only too prepared to claim that they would pass legislation that would "help" Facebook along that road. That also remains to be seen.

Whatever label one pins on Facebook's performance, it is at most a small part of a much broader problem. What is apparent already is that there are nations, various private groups and organizations, and a network of individual hackers who derive great profit, in many senses, from their efforts to use the Internet for misleading and often malicious purposes. This dark side of the Internet is an important part of our story. Along the way, we encounter nations like Russia that use the Internet to brazenly disrupt democratic processes and influence elections, not only in the United States but also in the United Kingdom and other major European nations.

At the same time, China has made an art form of stealing copious amounts of secret military and personnel data from governments it considers adversaries as well as equally large volumes of proprietary information from Western corporations. Large segments of China's economy are built on Western know-how. Iran, North Korea, and Syria have also exploited the vulnerabilities of the Internet for their own malevolent purposes. Not to be outdone, nonstate actors such as terrorist organizations have exploited the Internet, including use of the dark Web, for nefarious purposes, including for recruitment, fundraising, and educating adherents to create carnage in Western nations and beyond. The Internet is also used to further the global endeavors of organized crime.

It didn't start this way. In its earliest days, the Internet was seen as a (then) novel means of communication and data exchange, regardless of where the users were located. It was meant to be free and accessible for all and was seen as having boundless promise. In many ways, the promise of the Internet has been realized and perhaps in so many more ways than its original developers could have imagined. The technology and people behind it have served numerous positive purposes; millions lead better lives because of it.

As a snapshot, this is the current state of the Internet, a tool capable of enhancing the quality, efficiency, and effectiveness of countless governmental, business and private activities, all of which seem, at the same time, vulnerable to disruption, chaos, compromise, or worse.

There are glimmers of hope that nations and businesses are awaking to the problems that plague the Internet and taking action. The rare sight of a corporate icon like Zuckerberg being held accountable in a nationally televised forum for his company's failings could mark a sea change in the public's tolerance for abuses of the Internet. At the same time, as Nigel Jones illustrates, the often heavy-handed bureaucracy of the European Union may have taken a positive step with its General Data Protection Regulations (GDPR), another sign of willingness to hold accountable those corporate entities that fail to protect and report data problems.

Nations are also responding to the likes of aggressive cyber activities in Russia and China. Awareness is an essential start, and, as Nigel also points out, the British government has been highly active in responding to the challenges of cyber security, in part by developing a national cyber security strategy. I discuss a number of measures the Trump administration in America has taken in response to brazen Russian attempts to use cyber attacks to create chaos within American society as well as in its 2016 presidential election. The United Kingdom, France, and Germany have formulated their own responses to similar hacking efforts. At the same time, President Trump, as part of his seemingly endless love affair with Twitter, has called out China's efforts to steal government and trade secrets from the West as part of his justification to impose tariffs on Chinese goods and services, possibly triggering a trade war.

Within the private sector, my colleagues at Cymatus are tackling often overlooked but critical cyber security issues related to digital trust. In America, Europe, and Asia, countless other corporate entities, large and small, are tackling similar problems creatively.

There's more to the Internet than a global tug-of-war between forces that seek to use it for positive or malicious ends. The pace of change in the digital domain is extraordinary. In one of our chapters, we seek to discuss the implications for the future of the Internet of Things (IOT), the world of extreme connectivity that is already upon us and rapidly expanding, whether it is cars or refrigerators to the Internet. In addition, we have entered a world where big data and Artificial Intelligence (AI) are becoming increasingly ubiquitous. Zuckerberg claims, for example, that AI will be the key to improving Facebook's future operations. These developments are shaping the way we live, work, and play. Once again, how these issues evolve will tell us much about whether "the balance of (Internet) power is being held by those who desire a positive and productive Internet or those who wish to exploit its vulnerabilities and limitations."

At this writing, Mark Zuckerberg is in his early 30s and could conceivably be involved in these issues for another 50 years. Along the way, he will see and possibly shape the Internet world to come. Beyond him, the possibilities are endless. Perhaps the next Mark Zuckerberg is today throwing a baseball in Ohio or kicking a soccer ball in Milan or Manchester. For all of us, young and older, it will almost certainly be a fascinating and important journey. Whether it becomes a positive one will depend on our personal level of interest and engagement.

Jack Caravelli
Washington, DC
April 2018

CHAPTER 1

Cyber Terrorism and Covert Action

Jack Caravelli

September 11, 2001, marked a new and deeply troubling era in American life, ushering in the persistent threat, especially in cities like New York and Washington DC of terrorist attack. From a broader perspective and outside the United States, terrorism in its many forms is far from new, having been a presence in parts of the globe over the past two thousand years in Asia, Europe, and the Middle East.

We can identify three long-ago precursors to the terrorist movements we struggle against in the current era. The first were the Zealots who operated against the backdrop of the Roman Empire. They often used daggers and knives, usually in crowded gathering places, so that their vicious attacks could be observed by many. Their goal was the simple if wholly rejected demand that by using violence, they could make a political statement to force the Roman Empire to give up Palestine. The Zealots lasted only a few decades before being rooted out by Roman legions, but in that short period, they showed the power of their intense views by successfully mobilizing mass disaffection against Rome. Interestingly, in today's political lexicon, zeal is the meaning of Hamas, the Palestinian group.

The "Assassins," a word that is also still in our vocabulary, were Shia Muslims who operated in the Middle East from the eleventh to thirteenth centuries. Their stated goal was to "purify" Islam, a claim made in more recent times by terrorist groups also operating in the Middle East. As with the Zealots, the preferred weapons of the Assassins were knives, often used against moderate religious leaders. In an uncanny foreshadowing of what the terrorist group ISIS would seek hundreds of years later in our time, the Assassins sought to establish territorial control over large parts of the Middle East, welcoming those from outside the region who shared their messianic vision. The Assassins also, like their ISIS emulators, had a culture of martyrdom that was achieved, in a manner of speaking, when Arab and Mongol armies crushed them in vicious battle in 1275.

Finally, in India, the "Thugi" (a word that was modified slightly in referring to criminals as thugs) were Hindus who operated for nearly 600 years in defiance of local authorities before being defeated by the British in the 19th century. The Thugi had mainly religious, rather than political, goals at their core and, in their long history, managed to kill at least half a million people in the name of religion.

These historical excursions provide context to our discussion of terrorism, with particular emphasis on how terrorists operating in the current era have benefited in from exploiting cyber capabilities.

September 11, 2001 was a clear and sunny day in New York City and Washington, D.C. Summer vacations were just ending, and schools were back in session. On that day, a group of young Arabs carried out well-planned, brazen, and spectacularly successful attacks using commercial aviation against New York City's World Trade Center and the Pentagon in the nearby suburb of Arlington, Virginia. Another hijacking, this of United 93, ended with the plane crashing in a Pennsylvania field. The attacks left nearly 3000 dead while ushering in an entirely different and, in some ways, confusing security threat for the United States.

After decades of Cold War in which the adversary, the Soviet Union, was easily identified and its strengths and weaknesses were well understood, U.S. strategy and policies were well formed. Little thought among foreign policy experts was given to fighting terrorism at home. "Defense of the homeland" was a seldom-uttered phrase during the Cold War; combat between the superpowers, if it were to arise, was seen as being centered in Europe. If the homeland were to be involved, it would be as a result of a cataclysmic nuclear exchange, a fear that faded through the Cold War years.

From that perspective, September 11 presented barely understood challenges for the government and its citizens alike. The enemy did not appear as a military force in any way or possess large quantities of military equipment. The attackers were members of al-Qaeda (translated as "the base," a possible reference to Afghanistan training bases the group used in its early years) and led by a wealthy Saudi national, Osama bin Laden. They represented a small but virulent element of a religion, Islam, as opposed to the "godless communism" of the Soviet Union.

Bin Laden's intensely loyal followers did not wear uniforms or control vast armies or seek to conquer land. However, territorial conquest would occur in more recent years as their rival Islamic fundamentalist group, the Islamic State in Iraq and Syria (ISIS), aspired to establish a caliphate and succeeded in conquering considerable swaths of land in Iraq and Syria for a period of time. Radical Islam is not only an interpretation of an ancient religious faith but also a political totalitarian movement with secular goals. The duality of this threat was never fully understood during the presidencies of George Bush and Barack Obama.

In contrast, while the terrorist organizations lacked the traditional elements of military power and could never match the United States or other Western nations in such areas, they came to recognize a powerful counterbalancing tool, the use of the Internet. Notwithstanding how terrorists are using this new capability to further their aims, the war against terrorism—and that is the only realistic and proper description as the jihadists declared war on the West—also has many of the traditional elements of past wars. There has been significant loss of life on both sides; pitched military battles that lead to rampant and often wanton destruction, especially in parts of the Middle East and Afghanistan; religious persecutions; financial losses; and the destruction of countless and irreplaceable works of culture and art in Iraq and Syria.

As noted, the added and qualitatively different dimension has been the use of the Internet as a new weapon to advance the terrorists' agenda. For our purposes, we will define cyber terrorism as premeditated, politically motivated attacks against information, computer systems, computer programs, and databases that result in violence against governments, businesses, and individuals. We would add another dimension, noting the critical importance of the Internet in various recruiting and propaganda objectives.

At first, and through much of the 1990s and early years of the new millennium, al-Qaeda leaders and Osama bin Laden in particular mostly shunned the Internet and used simple means of communication such as audio and video tapes to send messages and issue instructions. Bin Laden's use of a trusted courier ultimately allowed the CIA to track him to Pakistan, where he was killed by U.S. Special Forces in 2011. In bin Laden's final years, the growing sophistication and use of the Internet coincided almost perfectly with the growth of the terrorist group's ambitions, which under bin Laden grew from striking the near enemy (Israel) to striking the far enemy and so-called great Satan, the United States.

While bin Laden operated in remote areas in Afghanistan for years, and then moved to Pakistan, he had to operate and exert leadership over an increasingly far-flung network while avoiding detection. Prizing security over the efficiency of other forms of communication, bin Laden often chose to send operational directives to subordinates by courier. At the same time, al-Qaeda, and later ISIS, like all military and political organizations, had various operational priorities that required timely and secure communications to advance their agendas and goals. Those priorities included publicizing successes on the ground, raising funds, and recruiting and training new cadres of adherents, while also carrying out operational instructions. The Internet emerged as a vital tool for supporting those activities.

Of particular importance was using the Internet securely. This was accomplished by using the Dark Web, the part of the Internet that is not accessed by popular search engines such as Google or Yahoo. Every day, millions of users access the Internet through those search engines, making them invaluable tools for government, industry, and consumers. Nonetheless, they provide a portal to only a small portion of a much-larger Internet. Some experts claim that as much as 90 percent of the information contained on the Internet is not accessed through conventional search engines.

The often "unseen" information is located through what are labeled the "Dark Web" and "Deep Web." The terms are often used interchangeably, which is somewhat misleading. In simplest terms, the Dark Web consists of websites that exist on encrypted networks. Any number of them, because of their anonymity, promote illegal activity such as drug sales or the purchase of firearms. There can be legitimate uses of the Dark Web as well, such as by groups in nations like Russia or Iran who may be trying to circumvent repressive government monitoring of their communications. For example, during the early 2018 Iranian protests, when the regime's law-enforcement entities were cracking down on social media, it can be safely assumed that protestors were looking for alternative means of securely communicating among themselves. In addition, there is the Deep Web, which includes the Dark Web but goes beyond that to include databases, webmail pages, and pages behind firewalls. Activity on the Deep Web may be legitimate or carried out for criminal purposes.

Use of the Dark Web by terrorist groups, along with associated techniques and tactics, have had a powerful effect in Europe, especially in France and neighboring Belgium. Gilles Kepel, a leading French scholar, pointed out the impact, dating to 2005, of the online publication "The Call for a Global Islamic Resistance," written by al-Qaeda member Abu Musab al-Suri. One of Al-Qaeda senior commanders, the charismatic Abu Musab al-Zarqawi, who later broke from that group to support ISIS, was particularly adroit at using the Internet. He regularly posted footage of roadside bombings as well as the beheadings of Egyptian and Algerian diplomats, among others, doubtless as a way to inspire his followers. Other footage posted on the Internet showed forms of gratuitous violence. His rhetorical flourishes were equally dramatic, speaking of the end of days and epic battles that would lead to them. He helped make ISIS and its struggle with the West the first tweeted war.

But it was ISIS that refined and expanded terrorist use of the Internet to the fullest in support of its goals. It is not an exaggeration to conclude that by the time ISIS came to prominence after the precipitous withdrawal of U.S. military forces from Iraq in 2011. This result was caused by the failure of the Obama administration to negotiate a Status of Forces Agreement with the Iraq government, just as the Internet was becoming an indispensable tool for the jihadists and extending its influence. Using the Internet took on early and grizzly elements when ISIS, like al-Qaeda, began posting graphic images of the mutilations of alleged enemies, including beheadings and burning of its victims. These images stoked passions in at least two entirely different ways, stirring fear and loathing in a West fixated on video while, at the same time, inciting followers and would-be converts to revel in the group's ability to punish the "infidels."

ISIS also took its use of the Internet into new directions. Perhaps ironically, but certainly cynically, one was to show the "human" face of ISIS. For example, the ISIS Amaq News Agency regularly shows images and stories of everyday life in the so-called caliphate, including children playing, people eating and casually chatting in restaurants, and ISIS members conducting charity activities known as *zakat*. These are intended to convey the illusory image of a group that can preside over normal events and maintain peace in areas it controls.

There also is a more malevolent side. In its earliest months, ISIS commanders didn't have legions of followers (or resources) compared to traditional armies, so they were always keen to recruit new supporters who were willing to come to the Middle East to train and fight and, if possible, return some of them to their homelands to carry out new waves of attacks. The Internet became the perfect tool for global recruitment. As one of us has written recently, jihadists in the Middle East have succeeded in recruiting an estimated twenty thousand jihadists from around the globe, including in the United States, Russia, England, France, Belgium, France, Germany, Sweden, Egypt, Jordan, Saudi Arabia, Japan, and other parts of Asia. How the ancient terrorist groups we discussed at the start of this chapter would have marveled at the capability to recruit globally!

ISIS was able to reach out to would-be adherents through its publications, including by using the Dark Net. ISIS has also been particularly successful in developing online publications, such as the above-referenced Amaq, to reach its supporters and recruit new ones. Jihadist recruitment was also supported by the use of social media such as Facebook and Twitter. The American born and educated cleric Anwar al-Awlaki was especially skilled at using the Internet for recruiting activities before meeting a timely end on September 30, 2011 as the target of a drone strike in Yemen.

The use of the Internet serves other terrorist purposes as well. *Inspire Magazine*, thought to be published by al-Qaeda on the Arabian Peninsula (AQAP), is an online, English language magazine. One notable issue from 2014 exhorts its followers to wage jihad against the West, writing, "He who terrorizes the enemies of Allah complies with the divine order of I'dad [preparation and training] and jihad."

That same issue also contains detailed instructions on how to make a car bomb, showing how the Internet is used not only to incite violence but to show adherents of jihad how to carry it out. This has become an approach of growing importance as terrorist incidents have increased in Western Europe. In most instances, new followers who come to the Middle East require on-the-ground training, often in formal training camps, in tactics, weapons, and explosives that cannot be fully replicated on the Internet.

Nonetheless, as we have discussed, the Internet can be a powerful tool for the type of training that resulted in the use of explosives in terrorist attacks in Belgium and France over the past several years. In no small measure through the Internet, al-Qaeda and ISIS are able to extend their reach across continents, even as they suffer significant and even devastating battlefield losses in the Middle East. This enables these groups to stay "relevant" in the eyes of their followers as well as the mainstream Western media. Publicity is the oxygen of modern terrorism, and the broad media attention generated by spectacular attacks in Western cities fully serves terrorist purposes. The Internet is central to this.

Terrorist supporters don't even need homegrown recipes for explosives to be supported by ISIS and al-Qaeda over the Internet. One of the favored uses of the online magazines and chat rooms is encouragement to violence by small groups or even individuals, many of whom will never see the Middle East. In addition, some Westerners traveling to the Middle East are being used to send jihadist inspirational messages to followers in their homelands. Without resource-intensive and extensive surveillance that raises privacy issues in Western democracies, this tactic is difficult for Western law enforcement to interdict.

One example was reported by the *Washington Post* in late 2017. At that time, ISIS released a video of an American calling on Muslims living in the United States to take advantage of lax U.S. gun laws as a way to gain weapons that can be used in attacks against citizens. The American, who used the name Abu Salih al-Amriki, spoke in English and was thought to have a New York accent. President Trump is described in the video as "a dog of Rome." The video may have been produced by the ISIS al-Hayat Media Center, which almost certainly works closely with the online magazine *Rumiyah*. It is unknown if al-Amriki broadcast from the media center or how long he may have been in the Middle East. Before the broadcast, there are no indications that he had come to the attention of U.S. intelligence or law-enforcement officials.

The Internet can be a powerful tool not only for inspiring violent actions but showing how to carry them out. One of the most dramatic examples of this came when Mohamed Lahouaiej-Bouhlel, a 31-year-old Tunisian, carried out a bloody attack on July 14, 2016, France's Bastille holiday. He had rented a 19-ton truck several days before the attack and had meticulously surveyed the area, a promenade in the southern French city of Nice where large crowds would gather in beautiful summer weather to celebrate the holiday and watch fireworks. Driving the truck at high speed down the promenade, Lahouaiej-Bouhlel was able to kill 85 and injure another 434. Hospitals overflowed with the wounded. The attacker was shot and killed in the act, but the carnage was immense. Several other brutal terrorist attacks occurred in Paris during François Hollande, the French president's term. He described the Nice attack as a having a "terrorist nature that cannot be denied." ISIS, the jihadist organization agreed, claiming the attack was carried out by one of its followers. The attacker was praised by ISIS as "a soldier of Islam."

In the aftermath, French law-enforcement authorities, deeply experienced in dealing with terrorist attacks after several tragic events in Paris, sought to understand the motive behind the carnage. What emerged was a realization that much of the "inspiration" for the attack came not as some might have expected, from years of Islamic study in mosques side by side with other jihadists. Rather, Lahouaiej-Bouhlel was "totally unknown" and was therefore never seen as a threat by French authorities, who concluded he had been "radicalized very quickly" in the words of a local prosecutor. This was accomplished through the Internet. For a few months before the attack, the jihadist looked at video postings of ISIS beheadings and conducted Internet searches on such topics as "terrible fatal accidents" to both inspire him and help refine the tactics he employed during the attack.

In mid-August 2017, another in what has become a long line of vehicular attacks against pedestrians in Europe occurred in Barcelona, Spain, when 15 innocent people were killed and over one hundred injured when a driver sped into a busy pedestrian mall. Hours later, a second vehicle rampaged through Cambrils, a seaside town about 60 miles southwest of Barcelona.

A few weeks before the attack, the Islamic State's online magazine posted, as it had done in the past, an illustrated article with advice on the type of truck best suited for attacking pedestrians. What the article termed the "ideal vehicle" would be "large in size and heavy in weight," with a raised chassis that can clear curbs and barriers. It should also be "fast in speed or rate of acceleration."

It is unknown if the attackers saw the article, but the vehicles used in the attacks were nearly exact matches to what the terrorist group recommended. As described in the *Washington Post*, "The group's still formidable propaganda machine, with its detailed prescriptions of how to kill large numbers of innocent people, remains a principal driver of terrorist acts around the world, even as the militants suffer crippling losses on the battlefield." The dead and injured came from at least 34 countries, another measure of the near universal price of terrorism.

In the United States, New York City was again the site of a similar terrorist attack. Since the 9/11 attack, national and local law-enforcement and intelligence organizations had broken up several terrorist plots around the city. New York remains a model for how terrorist threats to major cities can be substantially reduced, but, as events on October 31, 2017 demonstrated, such attacks can't be fully eliminated.

At that time, Sayfullo Saipov, a 29-year-old native of Uzbekistan, a central Asian country, who had been living in the United States since 2010, rented a truck in New Jersey. He drove it 21 miles to lower Manhattan and proceeded to head south, entering a bike path and deliberately striking and killing eight pedestrians and bicycle riders and injuring 12 more. He exited the truck, shouting, "Allahu Akbar" (God is great), and attempted to flee before being wounded in the abdomen by an NYPD officer.

An ISIS spokesman said Saipov was acting for the terrorist organization. That was probably an accurate claim; federal investigators later learned that Saipov had prepared to carry out the attack for a year, going so far as to carrying out at least one practice run along the route he would use. Authorities also learned that Saipov had been inspired by ISIS propaganda videos shown on the online magazine *Rumiyah*. That he could carry out his preparations for a year without being detected underscores the challenges for law-enforcement and intelligence professionals in protecting populations against terrorist activities.

These are the human faces of terrorism. The attacks are also reminders that ISIS is more than just a localized force seeking to occupy territory and establish Sharia law in the Middle East. Its larger aspirations are reflected in the resources it has poured into developing a virtual network with a near-global reach. After the attacks' successes in 2016 and 2017, it can be safely assumed that terrorist leaders will continue to use the Internet to advocate for more of the same. Moreover, that advocacy is probably not just tactical but rather a trend; as ISIS loses territory in the Middle East, it will seek to preserve its ideology in other ways and in other areas.

There is a flip side. The United States and its Western allies are demonstrating that they are not powerless against ISIS's exploitation of the Internet. One of the best examples has been the decision by former Secretary of Defense Ash Carter to push the U.S. Cyber Command, created in 2010 and headquartered at Fort Meade, Maryland, to expand beyond its original primary mission to protect the DOD information networks (referred to by the Pentagon as DODIN) by becoming more active against the ISIS use of the Internet from formerly safe havens in the Middle East. The result was the creation in 2016 of Joint Task Force Ares, a core element of Cyber Command's Combat Mission Force. Creation of Ares grew out of frustration in the Pentagon that Cyber Command had not been as active or effective at it could have been in disrupting ISIS use of the Internet and cell phones.

Things began to change in late 2016. Working in conjunction with the U.S. Special Forces Command, which has the lead in the fight against ISIS, Ares was described by Special Forces Commander General Raymond Thomas III as being an essential part "of an operation which had devastating effects on the enemy." Few details have been made available regarding how Ares operates, how it coordinates its activities with ground forces operating in the region, or what was achieved through actions designed to interdict ISIS's use of the Internet. What emerges from fragmentary information sources is the likelihood that terrorist access to the Internet was badly compromised and that past and often powerful postings of various atrocities, a favorite ISIS propaganda activity, were deleted from the Internet.

None of this happened overnight or without extensive planning, training, resource commitment, and coordination with other elements, not only of the U.S. military but also the, at times, highly fragmented intelligence community that has interest in how ISIS was using the Internet. At least for the time being, these bureaucratic obstacles are being managed satisfactorily.

In an era where the information environment is of considerable and growing importance, Ares may represent an opening salvo in how the U.S. military may conduct future combat operations, not only against terrorist organizations but also against more traditional foes. Ares represents nothing less than the first publicly acknowledged plans by a Western military to use digital weapons in conjunction with more traditional combat operations. Given these developments and what they portend for the future of warfare, the reactions, assessments, and resource commitments from Russia, China, North Korea, and Iran will bear close attention. As we have seen, those nations are fully cognizant of the importance for myriad reasons of developing and deploying digital capabilities in the information age, including in the service of military operations.

The power of the Internet as a tool for terrorists is undeniable, and, for years, major Internet and social-media service providers such as Microsoft, Twitter, YouTube, and Facebook often turned a blind eye to the consequences of its unfettered use. Claiming the demands of free speech were paramount, they took limited actions to restrict the access of terrorist organizations to the Internet. More needs to be done, perhaps including greater use of Artificial Intelligence in identifying "fake" or subversive postings from legitimate ones. As with many issues involving the Internet, striking a reasonable balance between freedom of expression and security is an evolving challenge.

A potentially important remedial step occurred on December 5, 2016, when one of the above-referenced groups, Facebook, agreed to "curb" the spread of terrorist propaganda on social media. Senior media officials agreed to collaborate by storing the digital fingerprints, known as hashers, of terrorist groups in a central database. The focus of the agreement was on images or messages that would incite violence. That's certainly laudable, but it is unclear if that approach goes far enough. As we have discussed, terrorists have been creative in their use of the Internet in myriad ways.

Two Facebook managers, in a June 2017 post, claimed their organization was trying to do better, harnessing the growing power of Artificial Intelligence to interdict terrorist Facebook use. As they note, this is a daunting task given that two billion users a month are on Facebook, and their postings are in 80 different languages. The managers detailed the new approaches as including:

- Image matching: if someone tries to upload terrorist-related photos, for example, those photos are matched against past known photos, theoretically limiting the dissemination of offensive material.
- Revolving terrorist clusters: the Facebook executives claim terrorists tend to work and radicalize in clusters so that when Facebook sees posts supporting terrorism, it "fans out" to identify related material. For example, this process might focus on identifying whether an account is friends with a high number of accounts that have been disabled for terrorism.
- Recidivism: detecting new fake accounts created by repeat offenders.

One of the more important ways to counter terrorist atrocities is to document them for posterity and even possibly for war-crimes trials. In August 2017, YouTube, host to hundreds of terrorist videos that graphically recorded those atrocities and other human-rights violations, announced that it had inadvertently deleted many of them. As quoted in the *New York Times*, Chris Woods, a London-based observer of the conflict, was quoted as saying, "What's disappearing in front of our eyes is the history of this terrible war."

The gaffe occurred when the company installed new technology that would flag and remove content that was inconsistent with their standards and guidelines, although some videos were returned to the site. The new technology is also based on machine learning—Artificial Intelligence— to identify videos placed by extremist groups. It is far from perfect and still relies on human intervention and judgment. Nonetheless, it may point to a new tool for those seeking to counter terrorist propaganda and Internet use.

While the word "terrorism" is usually and properly understood as focusing on subnational groups, the premeditated, political element of what we define as cyber terrorism brings us into discussion with how nations have waged what others may call covert action or cyber war, carrying out actions in the digital domain that have destructive consequences in some cases. These forms of cyber terrorism are of equal concern to U.S. security interests as is terrorist use of the Internet.

Hackers, almost certainly state-backed, have devoted extensive effort to disrupting elements of critical infrastructure, those essential parts of any advanced nation's economy, such as its energy assets, banking, transportation, and health care. Major disruption to any of those could have a devastating impact on the lives of millions for days, weeks, or even months.

One of the early manifestations of such a cyber attack began on April 27, 2007, in Estonia. Estonia, with Lithuania and Latvia, forms the Baltic states—small, vulnerable but prosperous and technically sophisticated nations. They had been forced into the Soviet Union in the communist era, and, for that and other numerous historical reasons, had built layers of enmity toward their imposing and often bullying neighbor. After the 1991 collapse of the Soviet Union, the Baltic states began to re-emerge from their neighbor's long shadow. On March 29, 2004, all three nations joined NATO, the West's military alliance. Russia, primary successor to the Soviet Union, expressed its outrage but was largely powerless to block the move. It would soon find more tangible ways to express its displeasure.

Symbols can be powerful tools of international politics, and, in 2007, the Estonian government decided to remove from a central square in the capital, Tallinn, a Soviet-era statue, the "Bronze Soldier," which honors the Red Army, and its war graves to a remote part of the city. Not all Estonians were supportive of the decision, but on top of Estonia's new NATO membership, the decision must have reverberated loudly throughout the Kremlin, including with the hypernational Russian president, Vladimir Putin.

Beginning on April 27, 2007, a major hacking attack, including numerous denial-of-service incidents, was launched against Estonian banks, the parliament, and various ministries. Massive waves of spam attacks by botnets (which hide the identity of the controller) also were launched. Customers couldn't carry out banking transactions, and government workers couldn't carry out basic e-mail exchanges with colleagues. As to be expected, the Kremlin never claimed responsibility for the extensive attacks against Estonia's infrastructure, which many speculated was timed as revenge for the statue's removal.

The disruption to Estonian daily life was considerable. In addition, the hackers learned not only how to damage a modern society, but also how its infrastructure worked and how that society operated in the face of a crisis. Those would be useful lessons for the future, demonstrating that cyber espionage, even if not the primary purpose of an attack, is a valuable adjunct to it. For Estonia and its Western partners, there was an upside. NATO experts studied the attack and, more than ever, came to realize that cyber security would be an indispensable part of military and societal security in the future. As a result, NATO formed and maintains a Cyber Center of Excellence, and Estonia formed a voluntary Cyber Defense Unit. They will almost certainly face future cyber challenges from Russia.

The combination of political motivation and infrastructure attacks are also playing out in Ukraine. This now independent nation was, after

Russia, the most prominent part of the former Soviet Union, with close links to Russia through culture, language, and history. Ukraine's ties to Russia through the centuries had been tumultuous, with periods of both productive and disruptive relations. Beginning in 1991, relations entered a new era. After the Soviet Union's breakup, Ukraine began a slow and sometimes shaky march toward integration with the West, which, for financial and security reasons, most of its citizens felt offered better future opportunities.

This integration would not be a simple matter. Long saddled with a well-deserved reputation for corruption, Ukraine's "reception" in the West was always mixed, especially among major European nations who were never entirely convinced it would become an important contributor to the West. Even fewer were willing to contemplate any sacrifice or expenditure of resources that would aid Ukraine in a time of crisis. Europe remains a self-satisfied continent in many ways. Nonetheless, the prospect that Ukraine might be integrated into Western Europe, including possibly joining NATO at some point, was viewed in the Kremlin as a bridge too far. In 2014, with swift and stealthy aggression, Russian-backed military forces annexed Crimea, including an important naval base used by the Russian fleet. That action would put on hold, perhaps indefinitely, any plans for bringing Ukraine into NATO—a major success for Russia. It also showed the markedly improved performance of the Russian military compared to the poorly conducted 2008 invasion of the Republic of Georgia.

President Barack Obama, a master at feigning indignation at unfavorable political developments and who had belittled Russia publicly by calling it only a regional power, soon learned that he was powerless to stop or reverse Russia's conquest, except for the imposition of America's favorite foreign-policy tool, economic sanctions.

Russia's victory in Crimea did not end the Kremlin's desire to punish the country, undermine its government, and terrorize its people. For example, just two months after the annexation of Crimea, in May 2014, a major hacking attack, using a program called Sofacy, hit Ukraine's Central Election Commission.

There was much more to come against Ukraine. The result was a series of cyber attacks aimed at Ukraine's infrastructure—in this case, its energy industries. On December 23, 2015, residents of the Ivano-Frankivsk region of western Ukraine lost electrical power and heating. The cause was the remote, forced opening of circuit breakers against at least 16 regional power substations. Ultimately, about 36 substations were forced offline, along with two major energy-distribution centers. In all, some 230,000 residents were left without power in what may have been the first hack attack to take down a power grid.

The U.S. FBI and Department of Homeland Security assisted Ukrainian authorities and cyber experts in investigating the attacks, uncovering some troubling aspects. Perhaps the most disturbing was that attacks' sophistication. Planning began months in advance, with phishing attacks against IT specialists and system administrators from parts of Ukraine's energy industries. Because the industries did not use dual-authentication procedures, the hackers were able to gain passwords and other useful information in planning the attack.

In addition, the attack, once launched, was accompanied by a telephone denial-of-service attack that blocked customers from calling emergency responders and energy officials, delaying their knowledge of and response to the attack. This type of operational and logistics planning implies the resources of a state-sponsored operation, presumably Russia in this case.

A similar but smaller scale attack against Ukraine's energy network was launched in 2016 and followed by an even more widespread attack in June 2017. Known as the NotPetya ransomware, the attack targeted not just the energy sector but government agencies, transport, and banks. Ukraine's security service, the SBU, immediately branded Russia as behind the attack. Other private-sector cyber security firms throughout the West agreed with the SBU.

For hackers and those nations backing them, the intangibles of the ongoing attempts to disrupt everyday life in Ukraine add to the value of whatever information is acquired or financial losses inflicted. Loss of electrical power, a staple of modern life, can not only terrorize citizens, but it also undermines their confidence in the competence of their government. It is easy to imagine that those behind the attacks, probably in Russia, were not terribly upset by those developments.

The U.S. and European energy-infrastructure companies also have been garnering attention of international hackers since at least 2010/2011. Since that time, an advanced persistent threat (APT) emerged in the form of a malware called Dragonfly, which used a Remote Access Trojan (RAT) to target U.S. and Western Europe defense and aviation companies. Particular focus soon centered on energy companies, including energy-grid operators, major electrical-generating firms, petroleum pipeline operators, and energy industrial-control systems. Similar entities in Spain, France, Germany, Turkey, and Poland also were targeted.

Subsequent investigations showed that Dragonfly's main purpose was to extract and upload stolen data—classic cyber espionage—as well as to install further malware in vulnerable systems and run executable files on infected computers.

These attacks continued in 2017. On June 30 of that year, U.S. media outlets reported that DHS and the FBI had issued alerts to energy-sector companies that "advanced persistent threat actors" (APT) were stealing network log-in password information to gain access to company networks, including nuclear power plants—of which there are about 100 operating in the United States. Advanced persistent threat actors most often refer to nation states.

Near Burlington, Kansas, Wolf Creek, a major nuclear-power plant in operation since 1985, was affected by the cyber attack. Business operations were disrupted, but like other nuclear-power plants, the company's operational computer systems are separate from company business networks, and control systems are also isolated from the Internet. At least another 12 U.S. nuclear-power plants, as well as some nonnuclear-power plants were affected.

The attackers, with a high probability of ties to Russia as in the attacks against Ukraine, used legitimate résumés from job applicants that were sent to system administrators and senior IT personnel. Log-in and password data were then collected as a way to sneak into the network.

One of the attack's enduring lessons is that there was no apparent attempt to disrupt operations or create, as was the case in Ukraine, widespread blackouts. The hackers appear to have had a different plan, using the acquired information as a precursor to a future major attack.

We would be remiss if there were not discussion of the first physically destructive capabilities of cyber attacks through covert action. The source of what would become known as "Stuxnet"—the word has no special meaning or definition—was not Russian or Chinese hackers. Rather, it was a highly successful effort by American and Israeli experts, with approval from the highest political levels in both nations, to disrupt the operations of Iran's uranium-enrichment facility at Natanz. Located in central Iran, Natanz is a centerpiece for Iran's uranium-enrichment program. The facility is home to a pilot-fuel enrichment plant and a hardened, underground fuel enrichment plant.

Since at least the early 1990s, the United States and Israel had watched the evolution of Iran's nuclear program amid concerns that it was being used as a cover for Iran to acquire nuclear weapons. Doing so would have been a violation of Iran's commitment to remain a nonnuclear-weapons state under the terms of its joining the nuclear Nonproliferation Treaty (NPT), which, in 1970, entered into force. That commitment notwithstanding, a growing body of evidence through the 1990s and the first part of the 21st century, including Iran's extensive reliance on external technical assistance from Russia, China, North Korea, and Pakistan pointed in a different and highly threatening direction.

Nations vote with their resources. In Iran's case, the allocation of its often scarce financial resources, which resulted from chronic government mismanagement of the economy and declining energy prices in recent years, was telling. It indicated a sustained commitment on the part of the ruling theocratic regime to not only invest in the international and domestic resources to acquire a nuclear-weapons capability, but a parallel commitment through a long-range missile program to develop the capability to deliver those weapons to targets.

Beginning in the mid-1990s with the Clinton administration, where one of us had direct responsibility for the issue at the White House National Security Council, and extending through the administrations of George W. Bush and Barack Obama, the United States sought to employ its foreign-policy tools in an effort to slow or, ideally, stop Iran's nuclear program.

Those efforts included extensive bilateral diplomacy between the U.S. and Russian governments, multilateral diplomacy, some of which included the British, French, and Germans with Iran; the equally extensive use of U.S. United Nations, and European financial sanctions against Iranian entities and individuals; the threat to use force against Iran in which "all options are on the table;" and covert action, including assassinations. This panoply of approaches over an extended period of time yielded almost wholly unsatisfactory results. Notwithstanding the sanguine views of some CIA officers who, for personal reasons, sought to undermine the more alarmist and far more prescient views of senior policy officials in the George W. Bush administration, such as State Department undersecretary and U.S. ambassador to the United Nations John Bolton, most observers of the Iran nuclear program were increasingly concerned about its pace, scope, and direction.

President Bush, who, in a 2002 State of the Union speech, had labeled Iran (along with North Korea and Iraq) as part of "an axis of evil," was deeply frustrated by the lack of positive results in stemming the progress of Iran's program. In addition to powerful voices within his administration, added pressure came from Israel that correctly and consistently reminded the president that Iran's nuclear and missile programs, warts and all, continued advancing.

There are two paths to acquiring the fissile material needed to make a nuclear weapon. The first is plutonium, which is a byproduct of nuclear-power plants or heavy-water production facilities. Iran lagged badly in these areas; its attempt to develop a commercial nuclear-power plant at Bushehr with Russian assistance had been little more than a colossal debacle for years.

The other path to acquiring fissile material is to enrich uranium to what experts term "weapons grade," which is defined as 90 percent enrichment or above in the isotope U-235. Iran had invested heavily in this process, beginning with the facility at Natanz. Natanz housed often inefficient as well as fragile centrifuges, long cylindrical tubes linked together in cascades, which were sourced to Pakistan and, in part, to the nefarious dealings of A. Q. Khan, a major contributor to Pakistan's nuclear weapons development.

Despite their inefficiencies and unreliability, the centrifuges were producing enough low-enriched uranium (LEU) to create concern in the

United States and Israel that if the Iranians chose the basic and well-understood process of making LEU, they could easily continue the process at higher enrichment levels until there were sufficient quantities of weapons-grade uranium to produce one or more nuclear weapons. Adding to these worries, Iranian president, Mahmoud Ahmadinejad, the voluble former mayor of Tehran, whose enmity toward the United States and Israel was boundless, had vowed to increase the number of centrifuges operating at Natanz from a few thousand to 50,000.

Around 2006, the midpoint of his second term in office, President Bush concluded that all policy options to date had not only failed to slow Iran's nuclear program, but the Iranians were advancing their program. Bush sought a new option, and that came from the U.S. Strategic Command, responsible for maintaining America's nuclear arsenal and the National Security Agency. Bush seized upon an idea they offered that it might be possible to use a cyber attack to disrupt Iran's nuclear program, potentially buying precious time. The concept was not entirely novel. About a decade earlier, the United States had carried out a less sophisticated covert action against Iran by tampering with the power supply coming from Turkey into Iran.

What Bush approved was of an order of magnitude that was more sophisticated. The intent was to insert commands into Iran's main computer at Natanz that would open the valves and force the delicate rotors, the heart of the centrifuges, to spin at hypersonic speeds, literally tearing apart the machinery. The concept was clear, but no one was quite sure if the idea would work in practice.

There was a way to test the concept. Thanks to the availability elsewhere of centrifuges similar to those used in Iran, the United States was able to acquire a set of Libyan centrifuges for testing after Libyan dictator Muammar Qaddafi shuttered his nascent nuclear weapons program out of fear of U.S. intervention in 2003. They were packaged and shipped to a U.S. national laboratory where U.S. and Israeli experts began extensive testing in preparation for the actual attack. In 2008, the cyber attack was ready for launch.

What senior U.S. and Israeli officials came to know by the code word "Olympic Games" had elements common to other cyber attacks. Those included the targeting of the Iranian supply chain to get a worm into a computer supporting operations at Natanz through a thumb drive, a period of intelligence gathering by the worm, and a prolonged period of deception whereby the Iranians did not know what was causing disruption to their centrifuges.

What was different from other cyber attacks was the scope of physical destruction that resulted from the Stuxnet attack. Stuxnet turned out to be the world's first physically destructive cyber attack, a collaboration of U.S. and Israeli scientists and computer experts. Its effects were dramatic; the Iranians for weeks were puzzled by what was destroying their machines.

Morale plummeted as fruitless searches for an explanation by scores of scientists provided no answers. Ultimately, 984 centrifuges were disabled, a large percentage of those operating at Natanz, setting back Iran's uranium-enrichment efforts for months, if not at least a year. Despite this success, Iran's nuclear program recovered and moved forward, showing that even a cyber attack of exceptional effectiveness was no assurance of long-term disruption to an adversary's plans.

Stuxnet also caused political problems for the administration of Barack Obama, who supported the initiative. Despite the new president's rather naïve demand that the operation be kept secret and impossible to trace back to American involvement, the Stuxnet worm migrated from Iranian computers and was analyzed by computer groups and presumably experts from other nations. For better or worse, the world came to know the emerging power of cyber attacks. In this respect, Stuxnet was a political game changer (whether Obama liked that outcome or not), even as it succeeded in imposing relatively short-term technical and financial costs on Iran's nuclear program.

In considering the future of countering cyber terrorism, we can easily envision a continuing cat-and-mouse game of growing sophistication. In addition to the work carried out by government entities such as the National Security Agency, CIA, and Britain's GCHQ, there exist many talented and dedicated cyber security firms such as Symantec, Frago, Crowdstrike, and Cisco. Some of these private firms have done excellent jobs in identifying the tactics and techniques of numerous cyber hackers as well as those sponsoring those activities. Their challenges will multiply in the future.

At the same time, cyber capabilities, for better and worse, are becoming more sophisticated. In 2014, what cyber security experts labeled Energetic Bear suddenly went silent. Shortly thereafter, a new threat emerged, dubbed Palmetto Fusion by experts. Palmetto Fusion had many of the same targets as Energetic Bear but operated in different ways.

Were the two groups different in fundamental ways, such as origin or what entity was backing or directing them? Was Energetic Bear, once identified, closed down so that a new hacking effort could be employed? If so, was the new organization and its methods designed to be deliberately different to mislead investigators? Answers to these questions, to the extent that they become available, will shed more insight into possible future hacker tactics.

As with cyber crime, an important element in countering cyber terrorism and cyber espionage is better training to reduce the number of human-error incidents—deliberate or not—that enhance the chances of success for hackers. Training and the accompanying message from senior executives that proper cyber security practices are demanded are essential elements of a good "defense" but are not sufficient. For example, there are numerous examples where the lack of a dual-authentication security procedure has created opportunities for hackers to access vital information. That simple process should never be overlooked by any organization claiming to be serious about cyber security.

Hackers, including those working on behalf of governments, are also becoming more nuanced in their methods. Based on the above cases, there is ample reason to conclude that in at least some of those cases, including in Ukraine where Russia almost certainly had a role in the hacking attacks, that some portion of the hard work, like coding, is being outsourced to private and crime-tainted individuals. Identifying those individuals—at least those working outside of but at the behest of such nations as Russia, China, North Korea, and Iran—whenever possible will be exceptionally challenging but worth the effort of law enforcement. Hackers know fellow hackers and often exist in de-facto communities. Tracking down one or two could lead to the disruption entire groups and would send a message to other hackers that they can't assume endless immunity.

This is especially important because there is likely to be a proliferation of operational links between governments, criminal organizations, and financially motivated individuals. Albeit certainly nefarious, the Russian government may well have had reasons to carry out attacks against Ukraine's infrastructure, for example, but criminal organizations could have profited from the resulting disruption as well. Criminal organizations, above all, seek to make money. Cyber crime and associated activities are highly likely to remain lucrative endeavors, virtually guaranteeing that those organizations will remain engaged in hacking activities. In turn, and even with their own cadre of hackers, nations such as Russia and China recognize the value of external assistance, when expedient, and are likely to seek future partnerships.

Western media is a powerful tool. Most discussions of hacking in the mainstream media focus on major incidents and consequences. That is understandable but ignores key parts of the cyber narrative. Media outlets exist in a competitive business, seeking to make money for owners and shareholders, often by resorting to sensational and biased reporting. Is it more than coincidental that the precipitous decline in journalism standards of the once legendary *Washington Post* largely coincide with its acquisition by Jeff Bezos, the billionaire, profit-driven owner of Amazon? The *Post's* and *New York Times's* war with the Trump administration, carried out every day on their front pages, is best carried out on the editorial pages, but the distinction between "news" and editorializing seems more blurred than ever.

Just as important as focus on the "blockbuster" stories is recognition of the importance hackers ascribe to exploiting vulnerabilities in the supply chain of energy companies and transport entities. As we have seen, this is a tactic used by Russian-, Chinese-, and American-sourced cyber attacks.

Government, industry, the media, and academics all have roles to play in countering cyber attacks. The power of their individual contributions is diluted because there is little if any coordination, where appropriate, between them. Those who have served in government understand how difficult it often is to develop coordinated efforts between various departments and agencies. Doing so across segments of society is even more daunting, including the reluctance of some societal entities such as academia or the media to coordinate its activities with government. That attitude is understandable and a useful standard to maintain in many areas. At the same time, there is nothing wrong with these entities collaborating productively in areas of common interest, including the security of the Internet, while maintaining their individual integrity.

For this reason, in a better future—and one that is needed urgently—there would exist the leadership to harness the power of these entities that serve a broader public good. That leadership requires multiple sources, including the executive and legislative branches of government, the media, academia, think tanks, and corporate America.

In this respect, we would spotlight the importance of Silicon Valley, which remains a shining example of American scientific and technological ingenuity and capability. In the 1970s, terrorism analysts sought to understand the weapons and tactics terrorists such as the Baader Meinhof gang in Germany or the Red Brigade in Italy might employ. For good reasons they focused on chemical, biological, and even nuclear scenarios. What they couldn't know in the pre-Internet era was that a possibly even more powerful weapon, the Internet, was about to change the face of national security, and, as we have seen already in the Middle East, warfare.

The Department of Defense has officially taken notice of the Silicon Valley. Again, under prodding from Secretary of Defense Ash Carter, in 2015 the Pentagon opened offices in the Silicon Valley and Boston as a way to develop ongoing relationships with some of the best technical minds in America. The result has been creation within the Pentagon of the Defense Innovation Unit (DIUx) which will invest in promising cyber technologies. This is also an important example of the type of public-private collaboration that can lead to enhanced cyber security for the U.S. military and, presumably, its civilian counterparts.

In the second decade of the twenty first century, the Internet tools and tactics terrorists use have proven effective but are still crude. By the end of 2017, the U.S. military and its allies inflicted battlefield losses resulting in destruction of the ISIS dream of creating a caliphate in the Middle East. That is a major accomplishment. Nonetheless, it is not synonymous with the destruction of ISIS. The terrorist organization continues to carry out operations in Africa and Afghanistan. Moreover, as long as it exists, it will almost certainly seek new capabilities to use against its hated enemies, the United States and Israel.

If this assessment is correct, we may look back on this decade as merely the opening salvo of the Internet as a terrorist tool. Technology is taking the developed world into new and even more complex directions. The Internet of Things, discussed later in our book, opens up not only new opportunities for efficiencies in our daily lives but also vulnerabilities that might be exploited. Similarly, many of our concerns about the vulnerability of our complex infrastructure focus on criminal activities such as attacks on banks. At the same time, parts of our infrastructure, such as the power grid, remain highly vulnerable to cyber attack and disruption.

Through our opening chapters on cyber crime, cyber terrorism, and the geopolitics of cyber, we have made reference and, in some cases, discussed the importance of policies and practices that can mitigate or counter malevolent cyber activity. We need to add a further dimension that is often overlooked among scholars and policy analysts with only passing insight into the workings of government.

The National Security Agency plays a central role in how the U.S. government defends its interests against cyber attack. We have also seen how one or two disgruntled employees can cause severe damage to NSA's work and, by extension, to U.S. national security. What we haven't focused on is the extent to which the general atmosphere at organizations like NSA affects its performance. In early 2018, reports were circulating of critical problems in NSA's morale.

A *Washington Post* article, for example, headlined how NSA is losing talent in its workforce of 21,000 over low pay and flagging morale. Senior officials trace the problem to 2015. The attrition rate is officially stated as 5.6 percent among some scientific cadres but is substantially higher among those on the front lines of NSA's mission, such as the daily operations center. This trend is likely to continue; the rise in cyber jobs in the better-paying private sector has soared, creating numerous career opportunities for well-trained cyber experts. At the same time, while NSA, of course, is working to replace departing cyber experts, it is difficult to quickly replace the gaps in experience and capability created by departing staff. It is these types of developments, not often seen by the public, that undermine the government's cyber security capabilities.

As important as these and related issues are, there remain even broader questions about how to respond to the challenges of cyber crime and cyber terrorism. As we have seen, the Internet was originally intended as an instrument of freedom and ease of secure communication. Will it remain so?

We have reached a point where broader questions should be asked about redefining the Internet. Much of its early promise has been realized; it is a tool that enriches our lives in numerous ways and makes government and business immeasurably more efficient. Personal relationships are enhanced in countless ways as well. Nonetheless, we see the abuse of the Internet in increasingly diverse and disturbing ways, with significant negative implications and consequences. Neither governments nor industry have found a panacea for these developments, and, in many ways, have not even scratched the surface of options for doing so.

BIBLIOGRAPHY

Adelson, Reed. "Anthem Hack Points to Security Vulnerability of Health Care Industry." *The New York Times*, February 5, 2015.

Baker, Al. "A Rush to Track Digital Villany." *The New York Times*, February 6, 2018.

Barrett, Devlin. "Chinese National Arrested for Allegedly Using Malware Linked to OPM Hack." *The Washington Post*, August 24, 2017.

Bernard, Tara Siegel, and Stacy Cowley. "Blaming One Worker for Breach." *The New York Times*, October 4, 2017.

Bisson, David. "Five Types of Cyber Crime and How to Protect against Them." *Compliance*, October 19, 2016.

Daniel, Michael. "Heartbleed: Understanding When We Disclose Cyber Vulnerabilities." The White House, April 28, 2014.

FBI. What We Investigate. "Cyber Crime." https://www.fbi.gov/investigate /cyber. Accessed October 15, 2018.

Gertz, Bill. *iWar: War and Peace in the Information Age*. New York: Simon and Schuster, 2017.

Jewkes, Stephen. "Suspected Russian-Backed Hackers Target Baltic Energy Networks." *Reuters*, May 11, 2017. www.reuters.com.

Johnson, T. A. *Cybersecurity: Protecting Critical Infrastructure from Cyber Attack and Cyber Warfare*. Boca Raton, FL: Taylor and Frank Group, 2015.

Kaplan, Fred. *Dark Territory: The Secret History of Cyber War*. New York: Simon and Schuster, 2017.

Kilgammon, Corey, and Joseph Goldstein. "Sayfullo Goldstein, the Suspect in the New York Terror Attack, and His Past." *The New York Times*, October 31, 2017.

Klimburg, Alexander. *The Darkening Web: The War for Cyberspace*. New York: Penguin Press, 2017.

Maass, Peter. "Does Cyber Crime Really Cost $1 Trillion?" ProPublica, August 1, 2012.

Morris, David. "The Equifax Hack Exposed Mora Data Than Previously Reported." *Fortune*, February 11, 2018.

Muskherjee, Sy. "Anthem's Historic Health Records Breach Was Likely Ordered by a Foreign Government." *Fortune*, January 9, 2017.

Nakashima, Ellen. "Russian Military Was behind Cyber Attacks against Ukraine, CIA Concludes." *The Washington Post*, January 12, 2018.

Nakashima, Ellen, and Aaron Gregg. "NSA Is Losing Talent over Low Pay, Flagging Morale and Reorganization." *The Washington Post*, January 3, 2018.

Newman, Lily Hay. "Equifax Officially Has No Excuses." *Wired*, September 14, 2017.

Peterson, Andrea. "The Sony Picture Hack, Explained." *The Washington Post*, December 18, 2014.

Popper, Nathaniel. "Hackers Hijack Phone Numbers to Grab Wallets." *The New York Times*, August 22, 2017.

Riley, Michael, and Jordan Robertson. "The Equifax Hacking Has All the Hallmarks of State Sponsored Pros." *Bloomberg*, September 29, 2017.

Sanger, David. *The Perfect Weapon: War, Sabotage and Fear in the Digital Age*. New York: Crown Publishers, 2018.

Seuker, Cath. *Cyber Crime and the Dark Net*. London: Arcturus Publishers Ltd., 2016.

Shane, Scott. "The Lessons of Anwar al-Awlaki." *The New York Times*, August 27, 2015.

Wired. "Inside the OPM Hack: The Cyber Attack That Shook the World." October 23, 2016. www.wired.com.

Zetter, Kim. "Inside the Cunning, Unprecedented Hack of the Ukraine Power Grid." *Wired*, March 3, 2016.

CHAPTER 2

Cyber Crime

Jack Caravelli

Confronting cyber security risks is a daily fight.
—Richard Smith, former chairman/CEO Equifax

Cyber crime, which we define as a criminal offense by use of the Internet and computer technologies, has grown into an enormous, persistent, expensive, and highly disruptive set of activities. We may further divide cyber crime into social cyber activities that usually have a particular target. These include cyber bullying, the use of online social networks to intimidate or cast in a negative light on a classmate or peer, and sexting, using text messages or networking technologies to send sexually explicit material. These activities are both harmful and hurtful.

For our purposes, we will focus on those cyber crimes that impact governments and business. For the above-cited reasons, cyber crime is drawing increasing manpower and financial resources from law enforcement in the United States and other Western nations. In this chapter, we also will explore how organized crime is exploiting new technologies to reap new profits and expand its criminal reach.

As the U.S. government's lead law-enforcement organization, the FBI has direct responsibility for investigating cyber crime and cyber terrorism. While its focus is on activities within the United States, the FBI also has strong liaison relationships with international law-enforcement partners such as Europol. The FBI website describes the bureau's view of cyber crime threats as "more complex, dangerous, and sophisticated than ever." Even that alarming description does not fully convey the magnitude of cyber threats to U.S. governmental and business interests.

Financial costs are but the tip of the iceberg. It is virtually impossible to quantify the scope or cost of cyber crime, as reliable and agreed-upon statistics either in the United States or internationally don't exist. In a July 2012 presentation in Washington, D.C., General Keith Alexander, then head of America's National Security Agency, quoting private sector figures, said the annual cost to U.S. business alone from cyber crime could be as high as $250 billion. Alexander added the global cost of cyber crime could be as high as $1 trillion. He described the situation as "the largest transfer of wealth in history." Some private-sector experts disagreed, saying that those figures were likely exaggerated, while acknowledging that they could also be understated. Whatever the amount, the figure is undeniably staggering, imposing not only huge financial costs, but also significant operational and reputational costs on victims.

Another way to reflect the scope and nature of the problem of cyber crime in its many guises is reflected in the 10th annual global fraud and risk survey produced by Kroll, a well-recognized security firm. We may conclude from Kroll and others that, for the first time, data theft surpassed the stealing of physical assets from corporations in 2017. During the same period, a staggering 86 percent of those surveyed admitted to a cyber incident or data losses, a figure that may not capture losses to those unwilling to acknowledge they were victims. That number may be even higher in some countries.

The list of government agencies and private-sector companies victimized by cyber attacks represents a veritable "who's who" in American life, including the White House, CIA, FBI, NSA, Department of Defense, Office of Personnel Management, state governments and law-enforcement organizations, Google, Bank of America, Anthem Healthcare, J.P. Morgan, Boeing, American Express, Home Depot, Equifax and Target. There are countless others. Behind those names are the personal data and financial interests of millions of Americans that have been compromised or put at risk. The list of European and Asian victims is just as long.

In response to these attacks and to best carry out its mission, the FBI's website claims that the bureau has established key priorities to guide its resource allocation. The first priority is *computer and network intrusion*. Noting that billions of dollars are lost every year repairing systems victimized by such attacks, these intrusions take down vital systems and disrupt and sometimes disable the work of hospitals and banks, among other institutions, around the country.

As described in the FBI's website, behind these attacks are hackers looking for bragging rights, businesses seeking competitive advantage over rivals, criminal rings, spies from other nations, and terrorists. In response, the FBI has taken a series of interlocking organizational responses. It has established a cyber division at its headquarters in Washington, DC. It guides and coordinate's the work of cyber squads at 56 field offices around the country and cyber action teams, which, when called upon, can operate globally to assist in computer intrusion cases. The FBI has also increased its cooperative work with other U.S. federal and local organizations with cyber interests, including the National Security Agency, CIA, Department of Defense and Department of Homeland Security, and the New York City Police Department.

While this looks impressive on paper and is a significant improvement from U.S. cyber-related law-enforcement operations ten, or even five years ago, as we have seen, the scope of successful cyber attacks against U.S. business continues to be daunting.

The FBI's second priority is the challenge of *ransomware*. As the word implies, ransomware is the process of encrypting or locking valuable digital files and demanding a ransom to release them. Once an e-mail is opened, the malware begins encrypting files and folders on local drives and potentially even on other computers on the same network.

The technique often works, as countless firms are tempted to pay to regain file access. This is understandable; the inability to access important data can be catastrophic in terms of the loss of sensitive or proprietary information on top of financial losses and disruption to operations. Home computers are also vulnerable to ransomware attacks. The future seems to hold promise of even more sophisticated attacks without the use of e-mails, whereby legitimate websites can be seeded with malicious code.

Under these conditions, a return to the basics may be the best, if imperfect, defense. It often makes little sense to pay the ransom, as there are countless examples of the data not being made available once the ransom is paid. Prevention—or at least attempts at prevention—remain important. Employee awareness is critical, as is robust technical protection. Finally, business-continuity plans should be developed and, in the case of a ransomware attack, implemented, including backing up data on a different server.

Given the scope and nature of cyber threats, we adhere to the importance for governments, businesses, and individuals of a standard known as CIA, a concept we introduced in chapter one. For our purposes, CIA refers to confidence, integrity, and availability of data.

If CIA is the ideal or gold standard, a closer look at a few cases underscores the breadth and impact of damage when government and business fall short of that standard. In February 2015, Anthem Healthcare, America's second-largest health insurer and parent to Blue Cross/Blue Shield, announced that the personal records of 78.8 million customers from its own and other health-care networks had been compromised through a computer attack.

Among other compromised pieces of information were full names, home addresses, social security numbers (SSN), birth dates, employment records, and income data. No individual or group claimed responsibility for the attack, but suspicion fell on China. The FBI conducted a sweeping investigation but did not come to any final judgment on the perpetrator. A U.S. cyber security firm, hired by Anthem, concluded that the attack's success was a result of phishing, a fake e-mail that may or may not have been deliberately opened by an Anthem employee with access to data stored by the company.

Most cyber criminals may not care if they learn someone was treated for a broken arm or serious illness, but there is considerable value in other pieces of stolen information. Access to social security numbers is of special concern, as, in the United States, SSN numbers, unlike, for example, a bank account number or PIN, cannot be changed. Stolen SSNs can form the basis of fake credit applications, for example. Because of its intrinsic value, one SSN can be sold for $300.

In the aftermath of the incident, which had probably originated at least several months before the theft was reported, there were few examples of anyone trying to use or sell the personal information. Nonetheless, losses of various types mounted in what is the largest compromise of medical data in U.S. history. For individuals, confidence in the confidentiality (our "C," as noted above) of their most personal information was shattered, and, by extension, Anthem suffered significant and unfortunately well-deserved reputational damage. Particular reputational damage resulted when it was revealed that the company's lack of preventive actions, including not encrypting company files, demonstrated indifference to cyber security threats in numerous ways to many.

There were more tangible costs as well. Subsequently, the company had to deal with numerous class-action lawsuits and decided to invest an unplanned $260 million in upgraded IT infrastructure. By all indications, cyber security was not a priority for senior Anthem management; both the company and its millions of customers paid a steep price.

In late 2014, employees of Sony Pictures and Sony Corporation, the international entertainment giant, began their day by finding sounds of gunfire, threatening language, and a fiery skeleton on their computer screens. This "greeting" was the manifestation of a major cyber attack. In the run-up to the attack, Sony Pictures was preparing to release an action-comedy, *The Interview*, starring Seth Rogen. The plot involved two journalists who were granted an interview with North Korean leader Kim Jong-un only to be approached by the Central Intelligence Agency with a fanciful proposal to assassinate the dear leader. Notwithstanding Rogen's comedic talents, it is unclear how Sony Pictures executives thought the movie's plot would have any commercial or artistic interest or value.

North Korean leaders, not surprisingly, came to the same negative conclusion, albeit for entirely different reasons. For North Korea's epically paranoid officials, the proposed movie was another reflection of the West's "arrogant" disdain for their leader. In the ensuing, and perhaps inevitable, cyber attack, which one U.S. law-enforcement official said he concluded, with 99 percent certainty, was carried out by North Korea, chaos descended upon Sony executives. Subsequent investigations revealed that the attackers breached Sony's cyber security with malware compiled on a Korean-language computer.

The attack was spectacularly successful, revealing copious amounts of proprietary and personal Sony files, which were distributed in nine batches to online sites, including to a website used by hackivists. As with the Anthem attack, a critical reason for this success was almost certainly poor internal security at Sony, possibly involving the seemingly innocent gesture of someone opening an infected file or e-mail.

Similar to the Anthem breach, personal information from the Sony files released to the sites included names, addresses, and employment information. Proprietary movie scripts were also posted, as well as four movies that had not yet been released in theaters. As many as 47,000 employees throughout the corporation were thought to have had their personal information compromised. Another estimate is that all the information on 3,262 of 6,797 computers owned by the corporation were either wiped out or otherwise compromised. If that estimate is close to the mark, the financial costs and disruption to business operations must have been staggering. It's hard to imagine how anything but the most destructive and widespread physical attack could have been more disruptive.

Trailing in the wake of the hacking incident, Sony compounded its misfortune by giving in to blackmail. It decided not to release the incendiary movie that had drawn North Korea's wrath. Even President Barack Obama, more respected for his personal decency than foreign-policy strength of leadership, was critical of Sony's decision. According to media reports, Obama explained, "If somebody is able to intimidate folks out of releasing a satirical movie, imagine what they start doing when they see a documentary they don't like or news reports they don't like...or even worse, imagine if producers start engaging in self-censorship." The Sony breach resulted in its cochair, Amy Pascal, resigning her position.

Sony is not the only entertainment conglomerate to be victimized by a cyber attack. Pay-television network HBO has also been victimized by multiple cyber attacks. One in 2015 exposed scripts for one of HBO's popular programs, demanding a ransom to stop further script revelations.

Perhaps even more damaging for HBO was the 2017 cyber attack for which Behzad Mesri, an Iranian, was indicted in a New York City federal court. He was charged with computer fraud, wire fraud, and extortion. Operating from a safe perch in Iran, which in practice means he will never face justice in the United States, Mesri is alleged to have demanded a ransom of $6 million in Bitcoin as he was preparing to release some 1.5 terabytes of HBO data, text, and video. This was an enormous amount of material, about seven times the data released in the Sony attack. The

HBO material released on the Internet included internal correspondence, e-mails, and unaired episodes of popular programming such as *Game of Thrones, Ballers, Curb Your Enthusiasm*, and *The Deuce*.

The federal indictment was careful in not claiming that Mesri was operating at the behest of the Iranian government, but Mesri is known to have done cyber work for the Iranian military in the past. He may have been acting on his own in this case, but proving that is nearly impossible and hardly matters to HBO.

Cyber crime and cyber espionage (which we discuss in more detail later) can also be closely linked. On Obama's watch, the government's Office of Personnel Management (OPM) was victimized by an audacious and fully successful cyber attack. OPM is the administrative and human-resources arm of the federal government and, as, its name implies, is the repository of the records and personal data of past and present executive-branch employees. The success of the attack is conveyed in one statistic; over 21 million OPM personnel files were stolen, containing a treasure trove of personal information on past and present U.S. government employees and contractors. This constituted nothing less than a nightmarish scenario both for U.S. government security interests, as well as for the individual interests of those victimized by the attack.

The attack on OPM started in March 2014, or possibly earlier. It was not discovered until April 15, 2015. During that lengthy period, the personnel records of those millions were stolen, a major disgrace for the Obama administration which prided itself on being technologically savvy. What was even more egregious was that at least one year before the theft, the Office of the Inspector General, an independent, watchdog organization within OPM, issued a report noting that the OPM computer network was highly vulnerable to attack. That the organization's most senior executives, beginning with its director Katherine Archuleta, failed to heed the warning by taking no effective or remedial action is another example of bureaucratic malfeasance and poor leadership. She was forced to resign after her shortcomings came to light, but the damage already had been done.

The data breach was first noticed by Brendan Saulsbury, a security engineer. As described by *Wired* magazine, he noticed that when decrypting the secure sockets layer (SSL), the traffic that flows across the OPM network, that outbound traffic was being routed to a site called opmsecurity. org. OPM did not own the domain. Saulsbury and the rest of the IT team began a deeper search, discovering the signal's source emanated from a file called mcutil.dil. This was common software used by the computer security firm McAfee but that was out of place, as OPM was not using McAfee products.

In the attack's aftermath, considerable interest was placed on identifying the attackers. As with so many other cyber attacks against U.S. interests, attention again turned to China. The Chinese maintain an army of cyber hackers, estimated to number some 100,000 specialists, such as those working for Unit 61398. Its members belong to the People's Liberation Army, using Shanghai as an important base of operations. Predictably, China denied any role in the incident.

There was strong evidence to the contrary. For example, OPM officials brought in the highly trained Department of Homeland Security Computer Emergency Readiness Team (CERT) to investigate deeper than the initial surveys conducted by OPM IT specialists. The DHS CERT team uncovered that the remote-access tool used by the perpetrators was PlugX, a malware used by the Chinese. Investigators found PlugX on ten OPM machines, which, at first blush do not appear overly troubling, except that one of the machines was the OPM central-administrative server.

There was extensive speculation regarding China's intentions or goals in carrying out the cyber attack. Sufficient evidence may exit to place the matter within our following chapter, which discusses cyber espionage. We have chosen the current approach because it was a cyber crime under U.S. law, and we have yet to see the use of the illegally acquired material in any national-security context. Nonetheless, China's brazen attack underscores the larger point that nations use cyber crime as another means of undermining their adversaries.

The global scope of cyber crime was driven home in May 2017 when computers around the globe, WCRY appeared at the end of file names. This became known as WannaCry, initiated through a remote code executed in Microsoft Windows. Microsoft had produced a patch for that vulnerability in March of the same year, but tens of thousands of users either didn't know of the patch or ignored its importance.

A hacker group had a different perspective. The software vulnerability was first discovered by the National Security Agency, which, ironically, apparently had its knowledge of the problem compromised and disseminated by the Shadow Brokers, the hacker group about which little is known.

The scope of WannaCry was staggering. Hospitals in the United Kingdom, universities in Asia, rail systems in the Republic of Georgia, and manufacturing plants in Japan were victimized. In all, tens of thousands of computers in 153 countries were compromised. What was disseminated was a ransomware attack whereby those with infected computers were ordered to pay $300 in Bitcoins, an anonymous virtual currency, within three days to free the encrypted files. If the ransom was not paid in three days, the demanded amount rose to $600, and if that was not paid, the promised punishment was deletion of the corrupted files.

What made WannaCry one of the more sophisticated and unique cyber attacks was that, unlike the problems that befell Anthem, Sony, and OPM, human error, not counting NSA's initial malfeasance, was not responsible for the spread of the malware. Rather, the "payload" from WannaCry contained its own network scanner that found additional hosts and could self-propagate to other systems.

Within a week of the WannaCry attack, analysts were warning of a second classified cyber weapon stolen from NSA. This was code named EsteeMaudit, and, like EternalBlue, the basis for WannaCry, the new code also exploits vulnerabilities in Windows software. Both former NSA hacking tools were thought to be part of a larger set of digital espionage capabilities available to NSA.

At the end of 2017, the Trump administration's homeland-security adviser, Tim Bossert, stated the U.S. government had concluded an investigation that showed North Korea to behind WannaCry.

In early September 2017, Equifax, one of the three major American consumer-reporting agencies, admitted that earlier in the year, hackers had gained access to company data. As many as 143 million American consumers, nearly half the U.S. population, may have had critical personal information, including driver's license and social security numbers stolen. Equifax also operates in 24 other countries. Initial reports focused on a security breach in May through July that resulted from software vulnerability. The company did not explain why it had waited more than six weeks before releasing information of the security breach. During that period, the company's chief financial officer, John Gamble, sold shares worth about $1.8 million, presumably betting that the company's stock would plummet once the company's problems surfaced. Several other executives also sold large blocks of Equifax, but a subsequent investigation found nothing improper in their actions.

Adding to the unfolding story of Equifax's apparent indifference to its clients' security, several newspapers reported in September 2017 that Equifax set PINs based on the date and time a credit freeze was established, making them easy to figure out. An Equifax spokesman claimed, without providing any evidence, that no PINs had been compromised.

The company issued the usual bland apology and offered one year of free credit protection through a website, an insult to the victims because their information could be used or sold by hackers for years. With the stolen information, hackers could, for example, impersonate people with lenders and service providers. Equifax also brought in an outside team of experts to investigate the cause of the attack. Senator Mark Warner, a Virginia Democrat and cofounder of the Senate Cyber Security Caucus, said the breach represents a threat to the economic security of Americans. While the identity of the perpetrators was not revealed immediately by Equifax, another massive data leak posed its own national security concerns as well.

The Equifax debacle, the only proper description of its malfeasance, caught up with some of those responsible for the massive data breach. The IT and chief security officers left their positions at the company.

In addition, chairman and CEO Richard Smith, who had directed the company since 2005 and whose thoughts on cyber security led off this chapter, agreed to an early retirement. His "punishment" was to receive an $18 million pension and other benefits reaching possibly $90 million following a review by the Equifax board of directors. Smith's departure would not shield the company from multiple federal investigations over the hacking incident as well as the timing of stock sales by Equifax executives. Myriad lawsuits were being prepared in late 2017.

His departure also did not shield him or the company from Congressional scrutiny. During formal testimony in an October 2017 meeting with the House Energy and Commerce Committee, Smith, who had vacated his position, made repeated apologies to the members. He also sought to downplay the severity of the problem while saying little about how the company would compensate its millions of customers whose credit and other personal information had been compromised. Greg Walden, a Republican congressman, said Congress could not pass a law to "fix stupid."

Smith also went to great lengths to demonstrate that the data breach was caused by a single employee. Months earlier, in March 2017, the U.S. Department of Homeland Security alerted the company and others that software vulnerability existed in the online portals used in customer complaints. The internal e-mail sent to Equifax technical staff, requesting the problem be fixed was not acted upon by the individual responsible for alerting the team charged with making the fix. In addition, the software used to verify vulnerabilities failed to find the unpatched hole.

The lessons from the Anthem, Sony, OPM, and Equifax cases are not hard to discern. All fell far short of the CIA standard, and much of the problems were a reflection of vulnerable conditions created by poor cyber security practices that were then exploited by their attackers. Within each of those organizations, human error mixed with indifference to fundamental cyber security practices at various organizational levels led to extensive damage and disruption. The obvious lessons going forward are that employees need better training in basic cyber security practices, given that cyber war is largely a function of and carried out through data mining.

Even more needs to be done. Nothing less than a revolutionary, cultural shift in government and industry is required to begin leveling the cyber playing field, but even that demanding approach would be just a starting point against the voluminous and voracious hacking community of predatory nations, criminal groups, and talented individuals. At present, most corporations have IT departments of often junior staff and perhaps a chief information officer (CIO) or chief security officer (CSO). Most have limited experience in facilitating effective cyber security practices and policies as, until recently, that was not a focus for IT professionals. Few CIOs or CSOs will ascend to the top of the corporate ladder because marketing or financial skills often garner much greater opportunities for career advancement.

In addition, the CIO and CSO do not always command the broad authority in corporations to impose the training and cyber discipline required to fend off cyber attacks. They also often lack the influence to command the resources needed to carry out their jobs unless the corporation is victimized by a cyber attack. Finally, even many of the most talented CIOs or CSOs lacks the experience and breadth of vision to develop a resilience plan in the case of a successful cyber attack. Doing so is time-consuming and hardly looks rewarding, at least until it needs to be pressed into service. In the contemporary world, cyber security and physical security are two sides of the same coin, and that is perhaps the best mind-set for all security professionals and their executives.

Within the highest levels of the C-suite—the CEO and COO—executives need to take personal interest in and commit to appropriate resources to cyber security. Moreover, while it is highly unlikely that any entity can fully inoculate itself from future cyber attacks, it is reasonable for the public, in the case of the federal and state governments, and shareholders and corporate board members in business settings to support their experts in developing a "Plan B" after a cyber attack so that damage is mitigated, and rapid recovery to normal operations is possible.

Unfortunately, some companies have chosen a different route in dealing with cyber problems. In November 2016, Joe Sullivan, chief security officer for the transport (and controversial) company Uber, opened an e-mail claiming the sender had identified a vulnerability in Uber's operating systems. Uber had instituted a "bug bounty" program in March 2016 as a means to incentivize payments to individuals who identified problems in its computer operations. Uber paid as much as $200,000 under its bounty program, and, on this occasion, officials paid the hacker $100,000 after a back-and-forth negotiation in which they first offered a $10,000 payment, and considered the matter closed. It wasn't.

In November 2017, a year after the initial e-mail, it was revealed that Uber had placed at risk private information of as many as 57 million customers. Mr. Sullivan lost his job. The company, no stranger to criticism for its labor practices and alleged assaults against passengers by several Uber drivers, again came under scrutiny arising from the lengthy delay in acknowledging the scope of the compromise of customer privacy.

Uber is not the only Silicon Valley company to pay a "bug bounty." The practice is sufficiently widespread that there is a bug bounty field manual on that Internet, which promises to guide the user through planning and implementing a bug-bounty program.

None of this guarantees success against attack, but these measures should be considered the minimum expectations for government, industry, and business of all sizes. The academic world also has a role to play.

A rapidly growing number of courses for undergraduates, law students, and MBA candidates address various aspects of cyber security. What used to be an IT focus in engineering departments, for example, is being re-imagined in ways that offer students a much broader perspective on cyber issues. The payoff may not come for years but is a reflection and recognition of the changing culture we call for of cyber awareness that can inculcate in the next generation of leaders commitment to aggressive cyber security practices.

At the national level, one major change was the announcement by President Donald Trump in August 2017 that he was upgrading the nation's cyber security operations located at Fort Meade, Maryland. That is the home of the National Security Agency (NSA) where the NSA director is "dual hatted," leading the NSA as well as the nation's cyber-defense activities. Under Trump's direction, which received broad Congressional support, a Cyber Command will be created within the Department of Defense, which will be the bureaucratic equivalent of the unified commands such as Central Command. In prepared remarks, Trump claimed creation of Cyber Command reflected his administration's resolve to confront various cyber threats.

The new Cyber Command will not be a panacea for America's ongoing lack of strategic planning to defend the nation against cyber attack. A new leader needs to be identified and confirmed by the U.S. Senate, a process that takes months. How will he or she and the new Command interact with the changes already in place at the FBI? In addition, the creation of new bureaucratic entities in Washington seldom translates into effective operations quickly. The smooth operation of the Department of Homeland Security, years after it was established in 2002, remains a work in progress and ridden with internal rivalries and dysfunction. Within the Department of Energy in 2000, the National Nuclear Security Administration was created, which has been plagued for years by a succession of incompetent and, at times, corrupt leadership.

In addition, one of the most compelling lessons from the WannaCry attack centers on how and whether the U.S. government should stockpile and hoard security vulnerabilities the way NSA did, which, once stolen, led to global havoc. Whoever is nominated by the president and confirmed by the Senate to run Cyber Command cannot ignore that the organization can, under certain limited but extreme circumstances, become part of the problem rather than part of the solution.

The United States, in both the public and private sectors, needs to commit more resources to cyber security work. Rob Joyce, White House cyber security coordinator, said in August 2017 that the nation needed an additional 300,000 cyber security operators in coming years, presumably from the growing number of students being trained across the nation. Nonetheless, those numbers will not be reached easily or quickly. Is there anywhere near that much talent available? Will the cyber field be viewed as an attractive career path for intelligent young individuals? Is government or industry even prepared to bring large numbers of IT professionals into the work force, even if those numbers can be found?

Much more also needs to be done to negotiate and implement international standards for cyber behavior. This will be difficult to accomplish. Russia, China, North Korea, and Iran, among other nations, have benefited enormously and in multiple ways from successful hacking attacks and, as such, have little incentive to engage in serious effort to control cyber attacks. Among other factors, those nations, which give shelter to hackers working on their behalf, make it difficult for the United Nations, as one example, to exercise any authority or even guidance on a growing international problem.

This is not to say that the UN has been ignoring cyber threats. In July 2017, the UN's Press Center issued a report drawn from work carried out by the International Telecommunications Union that concluded only half of all nations have a cyber security standard or are developing one. Only 38 percent were assessed as having such plans in place, while another 12 percent were seen to be developing cyber security plans. A senior UN official said cyber security "is an ecosystem," where all the elements of a cyber security strategy such as laws, organizations, skills cooperation, and technical implementation need to be blended in harmony.

It was impossible to know how well the referenced national plans were designed in various countries or whether the resources or expertise exist across the globe to implement those plans, underscoring the need for a much deeper look at how the globe is dealing with cyber problems. According to the UN press release, the countries that are most committed to enhancing cyber security capabilities are, in descending order, Singapore, the United States (a surprise given the vulnerabilities we have described in this chapter), Malaysia, Oman, Estonia, Mauritius, Australia, Georgia, France, and Canada.

Russia, one of the most aggressive users of cyber attacks to further its political ends, was ranked eleventh of all nations in trying to enhance its cyber capabilities. Could the Kremlin, ironically, be worried about cyber retaliation? This is not an overwhelming record of global accomplishment, but that doesn't alleviate the importance of the United States and other nations endeavoring to push toward an international standard of cyber conduct.

If there was another reason needed for accelerated efforts on the international level to confront cyber threats, the 2017 "WannaCry" malware attack provided it. The global phenomenon of cyber attacks and vulnerabilities was driven home by one number—the 153 nations whose businesses and operations were involved in the attack.

Beyond the threats to governments and industries, individuals will confront a growing range of cyber threats in their daily lives as well. The battle between hackers and those victimized by cyber attacks continues to rage. In August 2017, the *New York Times* ran a front-page story about how hackers have been using with increasing frequency the tactic of "calling up Verizon, T-Mobile, Sprint, and AT&T and asking them to transfer control of a victim's phone number to a device under the control of the hackers." The purpose is to "reset the passwords on every account that uses the phone number as a security backup as services like Google, Twitter and Facebook suggest." The Federal Trade Commission reports that these phone hijackings have more than doubled in frequency over the last several years. Those at particular risk have been users of virtual currency or anyone who is known to invest in virtual-currency companies, such as venture capitalists.

Beyond the details of the report and the near-term consequences of another emerging new threat, the broader implications for the future trends in cyber security come into focus. It is easy, and probably largely correct, to conclude that cyber hackers or attackers—the offense—will maintain the upper hand, perhaps for a considerable period. They have obvious advantages, including a low likelihood of being caught, as well as the fact that new technologies and capabilities coming online in coming years will almost certainly be more complex. Those complexities will create new vulnerabilities to users—the defense—as the *New York Times* article describes.

At the same time, while we may lament and embrace some aspects of new technologies, we may be entering an era—or at least approaching one—where the capabilities of the defense may increase. It is not unrealistic to imagine that within five years or so, new technology will be developed that can continue to operate after an attack. American technical know-how in these areas is considerable; the work in Silicon Valley, among other research centers, may hold the key to whether the challenges of confronting cyber crime become manageable.

Having discussed the scope, nature, and effects of cyber crime, it is easy—and perhaps simplistic—to conclude that the problem will continue and even increase. As we also have observed, what enables much—not all—of the cyber crime we have discussed is the almost shocking indifference of much of corporate America to the challenges of preserving sensitive data and its failure to train employees adequately to meet those challenges.

Training of personnel in cyber security and holding them responsible for that cannot be overstated as a first step for corporations and businesses. At the same time, we also cannot ignore the challenges tech firms confront when working in the same space. This aspect of cyber security was brought home forcefully in an early 2018 discussion in *The Washington*

Post. As the *Post* described, "The technology industry has been stunned to discover that the microchips powering nearly every computer and smart phone have for years carried fundamental flaws that can be exploited by hackers and yet cannot be entirely fixed."

The flaws are dubbed Meltdown and Spectre, and, while there is no evidence that these flaws have been exploited by hackers, there is broad consensus among exerts that it would be neither surprising nor difficult for these vulnerabilities to be developed. The result, as in so many other cases, could be the compromise of personal information, including credit-card number and passwords. Meltdown affects mainly Intel chips and will be addressed partially through patches. Malicious exploitation would be hard to detect because no record of intrusion is created. In the case of Spectre, which affects AMD and Arm as well as Intel chips, software patches will be difficult.

As these problems were surfacing, the process by which the U.S. government would provide information on software and hardware flaws to vendors and suppliers was being clarified by former NSA executive and White House cyber security coordinator Rob Joyce. Formally, this notification system is called the vulnerabilities equities process or VEP. According to a White House document issued in late 2017, the U.S. government seeks to balance notifying vendors and suppliers of vulnerabilities and the expectation they would be fixed against possibly restricting information on those vulnerabilities to government circles for possible exploitation for national-security or law-enforcement purposes. Central to the operation of the VEP will be a monthly meeting of a review board composed of representatives from throughout the federal government who can bring forward for discussion new cases of discovered vulnerabilities.

For years, NSA had been working quietly—before revelations from Edward Snowden, who betrayed a treasure trove of secrets—to negate Chinese hacking efforts, with at least moderate success. A number of successful blocks of Chinese hacking attempts underscore the possibility of disrupting at least some attacks. Nonetheless, as we have seen, China scored impressive successes against U.S. national security and business interests.

Beyond a behind-the-scenes technical war, the problems of cyber crime and ways to enhance cyber security also have broad ramifications for how international business is conducted, beginning with elements of the world's two largest economies, the United States and China. In early 2018, tech giant AT&T announced that it was not going to complete a pending deal to sell in the United States the phones of the Chinese firm Huawei Technologies, which, in 1987 was started by Ren Zhengfei, a former People's Liberation Army engineer. The newest phone, called the Mate 10, was reported to have an advanced screen and special artificial-intelligence features as companies rush to build for the upcoming 5G technologies.

The phones may still be sold in the United States, but without the backing of AT&T or other major wireless carriers like Verizon or T-Mobile, its sales will almost certainly be curtailed.

AT&T did not specify the reasons behind the changed plans, but there's little doubt that political factors, beginning with concerns about Huawei's ties to the Chinese government and Chinese cyber attacks in general were a major factor. Huawei has a global presence and conducts business in Iran and North Korea, which has not endeared it to U.S. officials. As the AT&T decision was being debated internally, a group of U.S. legislators issued a letter stating their longstanding concerns about the Chinese company and its work with its government.

Huawei is a private company and denied any collaboration with the Chinese government, claiming it had "delivered premium products with integrity globally." The AT&T decision was the most recent in a long line of similar refusals by Western firms to conduct business dealings with China after a spate of revelations about its predatory cyber attacks. Huawei is assessed by various U.S. government agencies as having the ties it has denied to Chinese intelligence organizations. For this reason, the company's core telecommunications business has also had a difficult time gaining traction in the U.S. market.

Alibaba Group, another Chinese entity, also pulled back it plans to acquire, for over $1 billion dollars, MoneyGram after a U.S. review panel questioned whether Alibaba would adequately safeguard personal data contained in MoneyGram transactions. The concerns of U.S. government officials regarding Chinese products is matched by similar Chinese government suspicions. Most American technology providers have had their own problems in gaining access to Chinese markets. These examples illustrate how politics remains a powerful factor in global business.

Concerns about data protection and protection of intellectual property also have spilled into the political arena at the highest levels. During most of his presidency, Barack Obama, a most conflict-adverse politician, ignored the repeated advice of experts, corporate leaders, his cabinet, and the U.S. Congress in taking few policy actions against the growing volume and seriousness of cyber attacks, including those emanating from China.

For example, as veteran reporter Bill Gertz recounts, in 2011, the Obama administration, reflecting growing concern about Chinese hacking against U.S. industrial targets, began assessing its policy options. They included conducting cyber counterattacks against Chinese industrial targets and use of America's favorite diplomatic tool, economic sanctions, against Chinese officials deemed to have been involved directly in cyber operations against the United States. Obama chose to do nothing, preferring not to possibly antagonize America's most important trading partner.

Obama, who enjoyed studying every dimension of a problem exhaustively often questioned whether the Chinese government or independent hacking groups were behind many of the hacking attacks. He should have known better, as there was more than ample evidence to suggest that parts of the Chinese government, such as elements of the People's Liberation Army, were operating with official cover and support. If he had taken a closer look and relied upon reporting, the president would have found that, as Gertz has illustrated, since at least 2006, Chinese hacking has targeted technical design details for Westinghouse nuclear reactors, U.S. Steel, Alcoa, and other major U.S. corporate entities. Ironically, and, as we'll see in a much different context, it would be with Russian, not Chinese, cyber hacking that Obama would have an epiphany moment.

Nonetheless, it was first with China that, after years of a see-no-evil approach, things began to change regarding Obama's direct engagement on cyber issues. In 2015, the accumulation of Chinese cyber attacks across a web spectrum of U.S. government and business interests led Obama to begin dialogue with Chinese President Xi Jinping. In a highly publicized agreement announced between Obama and his Chinese counterpart in the White House rose garden on September 25, 2015, they pledged to respect each other intellectual property and more closely monitor and control unlawful cyber activities on their soil.

It didn't take long for the Chinese to demonstrate their contempt for the agreement. The California-based cyber security company Crowdstrike issued a report concluding that, in the agreement's aftermath, there was no respite from Chinese hacking attempts against U.S. technology and pharmaceutical companies. The actions taken by the Chinese after a so-called agreement with President Obama go a long way to explaining the actions taken subsequently in the Huawei and Alibaba cases.

While much of our cyber crime discussion has focused on large corporations and the damage wreaked by cyber attacks on them, an often overlooked cyber threat is the vulnerability of small businesses, which we may define as having 100 or fewer employees. According to the highly regarded and nonpartisan Rand Corporation, there are approximately 28 million small businesses, and they employ about half of the entire U.S. workforce. They rely on IT to manage their inventory, track orders, and maintain customer relations.

They must at times be ruthlessly efficient in managing their resources, such as by sharing offices. For financial reasons, they almost always cannot afford to have an in-house IT department or cyber security expert. This only enhances their vulnerability to cyber attacks. What also encourages such attacks is an often laissez-faire attitude among senior managers. According to Rand, in one recent six-month period, about half of all surveyed U.S. small businesses admitted to some type of hacking attack, while a far higher percentage, about 90 percent, did not feel their companies were at cyber risk.

That head-in-the-sand approach carries obvious and considerable risk, not just to the individual companies but to broader networks that may also be attacked through what is termed supply-chain attacks. These vulnerabilities can be mitigated; employee training in effective and often simple cyber hygiene comes to mind. Congressional legislation is directing the U.S. Small Business Administration to support cyber training for small businesses. Prevention is the gold standard and the best antidote to cyber crime, and, while it is worth striving for, we recognize that companies are falling short of that standard for the above reasons. As a result, mitigating cyber threats—having prepared responses at the ready in case of a cyber attack—becomes an even higher priority when it is recognized that small companies, once victimized, have limited financial resources available to recover from attacks.

In early 2018, governments and large and small businesses around the globe had reason to be cautiously optimistic. At the World Economic Forum, the annual gathering of global political and financial leaders in Davos, Switzerland, it was announced during a panel discussion that there beginning in March 2018 in Geneva, a Global Center for Cyber Security would be established. In the press release, it was described as "the first global platform for governments, business, experts, and law enforcement to collaborate on cyber security." The Center will be supported by Interpol, the international law-enforcement entity. Alois Zwinggi, a managing director of the World Economic Forum, will serve as first director of the Center. Zwinggi said the Center's goals are:

- Consolidating existing cyber security initiatives of the World Economic Forum
- Creating a library of cyber best practices
- Enhancing knowledge of cyber security
- Working toward an appropriate and agile regulatory framework on cyber security practices
- Serving as a laboratory and early-warning think tank for future cyber security scenarios

Assuming the Center comes into operation, it may take years before an assessment can be made of its effectiveness of the stated goal of aiding governments and businesses in enhancing cyber security. There is no single "fix" to the many threats posed by cyber attacks. Nonetheless, the symbolic value of the Davos announcement should not be underestimated. There is a powerful message if the international community is truly prepared to work collaboratively on this problem. The challenge, among others, will be to ensure that nations that support and shelter hackers, such as Russia, China, North Korea, and Iran, do not undermine the integrity and credibility of the organization. If successful, the Center could be a harbinger of future global cooperation in enhancing cyber security.

Information from the 2018 Winter Olympics in PyeongChang, South Korea, demonstrates the global reach of cyber crime and the politics behind it in another way. At the 2014 Winter Olympics in Sochi, Russia, a lengthy investigation uncovered a broad and almost certainly Russian government-backed scheme to cheat on behalf of dozens of its athletes by tampering with their use of performance-enhancing drugs. Never the hallmark of integrity in dealing with the international sports community, the Russians vehemently denied the charges that included the use of Russian security officials in tampering with urine samples to cover the illicit drug usage. In the face of overwhelming evidence from a lengthy investigation that uncovered the cheating, even the epically timid international governing bodies for sports had to take action. The punishment was that Russian athletes would not compete under their national flag at the 2018 games, and many were banned from competing at all.

These actions enraged the hypersensitive Russian government. As a result, as the 2018 Games were opening, reports were circulating of months of Russian hacking of Olympic databases, presumably to gain information on non-Russian athletes who might be compromised or embarrassed. Some 300 Olympic websites had been attacked by the opening of the Games, according to a *New York Times* article. Such is not the spirit of the Olympics, but Russian actions, naturally denied by Russian spokespeople, represent the era of using cyber activities to promote national agendas at almost any venue or for any reason.

Meanwhile, within the United States, law-enforcement agencies are contending with emerging areas of cyber crime. An early 2018 article in the *New York Times* highlighted some of the new dimensions of cyber crime:

- In Philadelphia, inefficient and outmoded ways of confronting iPhone theft undermine efforts to disrupt stolen cellphone rings. Police are left without the tools to treat the thefts as part of a vast network of cyber crimes.
- In Nashville, local enforcement has seen a surge in what they call the "cheating husbands" e-mail scheme, "in which anonymous extortionists mass e-mail large numbers of men, threatening to unmask their infidelities. The extortionists have no idea if the men have done anything wrong." Some will pay, including through the use of Bitcoin.

Data for such crimes is virtually nonexistent, making it difficult for law enforcement to analyze them or develop strategies to mitigate their effects. In the digital era, criminals can make significant money without the risk associated with using violence. As the *Times* concluded, "digital villainy can be launched from faraway states, or countries eliminating physical threats the police traditionally confront. Examples such as identity theft, human trafficking and credit card continue to proliferate." Law-enforcement officials ask themselves: Who owns the crimes? Who must investigate them? What are the specific violations? Who are the victims?

Efforts are underway to modernize law enforcement at the national and local levels. Those efforts will take time to yield positive results. Technology-based crimes that span jurisdictions pose growing financial and psychological challenges for victims and law enforcement alike. These challenge's notwithstanding, there have been some successes. In early 2018, the U.S. Department of Justice announced it had filed charges against 36 people alleged to be members of an international cyber ring. The ring was said to have begun in 2010, trafficking in stolen financial data involving as many as four million credit cards and related data. Convictions on each charge could bring 30 years' imprisonment. Five Americans had been arrested to date, while international law-enforcement authorities were planning similar actions.

BIBLIOGRAPHY

Bernard, Tara Siegel. "Equifax Says Cyber Attack May Have Affected 143 Million in the US." *The New York Times*, September 7, 2017, p. A7.

Brewster, Thomas. "A Brief History of Equifax Security Fails." *Forbes*, September 8, 2017. https://www.forbes.com/sites/thomasbrewster/2017/09/08/equifax-data-breach-history/. Accessed October 15, 2018.

Chan, Kelvin. "What Caused the Global WannaCry Ransomware Attack?" *Christian Science Monitor*, May 16, 2017. www.csmonitor.com.

Cheng, Dean. *Cyber Dragon: Inside China's Information Warfare and Cyber Operations.* Santa Barbara, CA: Praeger, 2016.

Cheng, Ron. "Cybercrime in China: Online Fraud." *Forbes*, March 28, 2017. www.forbes.com.

Dasgupta, Saibal. "China Trying to Rope India, Russia in Cyber Pact against the West." *Times of India*, March 2, 2017. www.timesofindia.com.

Denning, Dorothy. "How Chinese Hackers Became a Major Threat to the US." *Newsweek*, October 5, 2017. www.newsweek.com.

Dobbs, Fred. "FBI Says Russians Hacked Hundreds of Thousands of Homes and Office Routers." *The Guardian*, May 25, 2018.

Elkind, Peter. "Who Was Managing the Ramparts at Sony Pictures?" *Fortune*, January 25, 2018. www.fortune.com.

Fung, Brian. "Equifax's Massive 2017 Data Breach Keeps Getting Worse." *The Washington Post*, March 1, 2018, p. A. 12.

Hatmaker, Taylor. "DHS and FBI Detail How Russia Is Hacking into US Nuclear Facilities and Other Critical Infrastructure." March 15, 2018. www.techcrunch.com.

Henderson, Lauren. *Tor and the Dark Art of Anonymity.* New York: Random Books, 2015.

Hess, Amanda. "Inside the Sony Hack." *Slate*, November 22, 2015. www.slate.com.

Kaplan, Fred. *Dark Territory: The Secret History of Cyber Warfare*. New York: Simon & Schuster, 2016.

Kennedy, Merritt. "After Massive Data Breach, Equifax Directed Customers to Fake Site." National Public Radio, September 21, 2017.

Krebs, Brian. *Spam Nation: The Inside Story of Organized Cyber Crime from Global Epidemic to Your Front Door*. Naperville, IL: Sourcebooks, 2015.

Nakashima, Ellen, and Philip Rucker. "US Declares North Korea Carried Out Massive 'WannaCry' Cyber Attack." *The Washington Post*, December 19, 2017, p. A1.

Perlroth, Nicole. "Boeing Possibly Hit by 'WannaCry' Malware Attack." *The New York Times*, March 28, 2018, p. A5.

Peterson, Andrea. "The Sony Pictures Hack Explained." *The Washington Post*, December 18, 2014.

Petski, Denise. "*Game of Thrones* HBO Hack: US Officials Charge Iranian National." November 21, 2017. www.deadline.com.

Seal, Mark. "An Exclusive Look at Sony's Hacking Saga." *Vanity Fair*, March 2015. www.vanityfair.com.

Shaffer, Claire. "HBO Hack Is Seven Times Worse than the Sony Hack." *Newsweek*, August 2, 2017. www.newsweek.com.

South China Morning Post. "Chinese Hackers Targeting US Firms' Financial Data, Report Says." April 5, 2018. www.semp.com.

Spangler, Todd. "HBO Hacks and Leaks: How Much Did They Hurt the Business?" *Variety*, August 17, 2017. www.variety.com.

Volz, Dustin. "US Blames North Korea for 'WannaCry' Cyber Attack." December 18, 2017. www.reuters.com.

Weisman, Aly. "A Timeline of the Crazy Events in the Sony Hacking Scandal." *Business Insider*, December 9, 2017. www.businessinsider.com.

Whitaker, Zack. "Equifax Hack Just Got Worse for a Lot More Americans." March 2, 2017. www.zdnet.com.

Zetter, Kim. *Countdown to Zero Day: Stuxnet and the Launch of the World's First Digital Weapon*. New York: Penguin Random House, 2014.

Zetter, Kim. "Everything We Know about How the FBI Hacks People." *Wired*, May 25, 2016.

CHAPTER 3

The Geopolitics of Cyber and Cyber Espionage

Jack Caravelli

For thousands of years, warfare has been a central element in how groups, and then nations, settled disputes and pursued territorial conquest, following the creation of the international system in 1648 by the Treaty of Westphalia. Whether with rocks and sticks, bows and arrows, rifles, or ballistic missiles and nuclear weapons, until recently war has been defined by kinetic, physical attacks designed to inflict damage and destruction. Every day, the headlines remind us that kinetic warfare involving nations and subnational groups remains a prevalent part of geopolitics.

The celebrated strategist Carl von Clausewitz famously wrote that war is a continuation of politics by other means. If the brilliant Prussian were alive today, he would see how his dictum remains relevant but with a twist. The means of advancing political agendas has been augmented in the digital era by another form of warfare, the use of cyber attacks.

Nations continue to compete for political gain at the expense of their rivals. What has changed in the digital era is that they now possess a new tool of political competition, with cyber as the centerpiece. Stuxnet notwithstanding, these new weapons may not be kinetic, but they are designed and intended to inflict extensive damage on an opponent's political, economic, and social systems. They have triggered a new arms race, this time in the digital domain.

In the new digital age, the battle for political advantage can take different forms. Perhaps the most obvious is cyber espionage. Espionage, one of the world's oldest professions, is driven by two objectives. The first is counterintelligence, the protection of a nation's secrets. The second is to pierce the veil of the secrets other nations seek to protect. Those twin objectives are now augmented with cyber tools that can be used to devastating effect.

Cyber tools used in service of the U.S. government have been developed in recent decades with the expenditure of billions of dollars and thousands of trained personnel. Other governments, both friendly—such as those in the United Kingdom and France—and adversarial—China, Russia, North Korea, and Iran—also devote financial and personnel resources to developing and employing a panoply of cyber capabilities. Unlike in the democracies, the governments of China, Russia, North Korea, and Iran operate in environments where the right to privacy for their own citizens has no practical meaning, although, as we will discuss, that concept is becoming increasingly blurred in the West.

By definition, geopolitics involves the actions and interactions of nations, but the geopolitics of cyber begins with a domestic element, reflected in several ways. For authoritarian and repressive nations, the Internet creates new opportunities as a powerful tool to weaken their opponents, but it is also a source of considerable fear within their own regimes. For the likes of Russia's Vladimir Putin, China's Xi Jinping, North Korea's Kim Jong-un, and Iran's Hassan Rouhani and their governments, what they can't control is a source of constant worry, as it implies there may be an alternative to their rule. Implied in that convoluted world view is that their citizens can't be trusted, leading to a series of domestic policies that seek to limit access to and use of the Internet.

For example, in October 2017, Xi Jinping gave a state-of-China speech at the start of a major Communist Party congress in Beijing. In a marathon three-and-a-half-hour speech, Xi covered numerous topics, while taking ample time along the way to bask in copious self-praise. He also took on a number of security topics, placing particular emphasis on domestic control. Promising to strengthen government discipline over Chinese citizens, Xi established a National Security Commission, which will, inter alia, seek to enforce greater control over the Internet, employing censorship to "oppose and resist the whole range of erroneous views."

Under Putin, Russia has also pursued for at least a decade extensive efforts to control domestic use of the Internet and the spread of antigovernment messages. Russia's 2008 invasion of the former Soviet Republic of Georgia was heavy-handed and politically tone-deaf. In the wake of the inevitable, if poorly executed, Russian military victory, a network of domestic Russian social-media users roundly criticized the Kremlin. This not only angered but shook Putin, leading to a more-focused government effort to control Russia's Internet. Russia has no problem using the Internet to provoke dissent in target countries and undermine their political operations, and, perhaps for this reason, it is highly sensitive to the domestic use of cyber by its critics.

For the Kremlin, the most potent domestic threat comes from Alexander Navalny, a young, charismatic political activist who has been challenging Putin and the alleged rampant corruption, documented by various brave journalists, of the president and his cronies, for years. Those charges have resulted in Navalny being sent to Russian jails on several occasions. Navalny appeals to a young generation that is increasingly cognizant that its future opportunities under the Putin regime—which may last at least another six years if he is reelected as expected in 2018—are highly circumscribed in an era where globalization is expanding not only international awareness but through the movement of people career opportunities. Navalny's activities remain closely monitored, and Russia continues to pursue efforts to discredit him. As Vladimir Putin was announcing in December 2017 that he would again run for president of Russia, the Russian election commission was announcing by a 12 to 0 vote that Navalny would be ineligible to run against Putin because of past crimes. That's Russia's version of freedom of speech and another reminder of Putin's fear of open competition, even in a system he dominates.

For years the Kremlin has gone to great lengths to limit Navalny's access to the mass media, and what coverage he gets is almost uniformly negative. He has not protested this, in large measure because he takes a different and highly modern approach. Navalny has bypassed traditional Russian media outlets, instead using the Internet to create a large political network that reaches 80 Russian cities, supported by 160,000 volunteers. He promises to use these to rally support for the government's refusal to allow him to compete for the presidency.

At the same time, albeit in far different ways, domestic issues involving the Internet have bedeviled Western governments as well. Article four of the U.S. Constitution, for example, protects Americans from unreasonable searches and seizures, but the Founding Fathers could never have imagined that the U.S. government would conduct mass surveillance of its citizens in the name of national security. To a large extent, it was Edward Joseph Snowden's revelations that the right to privacy of Americans was being violated systematically that brought this issue to national consciousness. Snowden maintained his espionage activities and subsequent mass disclosures regarding the U.S. government's surveillance programs were justified because of these "violations." Snowden was a CIA employee and subsequently Booz Allen contractor working for the National Security Agency. No person or event more powerfully represents the nearly incalculable domestic damage to national security than his 2013 revelations to London's Guardian newspaper.

Snowden was not a particularly strong student but, from an early age, had a passion for government service that seemed to match his conservative politics. He kept a copy of the U.S. Constitution at his workplace.

Snowden claimed to have wanted to fight in the Iraq war and volunteered to serve in the U.S. military. He also later claimed a training accident at Fort Benning, Georgia, left him with two broken legs, taking away his chances for a military career. A more accurate and rather less dramatic rendering of that event that federal investigators later uncovered was that Snowden suffered from shin splints.

When his military career plans were shelved, Snowden continued to seek government employment, beginning a career as a security guard at a secret NSA facility in Maryland. He proved to have exceptional computer skills and later rose to a position of trust with extraordinary access to highly guarded secrets as an NSA contract employee on Oahu, Hawaii. Snowden had a $200,000 annual salary; was living with Lindsay Mills, a loving girlfriend; and, by his own admission, enjoyed a privileged life in one of the most beautiful places on earth.

Material comforts and challenging work in Hawaii didn't compensate for what Snowden claimed was the violation of Americans' right to privacy. Some years earlier, while serving in Geneva for the CIA, he became disillusioned with the U.S. government's sometimes crass methods of compromising foreign nationals and developing them as sources of sensitive information. Those issues had nothing to do with privacy questions for Americans. Whatever his true motivation, Snowden took the job in Hawaii as a "sys admin" because it granted him almost complete access to NSA's most important secrets. In that job, Snowden could access countless NSA files without leaving a trace of his activities, becoming what NSA insiders call a "ghost writer."

From that position in Hawaii, Snowden took it upon himself to expose the secrets of massive and highly sensitive government programs designed to collect vast amounts of data. A sizable portion of that data was collected from the conversations of millions of Americans. Under a program called Prism, Snowden described to *Guardian* reporter Glenn Greenwald and documentary filmmaker Laura Poitras a U.S. court order to Verizon mandating the company provide U.S. telephone records to the NSA on an ongoing basis.

Snowden also documented how the National Security Agency tapped into the internal operations of nine Internet providers, including Google, Yahoo, Microsoft, Apple, and Facebook. Through the "Dishfire" program, some 200 million text messages were intercepted annually.

While NSA was collecting enormous amounts of information from Americans, often illegally, in Snowden's telling, it also was committing resources to nothing less than a global surveillance campaign against U.S. foes and friends alike. Through Snowden's revelations, it was learned that collection operations were conducted against officials in Italy, France, and Germany; European Union offices in Washington, New York, and Brussels; 35 world leaders, including German Chancellor Angela Merkel, and 38 embassies. This wasn't exactly a shining example of how friends treat friends.

At the same time, the British counterpart to NSA, the Government Communications Headquarters (GCHQ), had been conducting its own aggressive surveillance programs according to Snowden. On a daily basis, for example, GCHQ was accessing 600 million telephone conversations through "Tempora," a program that tapped into long-distance fiber optic cables. Much of the GCHQ collection was shared with NSA, part of the "Five Eyes" program of data sharing that also involved the Canadian, Australian, and New Zealand intelligence services.

The scope and nature of Snowden's revelations raised profound questions about the right of privacy in the digital era and whether there could be any longer an expectation of privacy in America. As noted, Snowden claimed to be acting on principle in exposing NSA and GCHQ activities. At the same time, as Snowden knew, he was also breaking espionage and data-protection laws that carried severe penalties because they put numerous U.S. government secrets, interests, and possibly human sources at risk.

While claiming to be willing to face his U.S. government accusers, Snowden first fled to Hong Kong, where he met Greenwald, Poitras, and a senior *Guardian* editor. He convinced them of his bona fides, leading to a series of explosive articles written by Grunewald, the editor accompanying Greenwald, followed by a book written by Greenwald. Snowden didn't remain in Hong Kong long, as he was paranoid about the possibility of capture by a CIA team. That paranoia turned out to be misplaced. Ironically, rather than being an all-powerful international espionage force, the occasionally notorious, Langley-based U.S. government agency was by most post-mortem accounts slow to realize what Snowden was doing or where he had holed up once he left Hawaii.

Nonetheless, Snowden fled to Russia on June 23, 2013; after some inevitable bureaucratic delays, which are also a staple of the Russian government, he was granted extended stay in the country, where he can remain until at least 2020. The irony, of course, is that Russia is among the world's worst nations at protecting the privacy rights of its citizens, the issue Snowden claimed was of greatest concern to him.

Relations between the United States and Russia had entered a period of increasing confrontation and polarization, resulting, in part, from the personal animosity between President Barack Obama and his Russian counterpart, Vladimir Putin. It should be assumed that Putin took unbridled pleasure in Snowden's arrival in Russia and the attendant public relations debacle for the U.S. government from Snowden's theft of so many important secrets and Snowden's subsequent escape from the United States. Adding fuel to this fire, while Snowden claimed to have never provided the Russians with any sensitive material, the deputy chief of the

Russian parliamentary committee on defense and security in June 2016 claimed, "Snowden did share intelligence."

In September 2016, after a two-year investigation, the U.S. House Permanent Select Committee on Intelligence (HPSCI) issued a damage assessment of Snowden's activities. The report said he had stolen 1.5 million classified documents and may have used thumb drives to remove them from NSA. The HPSCI report concluded that Snowden's actions caused irreparable damage to U.S. interests, including compromising ongoing intelligence collection operations and endangering the lives of U.S. troops. Those revelations again confirmed that Snowden's actions had little, if anything, to do with the privacy issues he claimed to have been protecting.

The scope of the damage inflicted by Snowden places him high in the pantheon of notorious individuals who have betrayed secrets entrusted to them by the U.S. government, including Aldrich Ames from the CIA and Robert Hanssen from the FBI.

Nonetheless, albeit perversely, Snowden can take some sense of accomplishment in opening the debate over the extent to which government can carry out surveillance operations against its citizens. The British have changed the laws that govern these activities. In late 2017, the U.S. Congress was debating and, in early 2018, approved extension of Section 702 of the Foreign Intelligence Surveillance Act originally set in place in 2008. Two U.S. senators, Ron Wyden and Rand Paul, were at least raising questions about the sweeping nature of the legislation. The section's raison d'etre is the collection of "foreign intelligence information." In practice, the innocent communications of millions of Americans has also been swept up under Section 702, as the government seeks ways to interdict future terrorist attacks. Nonetheless, there is scant evidence that large numbers of Americans have much interest in information their government is able to collect and access about their private lives. In the early part of the 21st century, the long-cherished right to privacy is largely in tatters in the name of collective security.

Others beyond Snowden with access to cyber secrets also did extensive harm. Harold T. Martin III, another NSA contractor working for Booz Allen, played a prominent role. Martin was arrested in August 2016 and charged in a 20-count federal indictment in early 2017 of "willful retention of national defense information." Each count carries a maximum penalty of 10 years in prison.

According to the indictment, for years, Martin carried out a deliberate effort to remove documents from his workplace at NSA headquarters in Fort Meade, Maryland and store them in his home. He was reported to have improperly removed information on NSA, CIA, and Cyber Command cyber-intrusion techniques, enemy targets, and counterterror operations. Less clear is whether Martin ever intended to distribute any of this material to outside individuals or parties. In the Snowden case, the deep wounds he inflicted on U.S. national-security interests were the result of harboring grievances, real or imagined, against the government and some of its most important tools for carrying out surveillance against U.S. enemies.

At the same time, there is a growing volume of evidence of how other nations are using cyber in espionage activities against the West to further political goals, centered on the primary objective of undermining U.S. national-security interests. One of the most serious surfaced in late 2017 when Lee Cheol-hee, a South Korean lawmaker, claimed North Korean hackers had, according to the *Washington Post*, "stole a huge trove of classified U.S. and South Korean military documents ... including a plan to decapitate or eliminate the leadership in Pyongyang in the event of a war."

The war against North Korea never officially ended; there is in place only a 1953 armistice that ceased hostilities. In the ensuing decades, North Korea has maintained a hostile and frequently provocative posture against the United States and its South Korean ally. Through 2017, tensions between North Korea and the United States and South Korea reached the boiling point in the wake of a series of nuclear and missile tests from North Korea, accompanied by various threats and insults hurled by North Korean leader Kim Jung Un and President Donald Trump at the other.

Lee said his information became available from the South Korean Defense Ministry through Freedom of Information requests. In all, some 235 gigabytes of military data were acquired by North Korea. The *Post* report added that Lee claimed among the stolen documents were OPLAN 5015, addressing allied plans for conducting a full-scale war against the DPRK, which included the decapitation plans, and OPLAN 3100 for responding to attacks by North Korean commandos. A spokesman for the U.S. Department of Defense would not comment on the validity of those reports, but stories had been circulating for months that the South Korean military had been victimized by a series of cyber attacks.

Adding credibility to the claims of North Korean hacking is the extensive resources the DPRK has devoted to carrying out such operations. Its spy agency, the Reconnaissance General Bureau, has been linked to numerous cyber operations, including myriad attacks on South Korean financial institutions.

As the Western media was unveiling North Korean cyber espionage activities, a separate late-2017 report revealed Russia was carrying out another in a series of hacking attacks to illicitly acquire U.S. secrets. Israeli intelligence officials informed their U.S. counterparts that Russian hackers had been searching globally for codenames of American intelligence programs. The Israelis knew this because they had been accessing computer networks since 2014 using antivirus software made by the Russian software company Kaspersky Lab.

According to a *New York Times* story, the Russian operation succeeded in accessing information, including classified documents, from a National Security Agency employee working in an elite part of NSA known as the Tailored Access Operations Division who had improperly stored documents at his home on a computer using Kaspersky software. By all reports, that act was foolhardy, reckless, and illegal but was never intended to be a way to provide information to a foreign power. Even if true, that would be of small comfort to NSA.

As a Russian company whose founder, Eugene Kaspersky, had worked early in his career for the Russian Ministry of Defense and had detailed knowledge of Russian cyber capabilities, questions were inevitably raised about his and his company's complicity in the hacking. At the very least, alarm bells should have sounded from the outset when it was understood that the firm's antivirus data routed through the Russian Internet. Kaspersky denied any suggestions of impropriety, saying it had never helped any government with its cyber espionage operations.

That did not satisfy officials at the U.S. Department of Homeland Security (DHS). Numerous departments of the U.S. government, including the Departments of State, Defense, Justice, Energy, and Treasury and the army, air force, and Navy had used Kaspersky software for years. A DHS directive on September 13, 2017 ordered that Kaspersky software was to be removed from all government computers within 90 days.

None of this should have surprised observers of Russia's use of the Internet to further its political interests. The 1991 collapse of the Soviet Union resulted in the steep decline of what transformed from the Soviet to the Russian military. In ensuing years, the Soviet political collapse also became a financial collapse, and, for years, the military was starved for financial support. Within Russia, both senior political and military officials saw Russia as prostrate and vulnerable at the feet of the victorious West. Sensing danger, Russian military commanders concluded that the relatively low costs of conducting information warfare such as disinformation—a long-time staple of Soviet-era intelligence operations— was a way to compensate for some of the shortcomings in other areas of combat capabilities.

That approach would bear fruit. In 1998, the Federal Bureau of Investigation uncovered Operation Moonlight Maze in response to a series of attempts to break into computers containing sensitive information on U.S. Air Force technologies at Wright Paterson Air Force Base in Akron, Ohio, an important research and development center. Attacks were also carried out at two of America's most important nuclear weapons facilities at Sandia National Laboratory and Los Alamos National Laboratory, both in New Mexico.

Over time, the FBI confirmed that four Internet addresses listed in Russia were involved in the attacks and that similar attacks had been carried out against targets in the United Kingdom, Canada, and Germany. In the German case, the hacking was similar to the computer thefts in the 1980s by Markus Hess, a German national who sold secrets to the Soviet Union.

Not long thereafter, Russia began expanding its hacking operations in ways that even more directly promoted its political objectives. In 2007, Russia began carrying out government-sponsored attacks against selected Western nations, including Estonia, Latvia, Georgia, Finland, and Poland. For example, in May of that year, Russian hackers launched cyber attacks against the Estonian government and financial institutions in retaliation for Estonia's decision to remove a Russian World War II memorial from a town square.

A year later, in June 2008, and in retaliation for similar "crimes," the Lithuanian government's official website was defaced, and the Russian symbol of the hammer and sickle was inserted on the webpage.

Ukraine was a much more substantial target. In 2014, the same year that Russia carried out a forced and illegal annexation of Crimea, a Russian hacktivist group known as CyberBerkut sought to interfere in Ukraine's presidential election. A cyber attack was launched that delayed the vote count, while the names and faces of ultranationalist candidates, shown as winning, were inserted into government websites. In addition, the West, especially the United States, was portrayed as fascists determined to start a war and kill Russian supporters in the eastern Ukraine areas of Donetsk and Luhansk.

These activities did not tilt the election. Nonetheless, CyberBerkut remains active; in 2017 it sought to link Ukrainian payments to Hillary Clinton's presidential campaign and Clinton Foundation. The good news is that in Ukraine, StopFake.org works to uncover fake news designed to support the Russian narrative and undermine the Ukrainian government.

None of this came as a surprise to astute observers such as Michael McFaul, a former U.S. ambassador to Russia. Speaking at a 2015 conference, McFaul noted for years that the Kremlin has looked for ways to disrupt democracies, to help people the Russians like come to power, and to undermine the credibility of the democratic process.

There is no reasonable doubt that those and subsequent Russian attacks against more formidable targets including the United States and Germany can be traced to official approval and direction. The GRU, the Russian military intelligence organization, and the FSB, the successor to the notorious KGB, maintain a dedicated cadre of cyber experts. Moreover, the foreign intelligence service, the SVR, closely monitors Western media and bloggers for insights that can be used or distorted to serve Russian political goals. Their activities during the 2016 U.S. presidential election would receive intense scrutiny from their U.S. counterparts, the media, and general public.

Russian hacking activities, aided by similar cyber attacks carried out within other parts of the Russian government, reflect a commitment to

---

Box 3.1 Serving Russian Political Goals in a Military Context: The Gerasimov Doctrine of Nonlinear War

The Russian view of competition with the West and the role of cyber in it were clearly expressed in a 2013 interview given by Valery Gerasimov, chief of the Russian general staff. In what has become known as the Gerasimov Doctrine, the general said that the lines between war and peace had become blurred and that covert tactics like cyber warfare were becoming increasingly important for military success. Noting the rules of war have changed, Gerasimov said the nonmilitary means of achieving political and strategic goals have grown and in many cases they have exceeded the force of weapons in their effectiveness. He termed this nonlinear war. In the West, this is referred to as information warfare, which cuts across political and financial lines as well as military. Russian political authorities are following much of Gerasimov's script.

The importance the Russian military attaches to cyber warfare was reflected in the February 2017 announcement by Russian defense minister, Sergei Shoigu, that the Russian military was creating a new, 1,000-personnel cyber warfare unit, to be known as *kibervoyska*. The unit will augment existing capabilities and will be tasked with adding to the effectiveness of Russian cyber warfare operations.

While Russia is highly aggressive in using cyber warfare against its neighbors, that has not always brought about desired results. The illegal 2014 annexation of Crimea was a stunning defeat for the Ukrainian government and those living in Crimea, as well as a largely napping West. The late 2015 attack on the Ukrainian power grid, for example, was a serious blow to a large part of western Ukraine. Nonetheless, while that was an impressive show of Russian capabilities, in retrospect, it also seems as much as an act of pique as intimidation. Putin wanted much more; Kremlin plans supported creating a Russian-speaking state in the east, which was to be called Novorossiya. That plan never materialized, in part, because of resistance by Ukrainian army and, in part, because of Western sanctions on Russia. Cyber warfare can be used to great effect, but, in the service of broader political goals, it is not always decisive. In addition, Russia evinces little understanding of the political costs and resentment arising from such attacks against civilian interests in Ukraine and other nations.

---

undermining U.S. financial and military interests. In late 2016, a joint U.S. Department of Homeland Security and FBI report titled, "Grizzly Steppe: Russian Malware Cyber Activity," singled out the Russian organizations that had been directly implicated in cyber attacks against critical infrastructure in the United States.

Before embarking on how Russia has worked to influence elections in the United States and other Western nations through the use of information warfare, understanding the overarching Russian motivations behind these activities speaks volumes about the importance the Kremlin attaches to competition with the West. One of the clearest expressions of this came in 1999 when Vladimir Putin, just emerging on a national stage with the blessing of President Boris Yeltsin, published a report, "Russia at the Turn of the Millennium." In it, Putin laid out nothing less than a national blueprint, his vision of how Russia was to re-emerge as a global superpower in the early decades of the 21st century. The report in fundamental respects is a historical successor to past Russian world views that see international relations, especially with the West, through a zero-sum prism. As reflected in the report, for Putin, all forms of competition were seen as contributing to an ascendant Russia, including the use of an old Soviet tactic, information warfare.

While this sheds light on Putin's aggressive thinking and world view, a series of global events revealed, in Putin's eyes, Russia's and his personal political vulnerability. Historically, Russia has long harbored the view that the "near abroad," those nations on Russia's periphery, should fall within its sphere of influence. The 1917 (and subsequent) formation of the Soviet Union reflected this attitude. After the Soviet Union's 1991 collapse, nations like Georgia and Ukraine, often harboring deep resentments at years of forced political subservience, moved into independent orbits.

In the post-Soviet era, what became known in those nations as the "Color Revolutions," with strongly democratic leanings, showed the depths of resentment of the Kremlin and Russian rule. For Putin, this was a possible harbinger of political turmoil that could come to Russia and threaten his regime. He was not prepared to sit idly by. It almost certainly is not coincidental that Russia used military force (including cyber attacks) against Georgia and annexed Crimea, part of Ukraine, in response to those fears.

There were other signs of trouble elsewhere for autocratic rulers. As we have seen, what would become known as the Arab Spring swept from power such long-entrenched strongmen as Egypt's Hosni Mubarak and Russia's ally in Libya, Muamar Qaddafi.

Similarly, in late 2017 to early 2018, the Iranian government was stunned by a series of nationwide demonstrations that focused first on the nation's economic stagnation before expanding more broadly to questions of governmental corruption and malfeasance. Major cities, including Tehran and the holy city of Qom, saw street demonstrations where scores of mostly young people shouted "Death to the dictator" and other antigovernment slogans. Iranian President Hassan Rouhani went on television to acknowledge the right of Iranians to demonstrate, but security authorities were taking no chances. Fearing the power of the Internet, Iranian authorities began closing down or blocking Instagram and the messaging app Telegram that many Iranians used.

Events in the Middle East fed the narrative of Russian leaders, including Putin and his prime minister, Dmitry Medvedev, that the Internet was somehow under the control of the CIA for the purpose of undermining or destabilizing Russia and other American enemies. Medvedev claimed that "they [the CIA] have been preparing such a scenario for us and now they will try even harder to implement it." Perhaps it was impossible for Medvedev, Putin, and their ilk to conjure, let alone admit, that they, and not outside powers, were responsible for their nations' problems.

For Putin, with or without CIA involvement, the power of "the streets" would soon find its way to Moscow. In 2011, a massive, 100,000-strong demonstration protesting Kremlin rule and alleged corruption garnered international headlines. Long suspicious that U.S. political and financial power had supported unrest in parts of the former USSR and Middle East, Putin turned his anger away from the CIA (at least temporarily) and toward U.S. Secretary of State Hillary Clinton for what he believed was her hidden hand backing of these movements, including the Moscow demonstration.

Putin's fears were largely misplaced; along with President Barack Obama, Clinton, beyond signaling a preference for Mubarak's ouster, possessed neither the vision nor financial support for political activities in the Middle East or Russia. Similarly, the CIA under its director John Brennan, former assistant to President Obama, would never have undertaken a major covert action without White House and congressional approval. Moreover, the ever-timid Obama administration, in refusing to support the 2009 political unrest in Tehran (the Green Revolution), had shown that it was not prepared to push for political change in those nations, let alone Russia, with whom it had differences.

Nonetheless, the 2016 U.S. presidential election, in which Hillary Clinton was the nominee of the Democratic Party, provided an irresistible opportunity for Putin to seek revenge. Adding to Putin's interest in seeing Clinton defeated was the belief that Donald Trump, who had stated an interest in working with Russia if elected, might be more amenable to Russian interests in the Middle East and on financial issues, including financial sanctions imposed during the Obama administration. One result of what would become a massive Russian attempt to influence the 2016 presidential election was that the integrity of the most fundamental of Western democratic processes, the election of its leaders, was about to become a centerpiece of debate in the geopolitics of cyber.

The November 2016 election of Donald Trump to the presidency was viewed in many quarters as a stunning development. His rival, Hillary Clinton, was far more experienced politically, had been tested in political campaigns, and had spent years raising hundreds of millions of dollars to fund her and the Democratic Party's political goals. As Bill Clinton's wife, she also had daily access to arguably the most astute politician of their generation.

In the month before the November election, Barack Obama, in a public statement, commented that it was virtually impossible for outside hacking or tampering to impact the national election. Despite this outward confidence, senior Obama administration officials, including those at the National Security Council, were aware of a growing body of evidence that Russia was indeed endeavoring to influence the election. Some NSC senior staff wanted a strong response or at least warning sent to Russia. However, national security adviser Susan Rice, whose bald-faced lies about the attacks and murders of U.S. personnel in Libya, including Ambassador Chris Stevens, had soiled her reputation, spiked any plans for a strong U.S. response. Rice ordered a "stand down" of plans to expose Russian activities, perhaps in the belief that Hillary Clinton would emerge victorious and there was no need to undermine her looming victory.

Events didn't quite unfold the way Rice or Clinton imagined. In the wake of the 2016 election results, myriad pundits sought to unravel the reasons behind Hillary Clinton's defeat. Many came to realize that Clinton had waged a mediocre campaign, often ignoring her husband's advice and failing to offer a clear vision of America's future that would appeal to voters. She lacked her husband's almost transcendent political gifts, as reflected in her failed outreach to middle class workers and young women voters. In a state as critical as Wisconsin for its electoral votes, she never spent a day campaigning there; it is no coincidence that Trump won the popular vote there.

At the same time, for all his coarseness and inability to grasp that presidential candidates might consider appealing to the best rather than the basest of American values, Trump was able to tap into the angst and frustrations of millions of mostly middle-class Americans who felt their government had lost touch with them and their interests.

That combination of factors under most conditions would amply explain the outcome and Trump phenomenon, but 2016 was not a usual political year. Almost from the first days following the election, stories began to circulate that another force had been instrumental in Trump's victory. During different stages of the campaign, a series of damaging "leaked" material emerged about Clinton's campaign, as well as the internal operations of the Democratic National Committee and related organization seeking to elect candidates to seats in the U.S. House of Representatives.

In September 2015, FBI special agent Adrian Hawkins contacted the Democratic National Committee (DNC) with the unsettling news that there may have been a massive breach of the organization's computer network. Hawkins believed this activity was tied to "the Dukes," a computer group with ties to the Russian government that the FBI had been tracking for at least two years and believed was the source of attacks on unclassified computer files belonging to the State Department and the Joint Chiefs of Staff of the Department of Defense.

The DNC files were ripe to be compromised. The DNC is a nonprofit organization and had not devoted sufficient resources to installing sophisticated and state of the art defenses against cyber attacks. There were personnel problems there as well. Then Democratic National Chairwoman Debbie Wasserman Schultz was widely viewed as a win-at-any-cost politician, bereft of a basic understanding in the digital age of the imperative of protecting her organization's internal communications and plans. Maybe that was too much to ask, but she also never asked others in her organization to take on those issues.

After Hawkins alerted the DNC, a comic but ultimately tragic series of events created one of the largest political scandals in U.S. political history. Hawkins was referred to a help desk, where a part-time employee from Chicago, Yared Tamene, suspected Hawkins was a prank caller. By all accounts, Tamene never took the obvious step of trying to authenticate Hawkins' bona fides. Instead, the young and inexperienced employee made a cursory check of the DNC files and concluded that there was nothing amiss. Tamene never asked for more skilled help in reaching his judgment. The combination of laziness and lack of computer savvy was one of the myriad reasons the hacking operation was able to continue unimpeded for seven months.

It did not help that Hawkins didn't visit the DNC during this period but rather tried to use a series of phone calls to arouse DNC officials to the lurking dangers. As a result, there were missed signals and missed opportunities to avert disaster. The result was a major crisis for the Democratic Party as it was planning to support Clinton's campaign, which fully expected to win the presidency. Some of the revelations produced from the stolen e-mails of campaign director John Podesta and other campaign officials included:

- Three days before the start of the DNC convention, the organization WikiLeaks, possibly working in conjunction with those who had illicitly accumulated the DNC files, released over 44,000 e-mails. Those included compelling evidence that then National Committee chairperson, Debbie Wasserman Schultz, supposedly a neutral arbiter between the candidates during the primary season, had, in fact, tilted the DNC heavily toward Clinton. This was confirmed by Donna Brazile who followed the disgraced Wasserman Schultz as DNC chair. According to Brazile's book, *Hacks: The Inside Story of the Break-ins and Breakdowns That Put Donald Trump in the White House*, in exchange for relieving DNC debt, the Clinton campaign would take over the de facto running of the DNC, including its media strategy and personnel decisions. The result was that Senator Bernie Sanders never had a chance to secure the party nomination. Brazile described Clinton's actions as "unethical." It was another confirmation of Clinton's willingness to pursue victory at all costs.

- DNC campaign strategy and budget information were released, a blueprint to guide and a treasure trove for the Trump campaign.
- In an e-mail to a friend, John Podesta wrote (and reaffirmed our view) that Clinton "had terrible political instincts."
- Perhaps inadvertently confirming Podesta's assessment regarding her lack of political skills, Clinton said she planned to "plant the seed of revolution" against the Middle Age practices of the Catholic Church, even though Catholics constitute a major voting bloc while John Kennedy, America's only Catholic president, was a member of the Democratic Party.
- Clinton admitted to taking different public and private positions on various issues, adding to voter skepticism about her honesty and credibility.

These revelations, and many more like them, were not only major embarrassments for the Democratic Party and Clinton campaign, they also caused a great deal of internal disruption including badly damaging campaign-staff morale. In her book, Brazile says she was deeply troubled by what she claims were Russian efforts to destroy voter data stored at the DNC. The DNC denied this occurred, adding to the uncertainties in assessing the scope of the cyber attacks.

At the same time, a handful of Democratic Party candidates in races for seats in the U.S. House of Representatives came under hacking attacks. Thousands of pages of documents from the Democratic House Congressional Committee, located in the same Washington, D.C. building as the DNC, had also been stolen. The hacking probably began in March or April 2016 but was not discovered until August.

Once the Russian hackers acquired that information, they used social media to contact journalists and bloggers. The material provided information on internal party strategy for elections around the country. The Russian hacker group known as Guccifer 2.0 also revealed the DNC's assessments of its own candidates in New York, Pennsylvania, Ohio, Illinois, Florida, North Carolina, and New Mexico. For example, one Florida candidate was assessed as being a poor campaigner and also weak at fundraising, an assessment that undermined her losing campaign.

The Russian hacking operations had both witting and unwitting accomplices. The hacking began as a simple attempt to gather information. The Russians almost certainly provided the information they acquired to Julian Assange. Living in exile at the Ecuadorian embassy in London, Assange has denied that the Russians were the source of the voluminous information his organization, WikiLeaks, released. Widely reviled over the years for leaking even more sensitive and, at times, classified U.S. information, WikiLeaks's track record of accuracy was undeniable. Other websites such as DCLeaks.com also received and disseminated material.

In turn, the websites publishing the leaked information became sources for major media organizations such as the *Washington Post* and *New York Times* as well as foreign media outlets. Many did a poor job of thoroughly and independently checking the information and its sourcing, an increasingly common failing of some. In essence, they became "useful idiots," as the Russians liked to use the term in spreading the stolen e-mails.

The contentious and at times toxic presidential election did not end when the votes were tabulated. Months of leaked and highly embarrassing information led to inevitable charges from Clinton and other members of her party that the leaks had tilted the campaign in Trump's favor. The Niagara of leaks were augmented, especially near the end of the campaign, by the continuing drama and commentary from FBI Director James Comey surrounding Clinton's reckless handling of highly classified information, which, while serving as secretary of state, she stored on an unsecured server.

Doing so was an egregious violation of the most fundamental of security requirements, and a handful of nations were judged to have accessed sensitive and classified U.S. government information surreptitiously. Almost any other U.S. citizen acting so recklessly would have been in severe legal jeopardy. Notwithstanding Comey's decision to exonerate Clinton from prosecution in the face of overwhelming evidence to the contrary, his remarks about her added fuel to an already incendiary campaign. It is unlikely to have galvanized the attention of many voters and, therefore, probably was not a decisive factor in the outcome of the election. Clinton's supporters seemed willing to forgive almost any political or legal sin; Trump's supporters would never have considered voting for her anyway. The 2016 election had enormous amounts of vitriol.

Because of the complex crosscurrents of so many issues, it is impossible to answer with certainty what factors most influenced voters when they closed the curtain and cast their votes for president. Was it dislike of Clinton? Was it her poor campaign strategy? Was it the appeal of Trump's promise to "drain the swamp" and remake a dysfunctional government? Was it the accumulated weight of the embarrassing leaks? These factors were doubtless important, but apportioning weight to each is a risky and unproductive endeavor.

Adding to this uncertainty were remarks provided in early 2018 by Jeanette Manfra, who, at the time of the 2016 election, was head of cyber security at DHS. She claims that an entity, almost certainly Russian, targeted the voting machines in at least 21 states, including Maryland, Pennsylvania, Virginia, Alabama, and Ohio. Presumably the attempt, assuming she was correct, was to learn more about voters in those states. Only officials in one state, Colorado, concluded that their voter rolls had been penetrated. Nor is there any evidence that the actual votes in any state were somehow manipulated. That may be good news, but it also underscores the importance of election officials taking all available measures to mitigate and, if possible, eliminate ways in which future elections may be hacked. Federal–state cooperation on these issues seems self-evident, although some states were described as skeptical of federal involvement in securing future election results.

We conclude that while it is undeniable that the flood of leaked information severely embarrassed and undermined the Clinton campaign, in the end, it probably was not the decisive factor in those who went to the polls and voted to elect Donald Trump.

The U.S. intelligence community also had a pointed view of Russian involvement in hacking during the presidential election. Notwithstanding Putin's repeated denials, something at which he has long excelled in defending Russian interests on various issues, the Department of Homeland Security and director of national intelligence issued a joint and tersely worded statement shortly before the election that concluded that they were "confident" that the Russian government was the source of the hacked information.

The report did not name Putin directly, but it left little doubt that the intelligence community believed that the most senior members of the Russian government had approved the attacks. That was only the second time the United States had singled out a foreign government as being involved in a cyber attack, the first being North Korea's cyber attack on Sony Corporation.

A far wider ranging and incendiary report from the entire U.S. intelligence community was prepared at Barack Obama's direction and shared with Donald Trump in his New York City office in early January 2017, shortly before he took office. Titled "Intelligence Community Assessment on Russian Activities and Intentions in Recent U.S. Elections," the lengthy 14-page public report, said to be consistent with a highly classified version, did not comment on the hacking's effect on the election but drew the following conclusions:

- We assess Russian President Vladimir Putin ordered an influence campaign in 2016 aimed at the U.S. presidential election.
- Russia's goals were to undermine public faith in the U.S. democratic process.
- We also assess Putin and the Russian government aspired to help President-elect Trump's election chances when possible by discrediting Secretary Clinton and publicly contrasting her unfavorably with him.
- We assess with high confidence that Russian military intelligence…relayed material to WikiLeaks.

- We assess Moscow will apply lessons learned from its Putin ordered campaign aimed at the U.S. presidential election to future influence efforts worldwide, including against U.S. allies and their election processes.
- Moscow most likely chose WikiLeaks because of its self-proclaimed reputation for authenticity.

The report also suggests that beyond Putin's personal assessment of Clinton and Trump and whose victory would best serve Russian interests, the Kremlin may have sought revenge for what it felt was U.S. targeting of Russian interests through embarrassing leaks such as the Panama papers that showed how wealthy individuals close to the Russian government may have sheltered their fortunes and the revelations of massive doping infractions among Russian Olympic athletes. Russian officials could not bring themselves to acknowledge the truth of those allegations, such as the International Anti-Doping Agency report on elaborate Russian efforts to falsify the results of urine tests from Russian Olympic athletes.

Russian cyber attacks were aided by the near total failure of the FBI to alert Americans, mostly former and current senior government officials, that their e-mail accounts were being accessed. An Associated Press (AP) report in late 2017 claims only two American officials, out of nearly 500 known by the FBI and targeted by the Russian hacking group Fancy Bear, were contacted and told of the attacks. That abject failure was attributed by some to a lack of resources at the FBI to cope with the panoply and persistence of the attacks. Ironically, within several months the AP was able to dedicate enough reporters to contact 190 names on the list.

Questions about the influence of the hacking operations also took on other dimensions. The most complex and important centered on whether members of the Trump campaign, or even Trump himself, somehow colluded with the Russians to influence the campaign's outcome. Former FBI Director Robert Mueller, who admitted he had leaked information related to Donald Trump and Mueller's firing as FBI director to a friend for wider distribution, was appointed as special prosecutor to investigate those allegations. By early 2018, Mueller had found no evidence of collusion between the Trump campaign and Russian officials. Collusion is not a crime under U.S. law.

At the same time, U.S. investigators were becoming even more convinced that those who hacked the DNC and Clinton's campaign e-mails were working on behest of the Russian government. Consistent with the earlier intelligence community reports, federal investigators have concluded that as many as five or six of the hackers worked directly for the GRU, Russia's military intelligence agency, and may have begun their efforts by early 2016. The work on the GRU link was carried out by FBI agents in Pittsburgh and Houston, while agents in Washington D.C. have been investigating private-sector analysts, known as APT29, linked to the SVR, Russia's foreign intelligence service. Assuming the accuracy of the FBI's findings, they represent another hole in Putin's attempt to build a firewall between his government and the hacking operations. If we look closely enough, we can discern a Russian government that, much like its Soviet predecessors, valued and cultivated opacity surrounded by patent falsehoods in many of its dealings with the outside world.

During his final weeks in office, President Obama wrestled with how to respond to Russia's cyber attacks against the United States. His presidency was not marked by many decisive foreign policy actions, but he summoned the resolve to take a series of steps against Russia's hacking operations. Saying that "all Americans should be alarmed by Russia's actions" and that "the United States and its friends and allies around the world must work together" in a major press conference on December 29, 2016, Obama announced a series of retaliatory actions.

The most dramatic was the expulsion of 35 suspected Russian operatives who were in working in the United States and their families. (The Russian government later retaliated similarly against U.S. personnel working in Russia.) Obama also imposed sanctions on the two Russian intelligence organizations, the GRU and FSB, linked to the hacking, a largely symbolic gesture. He penalized two Russians for alleged theft of more than $100 million from financial institutions. Finally, in what felt like something from a Cold War spy novel, he closed two Russian compounds outside the Washington, DC, area, one in Upper Brookville, New York and the other on Maryland's Eastern Shore.

Putin retaliated later by expelling 755 U.S. embassy workers from Russia. As a result, the U.S. embassy was forced to hire a Russian firm, Elite Security Holdings, linked to Viktor Budanov, a former senior KGB officer and head of counterintelligence as embassy security guards. That arrangement was formalized in a no-bid $2.8 million contract to provide security for the U.S. embassy in Moscow as well as U.S. consulates in St. Petersburg, Vladivostok, and Yekaterinburg. The embassy issued a statement maintaining that the hiring would not compromise U.S. security. A Russian commentator took a different perspective, saying that Russia would never have any U.S. firm that was tied to the CIA involved in any security operations around the Russian embassy in Washington. As one U.S. congressman stated in a different context, "You can't stop stupidity."

Albeit often overlooked, Russia's attempts to undermine and weaken the United States are not limited to its extensive cyber activities against the executive branch. The integrity of the judicial branch and its widely held perception for fairness and equal justice under the law also appears to be in the Kremlin's crosshairs. Putin has threatened to sue in U.S. courts for

Box 3.2 Harnessing the Power of Social Media

Exploitation of social media has been a critical element in the use of the Internet for various political objectives. One of the most dramatic examples occurred in Egypt during the Arab spring, which toppled dictators across the region. Egyptian President Hosni Mubarak had been at the center of his country's political life, ruling with virtually unchallenged power for 30 years. In doing so, he made many enemies, making him vulnerable to the years of pent-up frustration and anger among the middle and lower classes of Egyptian society. Years of grievances about police brutality, rigged elections and other forms of corruption, poor economic and educational prospects for the young, and lack of free speech coalesced to erode the government's credibility.

In 2011, the Egyptian government knew of the public's growing discontent and began another in a series of crackdowns as a means to stymie dissent. In the past, mass arrests and general intimidation may have worked in these circumstances. What the authorities didn't count on, never understood, and were powerless to counter were the massive demonstrations, often led by young Egyptians, staged in protest of Mubarak's rule. Protests raged across the nation but were centered on Cairo's Tahrir Square, where, on January 25, 2011, 50,000 protesters gathered in what sparked a series of events that pushed Mubarak from power. Much of this was accomplished through social media, enabling Mubarak's opponents to communicate where and when the protests would take place.

In the aftermath of the November 2016 U.S. presidential election, attention again turned to the role of social media. In testimony to a congressional committee in November, 2017, as reported by *The New York Times*, senior officers from social-media companies testified that "Russian agents intending to sow discord among American citizens disseminated inflammatory posts that reached 126 million users on Facebook, published more than 131,000 messages on Twitter and uploaded over 1,000 videos to Google's YouTube service."

Facebook executives also described how the company conducted an investigation, which revealed that at least $100,000 for as many as 3,000 divisive ads had been placed by the Internet Research Agency, a company headquartered in St. Petersburg, Russia, and linked to the Kremlin. According to Facebook chief executive officer Alex Stamos, the ads were tied to 470 fake accounts. Stamos said another 2,200 ads, costing at least $50,000, may have been linked to the same hacking effort. In addition, the executive described how "trolls," or social-media users, had used the site in publishing negative comments about Hillary Clinton. Beyond paid ads, Stamos added that 80,000 pieces of divisive content had been placed and viewed by 29 million people.

The scope of those efforts was nothing less than breathtaking, exposing the length to which Russian hackers, acting on behalf of their government, were prepared to go to drive Americans apart on inflammatory social issues. Those efforts included fueling racial divisions in the United States, which had been on the rise after a series of incidents involving several police departments, alleged to have committed unlawful acts against black suspects. Similarly, the ongoing, and often bitter, controversies over President Trump's immigration policies could be another area Russian hackers may seek to exploit.

the return of Russian diplomatic buildings that were seized by the Obama administration, part of its response to Russia's meddling in the presidential election.

Putin announced that he would "see how effectively the much-lauded American judicial system works." According to a *Washington Post* columnist, the next day, the Russian media outlet *Sputnik* ran an article headlined "Russia Unlikely to See Justice in U.S. Courts over Diplomatic Property." Putin may find himself in a win-win position on this issue. If Russia sues and receives a favorable ruling, its buildings will be returned. If an unfavorable verdict is rendered, Putin can almost certainly be expected to claim that the judicial system is rigged. Judicial rigging is a process he understands well, given Russia's historical disregard for the rule of law.

The United States may be the most prominent, but far from only, Western nation targeted by Russian cyber activities. France also experienced extensive and heavy-handed efforts to influence its 2017 national election. Two years before, in April 2015, France's popular news channel TV5 Monde was victimized by a major cyber attack that was traced to APT malware used by Russian hackers. The hackers defaced the network website and Facebook page. The motive for the attack was unclear, and initial French thinking was that it could have originated with the terrorist group ISIS.

That was not the end of the story. A subsequent French investigation traced the attack to APT28, closely linked to Russia. If the Russians were indeed involved, the motive remains murky. We can speculate that it was an opportunity for Russia to test its cyber offensive skills, intimidate an important NATO member, and propagate the idea that there was cyberterrorist involvement from the Middle East. In any event, the attack was successful, knocking the station off the air for hours. An alert technician literally pulled the plug on the system that was spreading the malware.

The immediate cost to the station to recover operations was over $5 million, with several million dollars more spent on security upgrades.

As the 2017 campaign in France unfolded, right-wing and pro-Russian candidate Marine Le Pen was the surprise winner of an initial runoff, which then pitted her in the final vote against upstart and largely unknown centrist candidate and former finance minister Emmanuel Macron. Within the Kremlin, Le Pen was the favored candidate, and, over the course of the election's concluding weeks, Macron was smeared in a series of social-media attacks, with rumors including that he was a CIA operative, stole money from the federal budget to finance his campaign, and was homosexual.

There was no proof to support any of the derogatory news items claims—Macron, for example, was married to a glamorous, older woman—and he proceeded to become French president, easily defeating Le Pen. Scandal and *kompromat*, the Russian term for attempts to smear and discredit opponents, played a role in the French campaign but did not yield the results hoped for by the Kremlin. It would remain to be seen how Macron, aware of the Kremlin's tactics, would deal with Russia during his presidency.

Germany offers a different case study of the scope of Russian interest in influencing Western elections. As expected, German Chancellor Angela Merkel was elected in September 2017 to a fourth term in office but struggled for months to form a governing coalition. There had been warnings that German politics also would be the target of cyber attacks. In late 2016, German officials admitted that numerous e-mail addresses of the nation's highest ranking officials were compromised, with suspicion centering on Russia as the culprit.

Related to this, one source speaking on the background claimed the Russians set up bank accounts in Switzerland to fund these influence operations. In late 2016, the German government also told the Bundestag, its parliament, that German computer networks were hit regularly in the past year by various foreign intelligence services, including from Russia. The same report also identified Russia as the source of computer attacks on the Bundestag and national political parties in May and August 2016. This was done through malware known as APT 28.

Somewhat surprisingly, and despite the above, the German election in fall 2017 was not heavily targeted by Russian hackers. A series of factors explain the differences between what the hackers sought to do in the United States and France compared to Germany. The first is that the Germans closely monitored hacking activities in those nations and was prepared for possible hacking attacks. By the time of the German elections, the hackers had lost the element of surprise. The second was the widespread use of paper ballots that were almost impossible to hack. Moreover, and in anticipation of possible efforts to influence the German election, the

Federal Office for International Security ran penetration tests to assess any vulnerabilities that could be exploited to insert false information into the campaign.

In addition, and unlike in the United States, the Germans largely trust their media. That was a well-placed confidence, as the German media formed teams of fact checkers to ferret out false information. Finally, there was no viable alternative to Merkel, leaving Russian hackers little incentive to spread information that may have helped a different or stronger candidate.

Germany's problems with the political and security implications of hacking extend beyond Russia. Germany's domestic spy agency, the Office for the Protection of the Constitution, issued a report in late 2017 condemning China for using LinkedIn to target as many as 10,000 people, mostly prominent German citizens. Fake profiles were created and sent to those individuals, presumably to enable China to garner useful business and political insights and contacts. As part of the approach, the Germans were offered a chance to meet and work with Chinese counterparts. LinkedIn said it would deactivate the accounts of those the German government identified as Chinese spies.

German efforts to fight back reflect a growing trend. Other European nations are undertaking efforts to mitigate the effects of Russian hacking. In Sweden, for example, there is a program in schools to identify Russian propaganda. The Swedish Defense Ministry, according to one report, also instructs its military in tactics used by the Russians. Lithuania, a frequent victim of Russian hacking, formed a group of citizens who patrol social media for signs of Russian hacking. In Brussels, there is a task force of staffers and various volunteers from academia and journalism who look for false stories.

In late 2017, the British parliament was also looking closely at whether the Russians used social media companies such as Twitter and Facebook to try to influence the British vote on leaving the European Union, known as Brexit. Russia has long opposed the European Union (EU)—viewing it as a competitor for influence with East European nations—and routinely favors actions that could undermine it. The Internet companies have yet to respond to the official British inquiry but promised to do so. The British vote to leave the EU passed by 1.3 million votes. The issue was highly contentious in the United Kingdom, and the credibility of the vote would be badly undermined if the Russians were found to have exercised influence over it.

In a November 2017 speech to a business group in London, British Prime Minster Theresa May said Putin was trying to "undermine free societies" and "sow discord" between the British and its European neighbors. May's remarks were at odds with those of her unpredictable foreign secretary, Boris Johnson, who said a few weeks prior that he had seen no evidence of

Russian attempts to interfere with the Brexit vote. May's comments were also dismissed as "baseless accusations" by a Russian spokesman. Two days after May's speech, however, a British team of researchers revealed that 100,000 Russian-language Twitter accounts posted tens of thousands of messages in English advocating support for Britain's leaving the European Union. Johnson was made to once again look the fool, but for May's Tory Party, the question was whether it would take on the Russian hacking more aggressively, which, if taken to its logical extreme, could be seen as undermining the integrity of the leave EU results.

The answer was supplied in the wake of the brazen attempt to assassinate former Russian-turned-British-spy Sergei Skripal and his daughter in the quiet village of Salisbury, England. Once Skripal was turned to work for the British, he became a marked man in Vladimir Putin's eyes. In March 2018, the Skripals were on a park bench when they slumped over and became seriously ill. Rushed to the hospital in life-threatening condition, both father and daughter were judged by medical authorities as having received near-lethal doses of Novichok, a powerful nerve agent developed by Russia some decades earlier.

Overwhelming evidence pointed to Russia or those acting on its behalf. That judgment was shared by British Prime Minster Theresa May, outraged that such an attack could take place in her country, as well as by President Trump and French President Macron. Only British Labor Party leader Jeremy Corbyn, ever-convinced of the follies of the West and never willing to stand up for its values against authoritarian figures such as Putin, refused to clearly cite Russia as the culprit.

That was not a surprise, given Corbyn's epic willingness to turn a blind eye to any form of aggression against his country. Nor was it a surprise that Russian spokespeople would deny any involvement in the poisoning, despite both opportunity and motive to harm the Skripals. It also wasn't a surprise that the Russians would turn to the Internet to use media to support their tortured version of events. Among the claims made by Russian trolls and media spokespeople was that Britain poisoned the Skripals to stoke anti-Russian sentiment. Ukraine was also described as wanting to place blame on Russia. Perhaps the Skripals were poisoned accidently by a British nerve agent produced at Porton Down laboratory.

These contradictory descriptions and assertions are not a weakness in the Kremlin's propaganda, but a feature. The disinformation campaign is intended to unsettle governments and citizens alike and is a tactic used during the 2014 annexation of Ukraine and the downing of Malaysian Airlines MH17. For Russia, the only "truth" is what it says it is.

This pattern was repeated several weeks later when a nerve agent killed scores in Syria in a repeat of actions taken by the Syrian government that led President Trump to order air strikes against Syria in 2017. Russia, once again, came to the defense of President Bashar Assad, who was responsible for perhaps 500,000 deaths of his own countrypeople. Once again, the U.S. president responded, this time in concert with British and French military forces. Once again, as these events were unfolding, Russian media figures, aided by trolls, took to the airwaves to claim that the overwhelming evidence for the airstrike was fabricated by Britain. As Dmitry Kiselev claimed, this was a "devilish plot" led by "petty Britain."

As audacious and brazen as were Russian efforts to influence various national elections as well as major events such as the Skripal case and nerve-agent attack by Syria, a late 2017 report from the cyber security company Secureworks showed the extent to which Russia wanted to go beyond them and monitor the activities of perceived enemies of prominent people in the United States, Russia, and elsewhere. A sloppy error by the Russian hacking group Fancy Bear exposed their actions, which, from March 2015 to May 2016 focused on as many as 4,700 targeted e-mail accounts of notable and important Americans and Russians who were seen as opposed to Russian policies. Americans in that group included former Secretaries of State Colin Powell and John Kerry; General David Petraeus; and Generals Philip Breedlove and Wesley Clark, former NATO commanders. Also included on the "hit list" were senior executives from defense contractors Boeing, Lockheed Martin, and Raytheon.

As 2017 was drawing to a close, Donald Trump and Vladimir Putin once again discussed the issue of Russian hacking during a meeting at an Asian conference. Putin continued to assert that he knew nothing of the extensive Russian hacking efforts, which, in the highly unlikely event was true, indicated the former KGB officer had lost control of his government and military.

For his part, and notwithstanding the overwhelming evidentiary base, the president said he deemed Putin's denials "sincere." It was a position that Trump has consistently maintained since he was briefed shortly before taking office by U.S. intelligence and law enforcement officials. The president's views almost certainly are not shared universally by his closest aides, a number of whom reportedly advised him to take the conclusions of his intelligence and law enforcement advisers seriously. Whether this was another example of Trump's epic naiveté on foreign policy or an ego incapable of even the slightest possibility that his election to the highest office in the land may have been shaped by outside forces is impossible to know.

We conclude that Russia did not succeed in influencing the outcome of the U.S. and European presidential elections, but we take little comfort in the discord Russian hacktivists were able to sow in the Western democracies. It would not be hard to imagine Putin concluding that the results achieved by what he set in motion, beginning with the election of Donald Trump, suited Russian goals immensely. Trump's refusal to acknowledge this likely perspective just adds an extra measure of satisfaction for Putin.

What is clear is that comments from the president about viewing his Russian counterpart as sincere in denying Russian involvement in the November election hardly serve as a deterrent to future hacking efforts by the Russians and those in China, North Korea, and Iran who do so with virtual impunity.

Going forward, Russia seems fully committed to more aggressive methods of cyber espionage. In late 2017 a major U.S. newspaper was reporting that Russian submarines "have dramatically stepped up activity around undersea data cables in the North Atlantic, part of a more aggressive naval posture that has driven NATO to revive a Cold-War era command...The apparent Russian focus on the cables, which provide Internet and other communications connections to North America and Europe, could give the Kremlin the power to sever or tap into vital data lines."

In an era where cyber capabilities are growing and international efforts to defend against cyber attacks remain far behind those carrying out such attacks, Western government and businesses face an uphill battle to protect critical data. Attacks from Russia and other nations will continue.

In Russia's case, a concerted effort will also be made to blur the lines between Russian activities and those of the West. In one of the great political ironies of the year—and proving Donald trump's assertion that there is fake news—a Russian foreign ministry spokesperson claimed that the United States was trying to "influence" the March 2018 Russian presidential election by allegedly supporting Putin's putative opponent Alexei Navalny, notwithstanding that he has already been declared ineligible to run by the Central Electoral Commission.

Adding to his paranoia, but tacitly acknowledging the power of social media, Putin said he wanted to monitor social media to learn which Russian companies are engaging in political activity in the run-up to the Russian election. In the digital age, there are countless ways information can be used for good and bad purposes, and the line between them seems more blurred every day.

One thing is almost guaranteed; Putin and his Kremlin colleagues have seen how their actions can be disruptive for the democracies. As such, it would be prudent, as the experts have suggested, to expect a more sophisticated and targeted strategy in coming U.S. and European elections.

The intelligence and law enforcement chiefs of the United States share that concern. In mid-February 2018, they provided testimony to the Senate Intelligence Committee in which they unanimously warned of Russian plans—already underway, they claimed—to employ a digital strategy based on social media to spread disinformation and disrupt the U.S. 2018 November midterm elections. As described by Director of National Intelligence Dan Coats, "We expect Russia to continue using propaganda, social media false flag personas, sympathetic spokespeople and other means of influence to try to exacerbate social and political fissures in the United

States…There should be no doubt that Russia perceives its past efforts as successful and views the 2018 U.S. midterm elections as a potential target for Russian influence operations."

Adding even more drama to the issue, several days after this testimony, Deputy Attorney General Rod Rosenstein, drawing from a 37-page document, announced that 13 Russians and three companies were being indicted by the federal government for seeking to subvert the 2016 presidential election. According to the *New York Times* report, "the Russians stole the identities of American citizens, posed as political activists, and used the flash points of immigration, religion and race to manipulate a campaign."

The Russian information warfare operation, dubbed by them the Translator Project, began in the first half 2014—shortly after the annexation of Ukraine—according to the indictment, well before the Trump candidacy for president was announced. At that time, two Russian women came to the United States on visas issued by the Obama administration to conduct research on political activities in as many as nine states, including Florida, California, Michigan, and Texas. No allegations were made against anyone in the Trump campaign, including Donald Trump. Albeit relentless, the Russian operation was not seen as influencing the outcome of the 2016 election.

The scope and brazenness of the Russian efforts is striking. Working from St. Petersburg, teams associated with the Internet Research Agency worked day and night, using mostly social media and posing, according to the *Times* report, as Christian activists, anti-immigration groups, and supporters of the Black Lives Matter movement. They sought to undermine the Clinton candidacy while supporting Bernie Sanders, her rival for the nomination, but also supported activities such as demonstrations against Donald Trump. Overall, they sought to "sow discord," according to Rosenstein. At the center of the effort was Yevgeny Prigozhuin, a close confidant of Vladimir Putin, who has been linked to Russian activities in Ukraine and Syria. The indicted Russians almost certainly will not have to face the U.S. legal system, as the Russian government, which dismissed the indictments as "blabber," will not allow their citizens to be extradited to America.

The indictments, consistent with the briefing Trump received from U.S. intelligence officials in January 2017, show the assault on U.S. democracy in the digital age. Mitigating the effects of Russian efforts to undermine the U.S. political process will take a concerted and expedited effort, involving probably new patterns of cooperation between federal and state officials, as well as the continuing involvement of intelligence and law enforcement organizations and nothing less than a sense of urgency that President Trump does not evince. As discussed, we also do not believe that Russia altered or shaped the outcome of the 2016 presidential race, but it certainly sowed great unrest and exploited social divisions. America and its government have ample resources to respond and, if necessary, use its own cyber defense capabilities to demonstrate its seriousness, including those used by the CIA, FBI, NSA, Department of Justice, and Department of Homeland Security.

During their congressional testimony, the intelligence and law enforcement chiefs admitted President Trump had not ordered them to devote major resources to safeguarding the electoral process. This was followed several weeks later by testimony to the Senate Armed Services Committee from U.S. Cyber Command and NSA Director Mike Rogers, who repeated that he had not received any White House instructions regarding how to respond to future cyber attacks from Russia or elsewhere. He added that he was sure Putin had little fear of a U.S. response in kind to Russian hacking. This is troubling. Presidential leadership, not unlike what the leaders of Germany and France demonstrated during their elections, will be essential. This is an unfinished story with one of America's implacable foes determined to continue pressing its advantages.

As the implications of hacking by Russia and others comes into sharper focus, efforts to use social media for illicit purposes, such as the Cambridge Analytica case we will discuss in another chapter, raise a set of other equally troubling questions about the future integrity and credibility of the imaginative and convenient way of mass communication we call social media.

BIBLIOGRAPHY

Alexander, Keith. Testimony before the House Armed Services Committee, Cyberspace Operations Testimony, September 23, 2010.

Applebaum, Anne. "Russia's Fury Is Proof the Sanctions Are Working." *The Washington Post*, October 29, 2017.

Arquilla, John. "Cyber War Is Already upon US." Foreign Policy, February 27, 2012.

Cunningham, Erin. "Iran's President Pleads for Peaceful Protests as Unrest Grips Nation." *The Washington Post*, January 1, 2018.

Geers, K., ed. *Cyber War in Perspective: Russian Aggression against Ukraine*. Tallinn, Estonia: NATO Cyber Defense Center of Excellence, 2015.

Greenwald, Glenn. *No Place to Hide: Edward Snowden, the NSA and the US Surveillance State*. New York: Macmillan, 2014.

Harding, Luke. *The Snowden Files: The Inside Story of the World's Most Wanted Man*. New York: Vintage Books, 2014.

Healey, Jason, ed. *A Fierce Domain: Conflict in Cyberspace*. Vienna: Cyber Conflict Studies Association, 2013.

Joint Analysis Report of the Department of Homeland Security and Federal Bureau of investigation. "Grizzly Steppe: Russian Malicious Cyber Activities." December 29, 2016.

Jones, Sam, and Max Seddon. "Hackers Have Second US Weapon Primed for Attack, Warn Analysis." *Financial Times*, May 16, 2017.

Koerner, Brendan. "Inside the Cyber Attack That Shook the US Government." *Wired*, October 23, 2016.

Kramer, Andrew, and Andrew Higgins. "In Ukraine, a Malware Expert Who Could Blow the Whistle on Russian Hacking." *The New York Times*, August 16, 2017.

Lewis, James. "How Russia Overtook China as Our Biggest Cyber Enemy." *The Washington Post*, December 18, 2016.

Libicki, Martin C. *Conquest in Cyber Space: National Security and Information Warfare*. Cambridge: Cambridge University Press, 2009.

McCain, John, and Mark Salter. *The Restless Wave: Good Times, Just Causes, Great Fights, and Other Appreciations*. New York: Simon and Schuster, 2018.

Miller, Greg, and Adam Entous. "Report Putin Ordered Cyber Intrusion." *The Washington Post*, January 7, 2017.

Morris, Dick. *Rogue Spooks: The Intelligence War on Donald Trump*. New York: St. Martin's Press, 2017.

Office of the National Counterintelligence Executive. "Foreign Spies Stealing US Secrets in Cyberspace." October 2011.

Pelroth, Nicole, and Scott Shane. "How Israel Caught Russian Hackers Scouring for American Secrets." *The New York Times*, October 11, 2017.

Rosenberg, Matthew, Charlie Savage, and Michael Wines. "Russia at Work on US Midterms, Spy Chiefs Warn." *The New York Times*, February 14, 2018.

Sanger, David E. *Confront and Conceal: Obama's Secret Wars and Surprising Use of American Power*. New York: Crown Publishers, 2012.

Scott, Shane, and Mark Mazzetti. "Indictment Bares Russian Network to Twist 2016 Vote." *The New York Times*, February 17, 2018.

Wong, Julia Carrie. "Cambridge Analytica-Linked Academic Spurns Idea Facebook Swayed Election." *The Guardian*, June 19, 2018.

Zetter, Kim. "Inside the Cunning, Unprecedented Hack of the Ukraine Power Grid." *Wired*, March 3, 2016.

CHAPTER 4

The Internet of Things: Systemically Vulnerable

Nigel Jones

Imagine your older self, say, in twenty years' time. Perhaps consider your older children or elderly parents. What digitally enabled world do you want for yourself and your family? How do we collectively maximize the benefits of smart-living and Internet of things technology while minimizing any associated harm? How do we allow society to benefit from smart-living concepts, like the Internet of things, without imposing restrictive regulation? How do we enable a competitive commercial environment without compromising personal data security? In other words, *How do we get the Internet of things (IoT) we want, rather than the Internet of things we get?*

This last question envisages an ability to shape the services we use now and in the future. It contrasts with the idea that we are passive and unquestioning recipients of "innovative technology" that locks us into patterns of behaviour by design (or lack of design), gaining benefits without regard for the risk of harm. To design, develop, and implement systems that minimize risk requires conscious engagement by users, consumer, and citizens or others acting on their behalf.

This chapter is a revised report that was developed in research conducted by the Information Assurance Advisory Council (IAAC), which has kindly allowed the use in this book of its text, authored by Nigel Jones of IAAC and Nick Price from the Association of Professional Futurists.

The research sought to examine the challenge of assurance for smart living and Internet of things technology, with a focus on the services and technology that will, and does, assist people in their business and private lives.

Smart living is described as:

a trend encompassing advancements that give people the opportunity to benefit from new ways of living. It involves original and innovative solutions aimed at making life more efficient, more controllable, economical, productive, integrated and sustainable. This is a trend that covers all the aspects of day to day life, from domiciles and workplaces to the manner in which people are transported within cities. In short, Smart Living involves improved standards in several aspects of life, whilst striving for efficiency, economy and reduction of the carbon footprint.[1]

This research was driven in part by concerns in the community of inadequate care in the development, deployment, and purchase of Internet of things devices, without regard for privacy, security, resilience, consumer rights, and choice. This is not an unfounded fear given stories of, for example, surveillance cameras and baby monitors containing malware and vulnerabilities that would allow them to be used for the invasion of privacy, spying, or attacks on other computers. Likewise, something as mundane as an Internet-connected kettle is found to "leak Wi-Fi passwords."[2] At the time of IAAC's research, the first death was recorded involving car autopilot technology. Although this particular incident was part of the test and verification process, there is a growing trend toward making technologies and applications available first, and managing the consequences afterward. There is no desire to impede the benefits and growth afforded by new technologies; rather, this chapter addresses the perception of a gap between a capability that appears superficially desirable, and that which is genuinely fit for purpose.

In years to come, people might think of recent years as a time when security professionals were frustrated with consumer and employee inability to remember long passwords, neglect their smartphone security settings, and ignore the acceptable-use policy. In the debates on privacy and data-loss, share-value of major companies was affected, while the engineering of trustworthiness and safety of technology-enabled services was too often overlooked. Perhaps as the IoT accelerates, people will cease to be users in the input-device and display-screen sense and will became participants in a system. In this context, what good will long passwords be when people are simply taking showers, taking their medications, or commuting? And all the time, data will be collected to monitor, bill, manage, audit, and heath-check. Moreover, because of levels of automation and opaque algorithms, nations and individuals may become increasingly vulnerable to attack without any consumer, user, or participant having sufficient awareness.

SECURITY, SAFETY, TRUSTWORTHINESS, AND HARM

One can see that the examples given above represent a series of safety, security, and privacy issues. In this chapter, we also refer to "trustworthiness" and "harm." It is worth noting how these terms are used here.

The Trustworthy Software Foundation (TSFdn) states that:

Our daily lives and industrial processes are now heavily reliant on a wide range of underpinning software, whether it be the tools we use to communicate, the methods of transport we use, or the infrastructure that is used to support us in both our professional and personal lives. This makes software trustworthiness an underlying concern for all those who commission, write or use it."[3]

TSFdn argues that trustworthiness in software has predominantly five facets: safety, reliability, availability, resilience, and security. Software that is produced and procured should "perform as expected," "when expected" and "how expected."[4] This chapter extends these concepts to include consideration of the hardware elements of the IoT, as much of the hardware will typically function because of its embedded software or control software. There is a trend to think about these elements as being designed-in and, by default, in good practice, rather than bolted on.

There is an overlap here with the standard information assurance concepts of confidentiality, integrity, and availability of information, as shown in Figure 4.1.

This overlap is, to a large extent, unavoidable when taking a whole system view of smart-living IoT, incorporating control systems, sensors, services, data collection, and processing.

Furthermore, privacy is not simply about confidentiality of information. It is about the appropriate management and use of personal data. In the smart-living context, privacy issues will extend to unwarranted surveillance through, for example, security cameras or game-console sensors, and not simply the management of personal data. We add privacy to the trustworthy facets above as something that is particularly of concern in the smart-living space. Consequently, smart-living systems blur the distinction between harm and damage. One might regard the distinction as being based on harm to an individual, such as that resulting from a privacy breach, versus physical damage to a system, perhaps caused by the malfunction of a component. It may be that one leads to the other. In this report, the term "harm" is used because of our ultimate concern for the users of smart-living IoT technology and services and should be thought of broadly.

We do not wish to recommend what specific technologies and services should be developed in the future, nor stifle innovation. Rather, we feel it is useful to develop a set of principles that at least provide a sense of direction for what a "good" IoT might be like. In this context, this chapter does not aim to provide a solution to a problem, but to develop principles to help improve a "problem situation." This approach is very much in keeping with Checkland's ethos behind soft-systems methodology, which aims "to foster learning and appreciation of the problem situation between a group of stakeholders rather than set out to solve a predefined problem."[5]

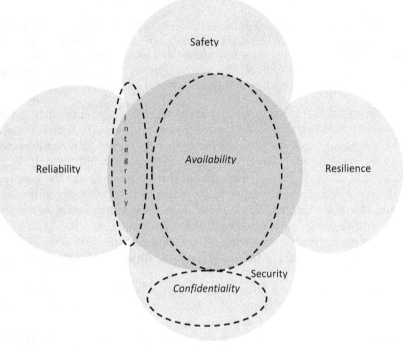

Figure 4.1

THE CHALLENGE

British Computer Society and Oxford Internet Institute

The British Computer Society (BCS) and the Oxford Internet Institute report on the societal impact of the Internet of Things (IoT) is comprehensive in highlighting the policy and governance challenges that emerge from the complexity of the connected environment. It notes the problem in being too specific about future developments because of the "assemblages of old and new technologies and the different viewpoints of the involved actors." Understanding of any particular system or requirement should be rooted in specific contexts of use. Moreover, the complexity and emergent nature of IoT systems may defeat the standard procurement process that assumes "the system can be fully envisioned and specified before it is built."

We therefore need to go beyond a technical focus, recognizing that involved actors extend to, for example, city governments who "worryingly lack the expertise to drive the design of public IoT infrastructures, relying instead on the expertise of technology vendors and development companies for much of the design, operations and maintenance."[6] This distinction between the government and commerce is an important variable that is explored further below.

In governance and regulatory issues, the BCS report notes that the scale of IoT and the data it produces requires a rethinking of security and data-protection policy. It notes that accountability and liability could become obscured in the case of failures. The report determines that "who sets the standards" and how local, national, regional, and global practices are aligned are key issues. Principles such as data minimization and privacy by design are advocated and form part of the policy challenges emerging in their workshop. Other challenges include:

- Industry is going ahead with this anyway and a common direction is needed between government, regulators and industry.
- Who is making the key policy and design decisions?
- Transparency and multi-stakeholder input is important.
- Who has jurisdiction over information flows?
- We need to consider impact of IoT on wider society.
- More expertise is needed in Government.

The BCS-OII report notes three ways forward. First, more research is needed that utilizes real-world application trials involving stakeholders. Second, there needs to be multi-stakeholder involvement at the design and development stage of applications and systems. Third, "there needs to be greater public understanding and discussion of the technology, its potential benefits, and related issues and challenges."

Cities2050

In March 2015, a "Cities2050" roundtable, chaired by Lord James Arbuthnot, now chairperson of IAAC, was held over two days in London, bringing 60 participants together. The event report discusses many of the upsides that technology can bring in making cities better places for people to live and work. It states that "cities must focus on the long term effects of technological change" and the ubiquity of smart-city technology. However, it also notes many of the same challenges discussed in the BCS-OII report. It recognizes that technology can bring vulnerabilities and "citizens may be reluctant to embrace a smart-city infrastructure," which, although "intended to provide ease of life, efficiency and protection for citizens, stirs up significant arguments regarding consent and privacy." It argues that designing for a city requires a holistic view to resilience so that, what the report calls the physical, compliance, supervisory, and insight layers, are seen as part of a wider ecosystem:

It is by taking this holistic and organic view of resilience, with interconnected layers and responsibilities, rigorously planned and tested in the face of wider global mega-trends, that we will be best prepared for the challenges of the future.[7]

Resilience and security are therefore set within a context of economic and social benefit, shaped by global trends in an interdependent ecosystem.

The report addresses the security and vulnerability issues under four headings: education, standards, incentives and governance.

Education—In terms of education recommendations, the report segments audiences by company, senior executives, and citizens. It highlights the need for the audiences to understand the benefits of smart technologies and their corporate/personal responsibilities regarding risk and security.

Standards—The report calls for standards in cyber security for smart technologies to "meet the required protection" and suggests that these standards are ensured through a combination of auditing and fostering "an environment of corporate social responsibility."

Incentives—The incentive's recommendations concern the influence of companies by consumers and by positive endorsement of their security efforts. The report proposes investment to create partnerships of consumers "to influence the providers of smart technologies."

Governance—The report calls for legislation by government to ensure companies meet security standards. It recognises the role of leadership in sponsoring security and taking responsibility for risk and "dangers" involved in new technology. It suggests providing autonomy to a local level in smart-cities to encourage "greater responsibility for implementation of cyber security."[8]

In terms of standards, more technical recommendations for security of IoT have started to emerge. Two such examples are from OWASP (the Open Web Application Security Project) and the IoT Security Foundation.

OWASP

OWASP has established an IoT project that provides information on a variety of topics, including attack surface and vulnerabilities. It offers guidance on the security of IoT as well as "Principles for IoT Security." It divides its guidance into general recommendations for manufacturers, developers, and consumers of IoT technology. For example, its guidance for product manufacturers regarding security of Web interfaces includes:

- Ensure that any Web interface in the product disallows weak passwords
- Ensure that any Web interface in the product has an account-lockout mechanism.
- Include Web application firewalls to protect any Web interfaces.

The manufacturer's guidance also includes advice on privacy:

- Ensure only the minimal amount of personal information is collected from consumers
- Ensure only less-sensitive data is collected
- Ensure a data retention policy is in place

The consumer advice is described by OWASP as helping "consumers purchase secure products in the Internet of Things space…[it] is at a basic level, giving consumers a basic set of guidelines to consider from their perspective." The examples below clearly indicate that a level of technical knowledge is expected of consumers in adopting this guidance:

Insecure Web Interface

- If your system has an option to use HTTPS, ensure it is enabled.
- If your system has a two-factor authentication option, ensure that it is enabled.

Insufficient Authentication/Authorization

- If your system has a local or cloud-based Web application, ensure that you change the default password to a string one and, if possible, change the default username as well.

Insecure Network Services

- If your system has a firewall option available, enable it, and ensure that it can only be accessed from your client systems.
- Consider employing network segmentation technologies such as firewalls to isolate IoT systems from critical IT systems.

Lack of Transport Encryption

- If your system has an option to use HTTPS, ensure it is enabled.

OWASP has also developed a series or principles for IoT security. Several demonstrate the particular properties of security relating to IoT, including scale, lifecycle, function when isolated from connectivity, and transitive ownership over an extended period. For example:

- IoT system designers must recognize that the extended lifespan of devices will require forward-compatible security features.
- Security countermeasures must never degrade in the absence of connectivity.
- IoT components must be stripped down to the minimum viable feature set to reduce attack surface.

- IoT components are often sold or transferred during their life-spans. Plan for this eventuality.
- IoT does not follow a traditional 1:1 model of users to applications. Each component may have more than one user, and a user may interact with multiple components.

IoT Security Foundation

The IoT Security Foundation, formed in 2015, provides a similar checklist to OWASP, organized around the following questions in a document entitled "Establishing Principles for Internet of Things Security":

- Does the data need to be private?
- Does the data need to be trusted?
- Is the safe and/or timely arrival of data important?
- Is it necessary to restrict access to or control of the device?
- Is it necessary to update the software on the device?
- Will ownership of the device need to be managed or transferred in a secure manner?
- Does the data need to be audited?

On its website, the IoT Security Foundation highlights what may be interpreted as its three key principles:

- *Security first approach*...designed-in at the start
- *Fit for purpose*...right-sized for the application
- *Resilience* ... through operating life

Asimov Revisited

So far we have charted a series of higher-level policy issues and principles down to bulleted lists of measures in technical detail. Among the material explored during the IAAC research was that of cyber specialists Daniel Dresner and Neira Jones, who have built upon Asimov's "three laws of robotics" to take us back to the higher-level principles. They, too, attempt to identify three fundamental principles among the plethora of checklists and bullet-point control documents that exist across cyber security advice and guidance. Dresner and Jones provide an example of how one might take a top-down approach of basic principles and then define a series of actions/states that are necessary for a system to be compliant with the top-level principle. Alternatively, it might be viewed as a bottom-up approach that attempts to make sense of the wide variety of security controls and checklists at their most basic and fundamental levels. As such, it is worth including here as a way of thinking about principles and their impact on what people might actually do.

Table 4.1

Asimov and Dresner/Jones Laws Compared

The Asimov Three Laws of Robotics	The Dresner & Jones Three Laws of Cyber and Information Security
A robot may not injure a human being or, through inaction, allow a human being to come to harm.	An information system may not store, process, or transmit an information asset in such a way that will allow harm to come to that asset, the subjects of the information asset, or the thrall of that system or, through inaction or negligence, allow any of them to come to harm.
A robot must obey the orders given to it by human beings, except where such orders would conflict with the First Law.	An information system must only store, process, or transmit an information asset as instructed by its builders or operators and by owners or custodians of the information asset with which the information system interacts, except where such orders would conflict with the First Law.
A robot must protect its own existence, as long as such protection does not conflict with the First or Second Laws.	An information system must protect its own existence, as long as such protection does not conflict with the First or Second Laws.

Source: Dresner, Daniel, and Neira Jones. "The Three Laws of Cyber and Information Security, 2014." First published in *Cybertalk*, Issues 6, Autumn 2014. http://www.softbox.co.uk/cybertalk-issuesix. Accessed March 31, 2018. Used with permission.

Building on Asimov, Dresner and Jones develop their own "Three laws of cyber and information security," as shown in Table 4.1.

For each of the laws, Dresner and Jones provide a series of conditions under which a law is either satisfied or its risk of being broken is increased. For example, they posit that:

The risk of system behaviour that will cause breaking of the Second Law is increased when:

- The system doesn't allow operators to apply patches on time due to operational release constraints.
- The system is operated in an environment where contractual or social constraints allow operators to bypass agreed controls either technical or procedural.
- The operators do not receive notification of configuration management changes which impact the service they are expected to receive or deliver.

They argue that early consideration of these principles in the design of systems is economically advantageous, over and above the harm reduction encapsulated in the "laws." This is through early removal of defects in the life cycle and the "likely emergence of increased quality maturity in the organisation required to achieve this."

EMERGENT PROPERTIES

Like in the publications outlined above, of particular importance is recognizing that the complexity of IoT has emergent properties. Consequently, the system as a whole is of interest with interdependence, shared risk, and emergent properties presenting much of the challenge of understanding the development of IoT services. This resonates with the ecosystem model highlighted earlier in the Cities2050 report.

We recognize that it is difficult, in these circumstances, to give very detailed advice to policymakers, architects, and designers that would address the specifics of any system. However, it is felt that it is useful to develop a set of principles that, while not giving a blueprint for future IoT, will, at least, provide a sense of direction for what a "good" IoT could be like, in terms of assurance, safety, trust, and security. These principles might even inform a capability maturity model for IoT smart-living development. However, it is proposed that the adoption of good practice and accountability when things go wrong are critical to improving quality and security in IoT development.

To help inform development of principles, there are two key questions that need to be considered:

1. What degree of control does any individual have in the development of the services and systems which they use or participate in?
2. What framework might be used to judge the societal impact of any IoT innovation in terms of the benefits and/or harm generated?

The first question allows us to explore the idea that principles give us agency—or the ability to change something. If we can't change it, then why have principles? The second question highlights the need for us to have a way of judging societal impact—or what is good and bad, better and worse, or beneficial and costly.

DEGREE OF CONTROL

At the heart of the control discussion is the distinction between having some degree of personal direction or influence over the selection and use of services and systems, and the environmental shaping of one's choices.

(In social science this is sometimes referred to as agency versus structure.) For example, one may choose to walk, drive, or go by train, but if a city is designed for cars, and sidewalks/pavements have been all but designed out, the decision not to walk becomes one of influence more by the environment than one's own preference. In terms of information systems, one might choose not to share information in exchange for a service, but if that is the only way to gain the service, choice has been reduced. In the case of autonomous vehicles, one might choose to maintain control of the car, not linked to another information system, but, in the future, the environment may be built for autonomous vehicles, where people don't even own their own personal vehicles. Instead, the context perhaps favors driverless taxi services.

GENERATION AND EXCHANGE OF DATA

If an individual chooses to participate in the autonomous vehicle system, this could produce a range of informational exchanges in a connected system beyond the mass surveillance of traffic already experienced today, certainly in the United Kingdom, through CCTV and automatic number-plate reading. This imaginatively could include:

- Personal identification of occupants through voice and facial recognition.
- Routines of occupants, including social connections, work, and social patterns of life.
- Preferred music and video services while in transit—personalization of experience.
- Web history while connected in vehicle.
- Health monitoring while in the vehicle—including weight, heart rate, temperature, and so on. Some health indicators have the potential to be used to infer mood and emotion. Possibly also the consumption of recreational mood modifiers.
- Speed, location, and route—log of departure and arrival times.
- Payment methods recorded.

It is worth reminding ourselves that there are likely to be multiple *concurrent* data exchanges taking places between different devices and parties at all times. These data exchanges will also *vary* in the degree of security negotiated between the parties involved.

At the [eco]system level:

- City managers can monitor traffic and manage flow, environmental, and infrastructure burdens by varying tariffs, speed, and route.

- Routes can be adapted by commercial enterprises to bring passengers past commercial and other opportunities.
- Driverless taxi companies can seamlessly cue electrically powered vehicles and transfer people between vehicles on longer journeys.
- Law enforcement can know who-was-where if needed, including all passengers in the vehicle.
- Content of the vehicle can be sensed for what is in transit.

Data about a subject can be generated and recorded. It can also be added to by crossreferencing from other sources, implied, and projected backward and forward. The ownership, quality, surety of algorithmic generation, and the reliability of the latter sources are difficult to guarantee. It is also worth noting that we are already in a highly data-driven society. It is less a case of not being represented somewhere by data, but more the degree of detail, granularity, and accessibility by whom. For example, a citizen who votes, earns money, uses the health system, has a mobile phone, makes cashless payments, drives, and travels overseas, has a large amount of Personally Identifiable Information.[9] People in the country without legal leave to do so may have little official data associated with them but can become part of an estimated figure of illegal presence.

A BURDEN ON SAFETY, SECURITY, AND TRUSTWORTHINESS

There is, arising from this view of the future, a burden on safety, security, and trustworthiness. For example, as people and wider society become more dependent on autonomous vehicle infrastructure, to the point where it is seen as a must-have utility like water and electricity, the property of dependability and trustworthiness becomes a high-impact item in risk assessment. One might consider a concept akin to a Universal Service Obligation of provision—a guaranteed degree of available service quality, nondiscriminating against individual circumstances or location, that is not compromised when other functions of a system are compromised. An example may be that where a driverless car loses network access, it will have sufficient onboard facilities for it to self-navigate and deliver its passengers to a secure terminus point.

MULTI-STAKEHOLDER PERSPECTIVES

In a system with emergent properties, different stakeholders will views costs and benefits in different ways and will have different degrees of control. For example, the city manager's ability to manage traffic will be set against the loss of autonomy of individual vehicle occupants. At one of the IAAC reservations workshop, two breakout groups tried to categorize stakeholders. The following are used to illustrate some of the discussion at

Table 4.2

Group One Framework

	Control Over	Influence Others	Context of Operations
Direct (1st) User/Citizen	Where and when to travel	Through consumer power	Responsiveness— high price trust
Indirect (2nd) Prime Supplier of Infrastructure	How the system operates/how to operate the business	Market dynamics	Responsiveness— medium cost trust
Collateral (3rd) Government/ Citizen at Large	How to regulate, tax, limit	Code of practice	Responsiveness— low

Source: IAAC

the workshop. While neither of these example frameworks is in any way complete or authoritative, they serve to show how different stakeholders have different motivations. They also point toward the utility of trying to capture a multi-stakeholder view in the design, critique, or operation of any service.

Group one used the framework in Table 4.2. Group two based their discussion on the framework in Table 4.3.

These frameworks highlight the benefit of taking multiple stakeholder perspectives into account in the development of smart-living IoT. Indeed, it is essential if one is to judge the impact of any smart-living IoT initiative, as it can only be judged by the stakeholders involved. This would mean adopting models that help think about the wider impact on economy and society. It is recognized that stakeholder views will not always be reconcilable. However, the identification and exploration of their different views at least allows explicit recognition of the risks and trade-offs in decision-making. Consequently, any principles that are developed must iteratively help decision-makers to take into account multiple stakeholder perspectives and an assessment of wider impact as systems develop.

FRAMEWORKS BY WHICH SOCIETAL IMPACT MIGHT BE JUDGED

One group at the same research workshop created a drawing that showed the hierarchy or "stack" in Table 4.4.

Table 4.3

Group Two Framework

R—Responsible	State Manufacturers Infrastructure providers Car owner	Motivated by?: Efficiency of the economy Environmental planning Cost Profit

A—Accountable/
Authority
	State and emergency
	   services
	Manufacturer
	Infrastructure providers
	Driver/system operator
	Miscreants
	Who's in charge?
		Motivated by?:
		Reducing autonomy to reduce
		   accidents.
		Profit of crime

C—Consulted/
Committed
	Driver and passengers
	State in transport planning
	Manufacturers and
	   suppliers
	Insurance providers
	Driving instructors?
	Universities
	Other road users
		Life benefits/health benefits/
		   productivity benefits.
		Economic opportunity

I—Informed/ Involved	Passengers Pedestrians Other road users	Safety

Source: IAAC

Table 4.4

Philosophy (e.g., individual autonomy/collectivist views of society)
Social (e.g., state, market, vulnerable and disabled, uninterested, etc.)
Hard infrastructure

Source: IAAC

The discussion that followed generated a relativist perspective in that the infrastructure of the IoT could only be judged by the impact on the groups it affects and their views, as highlighted above. This, in turn, would be influenced by the overall philosophy of the society in which the system is deployed. For example, in a society marked by individuality, a smart pill that allows an older dementia sufferer to live an independent, but remotely supervised, life for longer may be viewed positively. However, in a culture where extended families are the norm, this approach may appear cold-hearted and isolating. Likewise, different views on privacy and surveillance will result in different stakeholder perspectives on the collection, processing, retention, and security of personal data. The collective benefits of aggregating data from dementia patients may be debated differently in different cultures. In other words, there was no absolute standard by which impact could be judged.

Whether deliberately or not, the "stack" noted above evokes Sommerville's stack (2011) for socio-technical systems, which places equipment, operating systems, communications and data management, application systems, business processes, organization, and society, in ascending order.

This, in turn, is evocative of the technical-standard OSI model as in Table 4.5, which has physical equipment at the bottom, with data connections, logical processes, and applications built on top in a hierarchy.

In addition to the seven-layer OSI model, there is already a debate about a layer eight and beyond, the "user" or "political" layers.[10] Note that some parts of the Internet refer humorously to this as layers akin to political interference or stupidity in an otherwise good design. The adoption of such a framework might, however, allow the extension of principles relating to the interrelationship of weaknesses in one layer and its impact on others. It also hints at how vulnerabilities in software at a fundamental level can resonate at the societal level.

It is worth noting that with any of these hierarchies, a vulnerability at a lower level compromises the layers above, and a compromised layer may affect the system at another layer. The social and political layers can conceivable undermine the whole system, and vice versa.

Table 4.5

The OSI Model

Application layer

Presentation layer

Session layer

Transport layer

Network layer

Data-link layer

Physical layer

Source: Drawn from text at Open Systems interconnection project at the International Organization for Standardization (ISO/IEC 7498-1)

DEVELOPING PRINCIPLES

A number of factors lie at the heart of the IoT development engine, something that principles developed need to target them. These include the scale in connectivity, data collection, data aggregation, and incremental re-purposing of technology and services toward other innovative offerings and uses. In discussing these factors in a deployment context, the IAAC research sought to combine a game-theory type approach with design-thinking scenarios. Principles would only be worthwhile if they impacted movement toward a beneficial IoT with harm reduction. There are benefits to adopting a game-theory type approach, in that it can focus on key variables in order to understand some of the factors at work in a more complex reality.

Someone who plays the "development of IoT game" well would, in the end, be judged to have succeeded by maximizing benefits and reducing harm. Recognizing that there are commercial, government, and consumer stakeholders "playing the game," there would have to be measures or circumstances that shape the behavior of the stakeholders toward playing the game well.

This would require two key elements that would form the basis of the game. First, there is the distinction between the value system of the guardian (ideally acting on behalf of the citizen/consumer) and the value system of commerce. We define a "principled commercial actor" as a proposition developer who wishes to market and sell sufficient numbers to serve a business, while promoting comfort and convenience. Comfort and convenience are extended by the authors to include safety, security, and trustworthiness. In other words, principled commercial actors will only continue to thrive if they reduce harm to their customers.

We defined a "principled guardian actor" as a governing body of a country or administrative area that wishes to balance freedom of citizen choice, citizen safety, and the greater economic and social health of the populace as a whole. In the game of IoT development, the roles of guardian and commerce should be explicit and separate. This is similar to the separation-of-duties concept. For example, someone responsible for managing an account is not the person who audits the account. This allows the consumer/citizen a process of redress when unhappy about a service provided by a commercial entity or another part of government. It also allows a guardian to be engaged in specification of standards.[11]

Second there is the awkward distinction between security and productivity (productivity here is taken to mean the primary function of a device or system and good things such as innovation and efficient function). Often they are shown in opposition and in zero-sum relationships. That is, if security is enhanced in some way, productivity is reduced, and productivity is enhanced when freed from security controls. For example, in the context of enterprise information assurance (as opposed to our smart-living context), one can see where security procedures can place a burden on what employers and employees view as their "primary duties." As stated in the Hewlett Packard Enterprise/RISCS white paper that emerged from the RISCS project at University College London:

In modern organizations today, employee attention and efforts are consumed with messages about health and safety, sustainability, sector-specific regulation, and security. All of these are secondary activities that take time and attention away from primary productive activity.

The RISCS paper argues that there is a balance to be struck between security, productivity, and cost. There is, however, a question as to whether this is also true of the design and function of control systems and smart-living IoT. For example, can a product or system be described as functional if it causes harm, even if it appears to operate correctly on prima facie observation? For the purposes of this research, a person or entity that plays the game well will seek to reduce the difference between these concepts—security and productivity. This is different from balancing security and productivity, which maintains a sense of oppositional distinction.

It is worth noting that the UK work on Trustworthy Software, as coordinated by the Foundation (TSFdn), deliberately makes a distinction between "explicit" and "implicit" requirements for software. These are also referred to as "functional" and "nonfunctional" requirements respectively, the distinction being between "what the software is supposed to do, as in its specific behaviour and/or functions" and "specific requirements relating to Safety, Reliability, Availability, Resilience, Security, Usability and Performance." It would be poor software if it wasn't safe or available in performing its explicit primary function. However, TSFdn recognizes that:

No software asset can be proven, or even be expected to be completely free of all defects, i.e. free from conditions which could cause it to fail or behave in an unexpected manner. However, it should have a level of "trustworthiness" commensurate to the purpose for which it is used…[TSFdn] recommends a risk-based approach…whereby the reliance on the software to provide trustworthiness (in particular the 5 facets of trustworthiness) is considered together with the purpose of the software and the maximum impact of a defect/deviation in the software.[12]

TSFdn advocates a risk-based approach, which requires:

- A prescriptive, reasonable-endeavours[13] approach, with the aim of achieving a "Pareto" baseline of trustworthiness, as detailed in their Trustworthy Software Essentials guidance.

- A descriptive, best-endeavours[14] approach "with the aim of achieving a Comprehensive level of Trustworthiness, as defined in the UK Publicly Available Specification PAS754:2014."

TSFdn recommends a systematic approach to producing and procuring software; for example, requiring that governance arrangements are documented to cover areas such as:

- Roles, responsibilities and accountabilities
- Communication plans
- Risk management—documenting level of trustworthiness
- Formal assurance processes
- Trustworthy software controls

So clearly, while in our "game," we assume that productivity and security should be closely aligned (even to the point that they are the same concept), we acknowledge that in practice how much harm, what type of harm, and for how many, will be questions affecting risk, cost, and viability.

However, there is perhaps a bigger problem in recognizing that "no software asset can be proven…to be completely free of all defects," and that is the burden of proof relating to any liability in a future regulatory regime, whether viewed through a reasonable-endeavours or best-endeavours lens. We will return to regulatory issues later in the chapter.

The diagram in Figure 4.2 represents two key factors at work in our "game" of IoT development.

The preference is that we develop principles that help us move toward the state in the top left-hand corner in each diagram. If the IoT development game is played well, security and productivity will be aligned, almost as the same concept (1,1). Principled guardian roles and commercial roles will also be aligned (1,1). An IoT that is developed without principle from the perspective of guardian or commerce is represented in the bottom right as (0,0). Likewise, a system without security or productivity is in the bottom right (0,0), arguably a state we might occasionally observe regarding IoT devices. For example, this might be because commercial drivers run ahead of any regulation or thought for societal impact in the area.

Role-play scenarios in smart-living product development from the viewpoints of "principled guardian," "principled commerce," and "potential customer" drove the game-play in the research. As a result, a number of candidate principles emerged in discussion. This included the idea that a guardian should take responsibility for categorizing all potential issues that consumers may or may not have thought of, and identify how products or services conform to these. The guardian has to think for the consumer, rather than rely on the expectation that consumers will develop sufficient expertise and authority to act on their own behalf. Furthermore,

Variables in our Game

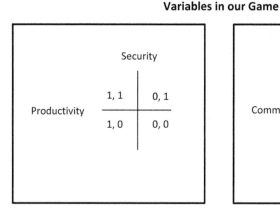

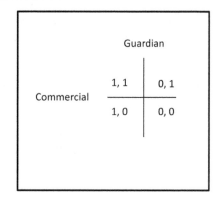

1, 1 = win-win

0, 1 and 1, 0 = zero sum, e.g., the
more security, the less productivity

1, 1 = principled commercial and
principled guardian

Figure 4.2

Game Variables (IAAC)

identification of issues needs to be done at each life-cycle stage and reiterated on an appropriately regular basis to deal with changes in environment or service. Actions against identifiable issues can vary and may fall to the guardian. For example, to document, do nothing, or do something—tolerate, terminate, transfer, or treat—are, of course, standard approaches in risk management. There was an attempt to categorize issues that arose as follows:

- Environmental; for example, power consumption and thermal properties
- Functionality (impact)
- Availability (impact)
- Privacy
- Safety
- Software updates (changing settings)
- Data sharing—how often and mechanisms
- Compatibility—technical and control

The relationship between liability regarding safety and security and "data for profit" in exchange for service access needed to be managed. It was felt that, in a manner analogous to health and safety regulation, liability lies with those who generate the risk. Analogous to environmental regulation was the notion that the "polluter pays," in relation to the production of services and products that cause harm. For example, aggregated data would be suitably anonymized; otherwise a sanction for "pollution," akin to spillage, would be appropriate. A number of specific guardian roles were identified:

- Guardians should intervene in the event of market or service failures.
- Guardians will make environmental information available to all providers.
- Guardians influence the decision-making for effects at system-of-systems level and for network and infrastructure carrying or delivering services.
- Guardians enforce legal requirements.

Overall, the games helped show that principles would need to help decision-makers focus on the identification and cataloging of issues of concern and developing mitigation strategies as part of the design and development process. They would help shape the context for good practice adoption through a series of incentives and would normalize reduction-of-harm thinking in design and development.

Before proceeding to a discussion of principles based on these factors, the next section briefly examine two topics persistently raised in discussion in the IAAC community, regarding software quality and liability. These are the extent to which health and safety provides an analogy for shaping behaviours in the design and development of smart-living IoT, the current state of consumer-protection legislation, and the alignment with engineering ethics.

Health and Safety as an Analogy?

In the United Kingdom, the primary piece of legislation regarding health and safety in the workplace is the Health and Safety at Work Act 1974. The Health and Safety Executive (HSE) is the body that oversees the enforcement of the act through a comprehensive suite of "internal operational procedures," including inspection, investigation, complaints, enforcement, notice, prosecution, major incident, penalties, and work-related deaths. It produces guidance and offers "essential principles" to underpin the guidance. These are included in Box 4.1.

The HSE published further principles relating to, for example, effective risk management and control of substances that are hazardous to health. It also produces a list of "principles and guidelines to assist HSE in its judgements that duty-holders have reduced risk as low as reasonably practicable." This includes definitions of key concepts such as ALARP (as low as reasonably practicable) and SAFIRP (as far as is reasonably practicable).

Box 4.1 Essential Principles

These principles are intended to underpin the actions in this guidance and so lead to good health and safety performance.

Strong and active leadership from the top

- visible, active commitment from the board;
- establishment of effective "downward" communication systems and management structures; and
- integration of good health and safety management with business decisions.

Worker involvement

- engaging the workforce in the promotion and achievement of safe and healthy conditions;
- effective "'upward" communication; and
- providing high-quality training.

Assessment and review

- identifying and managing health and safety risks;
- accessing (and following) competent advice; and
- monitoring, reporting and reviewing performance.

Source: UK Health and Safety Executive

It highlights "transfer of risk," where taken measures may transfer risk to other employees or members of the public and takes note of the impact of "changed circumstances" where companies may need to alter their controls and practices to maintain risk ALARP.

It has a number of key components that aid its effectiveness as an approach to regulation. Companies and their employees are answerable to an act of parliament that underpins it. It has the HSE as a body that is set up to enforce the act. It has simple guidance and principles, which have driven behaviors in the workplace. Since 1974, fatal injuries in the workplace have fallen by 86 percent.[15]

Others have tried to relate a safety approach to security. For example, Brostoff and Sasse outline how the argument that the safety and security domains are different because the former deals with accidental failures, while security often deals with deliberate breaches. However, they overcome this in their paper by placing both domains in a singular "dangerous world" context, according to outcomes. They cite the following example:

Crossing the street is dangerous whether or not drivers are trying to run you down. In both the safety (unintended collision) and security (assassination by car) versions of this scenario, the way to avoid the breach is to cross when there are no cars coming.[16]

They point out that the problem with adopting the safety model in a security context is that it requires a precondition of "reliable equipment of the right kind." Whether this can be found in an unconstrained IoT or in system with so much connectivity and complexity is a problem for further investigation. However, their argument draws on "Reason's Generic Modelling System" to show how weaknesses, "latent failures" that have been built into a system, promote insecure acts and weaken defences, making incidents more likely. Interestingly, they also point out that latent failures are more likely if the system is more complex.

Salim and Madnick have argued that a systems approach to security that adopts a cyber-safety model, treating cyber security risks akin to accidents, has a number of advantages over traditional technology-focused security frameworks. It encourages a holistic view of security that includes "people, processes, contract management, management support, and training to name a few dimensions." It involves people other than the security-technology department and, in the "eco-system," has to take account of "interactions with other systems/sub-systems operating beyond an organizational boundary."

There is much to learn by thinking about security from a safety perspective. The HSE approach demonstrates strong regulation, principles, guidance, and effective management. In other words, it provides a robust and comprehensive set of measures to shape behaviours toward good health and safety outcomes: there is education and enforcement. Principles should aim to foster a similar comprehensive approach. However, questions remain about cost and practicalities of implementation in smart-living, particularly if the IoT supply chain is set in a complex ecosystem that are beyond organizational boundaries in an international context or involves millions of lines of code. In these circumstances, establishing liability requires navigation of a highly connected set of relationships. There also remains the problem of people taking responsibility for the impact on others beyond their immediate contractual and legal obligations. Consumer-protection frameworks may describe some of these obligations. They are discussed in the next section.

CONSUMER-PROTECTION REGULATION

For some time, there has been a debate about whether consumer protection regarding digital products is weaker than that for other products such as cars. Principles in an IoT context should extend to digital products, services, and the systems in which they operate. As previously discussed, even the car is quickly becoming another part of a connected system. The UK Consumer Rights Act 2015 attempts to bring consumer protection up-to-date and includes sections on "digital content" for the first time. It defines digital content as "data which are produced and supplied in digital form." While the act makes no mention of "software" per se, UK government guidance on this provides examples of digital content as "software, games, apps, ringtones, e-books, online journals and digital media such as music, film and television." This guidance also states that "you are liable for the digital content if you are the *trader*—that is if you supply (sell) the digital content to the consumer." It clarifies that:

Digital content is not services delivered online, such as online banking or the website for online grocery shopping. In the same way as the use of a physical bank is not seen as the supply of goods, the use of an online bank is not the supply of digital content. The exception is where a consumer has separately paid for an online banking app—the app itself would be digital content…When a consumer contracts with an ISP 9 [Internet service provider] or MNO [mobile network operator] they are contracting for a service (access to a network). The ISP or MNO is not therefore liable for content which is faulty, but they would be liable in relation to the general quality of the network service provided.

The consumer has a right to a refund, a right to repair or replace, and the right to price reduction in instances where the digital content is shown to not meet satisfactory quality standards or is not reasonably fit for its particular purpose. Quality includes its state and condition regarding:

- fitness for all the purposes for which digital content of that kind is usually supplied
- freedom from minor defects
- safety
- durability

The guidance caveats questions of reasonableness. It gives a specific example of third-party software in digital content that is "later found to have an inherent security weakness." Reasonableness and judgment are at the heart of the advice quoted in the UK government guidance below:

- To be of satisfactory quality, digital content must meet the standards a reasonable person would consider satisfactory taking into account all relevant circumstances.
- The security of digital content is a relevant circumstance that could form part of the judgement of whether digital content is of satisfactory quality.

- If the security weakness had already been identified, the fact that you did not know about the security weakness when you supplied the digital content would not affect the question of whether the digital content is deemed to be of satisfactory quality. However, if the security weakness had not been identified, it may not be a reasonable expectation that the digital content should be secure with respect to that weakness.

Other guidance examines issues of "particular purpose" and technical incompatibility and provides advice to traders such as:

You are not responsible for quality issues that are the fault of a trader under the control of the consumer, such as their ISP, mobile network operator or cable provider, or due to problems with the consumer's device.

Guidance is provided on the issues of the digital content operating in a complex environment where, for example operating systems change. The guidance is tailored around providing clear information to the consumer and striving to maintain updates in such an environment. However:

The quality rights are judged on the day the digital content was first supplied. As long as the digital content that you supplied met the quality rights at that point, then if the consumer does something they should not have done or does not do something they should have done, which results in the digital content no longer being of satisfactory quality, you may not be liable.

There are also clauses in the act that relate to protection where digital content causes damage to a device or to other digital content. However, government guidance to traders notes that:

if the consumer makes a claim for damage caused by the digital content supplied by you, it is for the consumer to prove what caused the fault and that you failed to use reasonable care and skill to prevent it.

The UK government guidance encourages traders to be as helpful as possible in assisting the consumer to identify the cause of the damage.

The guidance recognizes a concept of risk in relation to testing, as shown in the document FAQ and response below:

Am I required to exhaustively test every possible configuration of software on a consumer's device?

- You are only likely to be required to conduct this type of exhaustive testing if this is considered to be the industry standard. In this case, it is likely that in not doing so you would not have taken the care and skill that is reasonable.

- As exhaustive testing is only the industry norm for very essential types of (business) software (such as in the nuclear power or space industry), you should take reasonable care and skill as and when problems with a particularly unusual software configuration do come to light.

The act certainly shows progress in consumer rights regarding digital content. However, it is perhaps limited in its application to singular products, such as a television or a particular application. How a citizen will have protected rights in a more-complex networked system of devices, software, and services may be more difficult to establish, particularly when a trader places a burden of proof on the consumer. Consumers International produced a report in April 2016, "Internet of things and challenges for consumer protection." It lists a number of challenges including:

the development of hybrid products; the erosion of ownership norms; remote contract enforcement; lack of transparency; complex liability; lock-in to products and systems; locked out of alternatives; and data, privacy and security.

Due to problem such as "complex liability," Consumers International is skeptical about the effectiveness of consumer-protection approaches that do not adequately take into account "what it means to be a consumer of highly networked products and services." Some IoT devices and services will fall foul of the UK Consumer Protection Act 2015, though exploring this, along with failures under privacy and data protection regulation, is something that merits further discussion and research. In particular, more work needs to be done on:

- How are judgments formed regarding highly networked products and services?
- What is reasonable in terms of what can be expected of consumers, users, developers, and others?
- How do we take account of other types of relationships beyond consumers and traders, for example, in business-to-business supply-chain relationships and complex systems?
- How are user rights protected in systems of shared data across multiple services?

Examination of these issues forms one of the recommendations in the IAAC research. Naturally, guidance already exists on what can be expected of professional engineers.

ENGINEERING ETHICS AS AN ANALOGY?

In the United Kingdom, all professionally registered engineers and technicians have committed to working in an ethical and socially responsible manner according to their professional engineering institution's code of conduct, issued in line with guidance from the Engineering Council.

Together with the Royal Academy of Engineering, the Engineering Council has produced a statement of ethical principles to guide engineering practice. This statement summarizes the fundamental principles and is designed to supplement the codes of conduct published by the engineering institutions. The statement draws on discussions with engineers from a range of engineering institutions and philosophers who specialize in applied ethics. It is underpinned by four fundamental principles to guide engineers and technicians in achieving the high ideas of professional life:

- Acting in a reliable and trustworthy manner
- Giving due weight to all relevant facts and published guidance and the wider public interest
- Identifying, evaluating, and quantifying risks
- Being alert to ways in which work might affect others, holding health and safety paramount

Principles developed in this work should support professional engineers in adopting their own ethical guidelines and standards.

DISCUSSION—FACTORS THAT SHAPE THE DEVELOPMENT OF PRINCIPLES

One of the key problems in this research is trying to move beyond a series of long lists into a more systematic approach to principles. Dresner and Jones above, in their paper on the laws of cyber and information security, have tried to do this through borrowing the concept from Asimov. What is clear is that when one takes the idea of trying to shape the IoT we want, one needs to plan for intervention on the basis of the principles. The number of bullet points available from multiple sources suggests that the community knows, to a large extent, what needs to be done at a detailed level. The challenge, therefore, becomes one of adoption of good practice, though some fundamental revision of core concepts, such as privacy in the scale of IoT, will require much more research. Consequently, in developing helpful principles in the context of smart-living, they will need to:

- Be simple at a high level and help people navigate the plethora of bullet-point guidance that might be employed in any given smart-living context.
- Drive and sustain the adoption of good practice that maximizes the benefits of IoT technology while minimizing harm.

So far, this report has proposed that any principles developed for smart-living IoT should:

- Provide a sense of direction for what a "good" IoT might be like…not aiming to provide a solution to a problem, but to develop principles to help improve a "problem situation."
- Encourage early consideration of principles in the design stage.
- Take into account multiple stakeholders' views in the iterative development of systems of systems.
- Recognize that different stakeholders may not have reconcilable views but that their identification and exploration at least allows explicit recognition of the risks and trade-offs in decision-making.
- The principles have to address the scale of IoT connectivity, data collection, data aggregation, and incremental re-purposing of technology and services toward other innovative offerings and uses. This was seen as being at the heart of the IoT development engine, and therefore something that principles would need to shape. It was also seen as being the driver of complexity not only in technical terms, but also in terms of shared risk and liability for when things go wrong. Traditionally, consumer rights have focused on singular products and services. The recent Consumer Rights Act 2015 includes new sections relating to "digital content," but difficulties in protecting the rights of consumers and traders in highly networked environments remain.
- Principles should encourage alignment of security and productivity, almost as the same concept. This is because a device or system that causes harm should not be considered functional. The principles should also encourage alignment of guardian (or governing) roles and commercial roles while maintaining a separation of duties.
- Help decision-makers focus on normalizing reduction-of-harm thinking in design and development through:
  - Identifying issues of concern.
  - Cataloging issues of concern and developing mitigation strategies as part of the design and development process.
  - Shaping the context for good-practice adoption through a series of incentives.
  - Guardians intervening on behalf of citizens and consumers when necessary.
- Principles developed in this work should support professional engineers in adopting their own ethical guidelines and standards.

Some of this may require regulation, but at the HSE example demonstrates, it needs to be a whole system and a comprehensive approach. It is managed and enforced. In the case of the IoT, the personal data aspects fall within the purview of the Information Commissioner. It could be argued that, given the dependence on telecoms platforms for the IoT to be effective, the key regulator would logically be OfCOM. However, it is largely focused on consumer demands of existing telecoms provision and on issues relating to media content. Other regulation will play a part, such as consumer rights, but having a law is not enough on its own. Any principle that envisages an empowered guardian must think about accountability, liability, and enforcement in the round. The Dutch "table of eleven" is a tool for assessing the regulatory regime and assessing the level of compliant behaviours. It consists of eleven dimensions that are grouped under two headings, as in Table 4.6.

Spontaneous compliance dimensions are those that are focused on the compliant behaviour of a target group, while the enforcement dimensions are focused on those elements that are "government activity aimed at encouraging compliance with legislation." This tries to capture wider elements of compliance, such as "nonofficial" control, an example of which would be the norms of a group and the social pressure it brings on its members to comply. Other spontaneous compliance issues include "knowledge of the rules"—people are unlikely to comply if they do not know there are rules or how they should be applied. Cost and benefit analysis acknowledges the logic at work on people's compliance calculations. Is it cheaper to pay the fine than to pay the cost of being compliant? The enforcement dimensions show a more nuanced appreciation than simple punishment for noncompliance. It recognizes that people may take risks such as detection, sanctions, and whether some groups are more likely to be selected for investigation than others, into account. An issue briefly discussed above was whether someone could prove an IoT system was free of defects or that it contained defects to which blame might be attributed regarding

Table 4.6

"Table of Eleven" Dimensions

Spontaneous Compliance Dimensions	Enforcement Dimensions
Knowledge of the rules	Risk of being reported
Costs/benefits	Risk of inspection
Extent of acceptance	Risk of detection
The target group's respect for authority	Selectivity
Nonofficial control	Risk of sanction
	Severity of sanction

Source: Netherlands Ministry of Justice, "The Table of Eleven: A Versatile Tool."
November 2004

liability. A judgement about this will impact on some view of their ability to be compliant or suffer a sanction.

The BCS-OII report provides a case study of the development of an RFID (radio-frequency identification) privacy recommendation by the European Commission. It received endorsement in January 2011 with the intention of it being part of self-regulation of industry and civil society. It was assessed as positive that the informal groups involved in its development had reached agreement. However, according to the report, it was not taken seriously by industry in member states for a variety of reasons. These included lack of sufficient representation from industry partners in developing the recommendations, no formal procedure or reporting responsibility, and the unclear status of the informal working group.

Clearly the fact that a regulation or law exists is not enough. It must sit in an ecosystem of compliance, supported by management, sanctions and rewards, and perceptions of legitimacy and social buy-in. A similar recommendation, but from the perspective of security-awareness training, is made in the Hewlett Packard/RISCS white paper, "Awareness is only the first step." That is, awareness on its own will not bring about desirable behavior. Rather the behavior of individuals is shaped by, for example, the example set by senior leadership and colleagues and the sort of nonofficial control measures mentioned regarding the table of eleven above. The Hewlett Packard/RISCS paper notes that the requirement for good security measures design in the enterprise. Communications, education, and training "cannot compensate for security polices and implementations that are impossible to comply with—removing impossible security tasks is essential security hygiene."

If good design of processes is a requirement at the enterprise level, it must also be true of information systems for consumer and citizens, particularly when they face harm or damage as individuals.

IN CONCLUSION: TOWARD PRINCIPLES FOR DEVELOPING SMART-LIVING IOT

Given the factors shaping the development of principles outlined above, the following principles are offered with a view to engaging the community on their further development. This reflects the word "toward" in the title above, recognizing that much more iteration is required. Further discussion is needed, as some principles may be easier to achieve in some contexts than others. Some may be contingent on others being adopted first. For example, liability depends on some pre-existing rule set. How some principles are enacted needs more consideration. For example, an independent architect for major IoT programs might be able to act in a role, similar to that in the construction industry. This was considered in this research as a principle in its own right but was rejected at this stage, as it falls more into the category of "how to" rather than a principle.

It is envisaged that principles may operate:

- "At the front of the mind" during system requirements setting in design, development, or procurement.
- "At the back of the mind," through becoming a way of doing/part of the culture, normalized through education, learning, and habit.

It may be best to think of these principles not so much as being "used" as traded in or out in decision-making. Ideally the aim should be to preserve all principles if at all possible, and only to trade-out certain principles when they are untenable.

In terms of by whom the principles might be adopted, a multi-perspective approach is suggested with the "we" in the title of this report being an inclusive, but varied, group. It extends from coders to system managers, procurement staff to consumers, and guardians to citizens.

The principles are organized around the contribution they make to better design, development, and sustained implementation of smart-living IoT systems in the round. Acting together will then help "improve the problem situation."

Table 4.7

Principles

Principle	Comment
A: Preservation	
1. A system should be designed to preserve safety, security, privacy, resilience, availability, and reliability by default. In the case of information and data generated by the system, it is confidentiality, integrity, and availability.	By default—the preservation of these properties remains in effect unless deliberately changed. The aim is to encourage thoughtful design.
B: Design & Development	
2. A by-design approach throughout the life cycle should be adopted, taking into account the views of the stakeholders affected by the system—a multistakeholder approach.	A complex system with emergent properties can only be judged through the eyes of its various stakeholders over the life of a system on an ongoing basis. The aim is to encourage discussion and collaboration in design and development.

(continued)

Table 4.7
Principles *(continued)*

Principle	Comment
3. Harm and damage reduction should be assessed and treated early in the system life and on an ongoing basis.	This assessment should be done along with an understanding of the benefits that the system will bring to the various stakeholders. The aim is to encourage a comprehensive view of the upside and downside of any innovation as well as accrue the economic benefits of getting it right early.
4. Functionality without the necessary security, safety, and trustworthiness should not be considered functional.	
5. Apply existing standards.	Due consideration should be given to existing standards, including PAS754:2014 on trustworthiness, which acts as a domain-neutral capstone for good practice; ISO/IEC25010:2011 on quality; the ISO/IEC27xxx security standards; and new standards as they emerge. The aim is to encourage people to apply what is known already.
C: Governance	
6. There should be explicit guardian and supplier roles in any smart-living service. Where they are unknown, unclear, or not-sufficiently separated, parties should seek to address shortcomings.	The aim is to encourage effective oversight, a necessary part of any compliance, redress, and grievance regime.
D: Transparency	
7. Consumers of services should be readily able to know what data a service collects and how it is used, updated, and stored. The consent principle should be maintained.	The aim is to encourage innovation in design and human interaction. The principle is consistent with today's data-protection regulations but remains problematic in highly connected data-driven systems.
8. Supplier claims about the security, safety, and resilience of a service should be substantiated with evidence.	The aim is to discourage lip service being paid to security claims and encourage best efforts on the part of the supplier and adoption of standards.

(continued)

Table 4.7
Principles *(continued)*

Principle	Comment
E: Adoption of good practice	
9. Good practice should be normalized at every opportunity, through obligation, education, and by example.	The aim is to encourage standards and good practice to live in policy and by example in education, work, and the effective application of oversight.
10. Engineering ethics are traded out at one's peril.	The aim is to encourage developers and procurement staff to be explicit about ethical issues, what is being traded out, and for what.
11. Government or service-procurement staff should act on behalf of consumers, adopt these principles, and ask critical questions of suppliers.	The aim is to encourage a critical view by examining risk and impact in a multistakeholder context. Technical guidance from OWASP and others acts as a spur to focusing on security and trustworthiness questions.
F: Regulation and legislation	
12. Compliance and regulation is only effective when it sits within an ecosystem of measures, when it can be enforced, and when it generates buy-in.	The aim is to encourage a whole-system approach to behavioral change. It is required if good practice is to become part of culture, combining softer social controls as well as hard enforcement measures.
G: Liability	
13. Liability lies with those who generate the risk.	The aim is to encourage developers to think about how technology and data is used and repurposed in complex systems and how it may generate and transfer risk. It provides a bottom line in trying to make a difficult judgment. The nature of the risk will determine whether reasonable endeavors or best endeavors are required by the provider.
14. A service provider takes responsibility for its suppliers.	This is to discourage quality issues in the supply chain being taken for granted and encourage inquisitiveness about the standards of those upon whom others rely.

Source: IAAC

NOTES

1. Lauren Probst et al., "Smart Living, Smart Construction and Processes, Case Study 17," Business Innovation Observatory, European Commission, February 2014.

2. Barbara Speed, "Kettles Are Leaking Wi-Fi Passwords (and other failures of the Internet of Things)," *New Statesman*, October 22, 2015, http://www.news tatesman.com/science-tech/future-proof/2015/10/kettles-are-leaking-wifi-pass words-and-other-failures-internet. Accessed March 31, 2018.

3. Trustworthy Software Foundation, "Trustworthy Software Essentials," Issue 1.2, February 2016, p. 8. http://tsfdn.org/wp-content/uploads/2016/03 /TS502-1-TS-Essentials-Guidance-Issue-1.2-WHITE.pdf. Accessed November 4, 2018.

4. Ibid., 16.

5. For a short overview, see University of Cambridge, "Soft Systems Methodology," http://www.ifm.eng.cam.ac.uk/research/dstools/soft-systems-methodo logy/. Accessed July 17, 2016.

6. "The British Computer Society (BCS) and the Oxford Internet Institute report on the societal impact of the Internet of Things (IoT)," 7.

7. Cities2050, "Securing the Future in a Connected World," *Cities2050 Roundtable Event report, London, May 19–20, 2015.* Aquan Limited, 2015, p. 8.

8. Ibid., 6.

9. "Personally identifiable information" is a term used in data-protection legislation in several nations, including in the United Kingdom and the European Union General Data Protection Regulation 2016.

10. CISCO, "Ever Heard of Layer 8?" Forum Post by "Jared," January 7, 2012. https://learningnetwork.cisco.com/blogs/vip-perspectives/2012/01/07/ever -heard-of-layer-8. Accessed March 31, 2018.

11. This idea of separation of guardian and commerce and concepts such as promoting comfort and convenience draw in part on Jane Jacobs's work on the guardian and commercial "moral syndromes." Jacobs defines a moral syndrome as coming from the Greek, meaning "things that run together." She presents the guardian and commercial moral syndromes as a series of traits "that run together" and argues that they are each a collection of traits with its own internal logic, but they run into moral problems when they become mixed. For example, guardians should "shun trading," as it becomes unclear to others for whom they are ultimately working. A commercial actor should "shun force" (only guardians should have monopolies on force) because fair trade is preferable to cartels and lack of choice. This, of course, may seem at odds with politics that encourage markets and commercial suppliers in the delivery of government services to the public, for example. in prisons, the health service, and education. However, given that governance and running of such arrangements are subjected to continual scrutiny, the idea of separation of duties regarding oversight and auditing at least gives weight to the general distinction. See Jane Jacobs, *Systems of Survival* (New York: Random House, 1994).

12. Trustworthy Software Foundation, "Trustworthy Software Essentials," Issue 1.2, February 2016, p. 15, http://tsfdn.org/wp-content/uploads/2016/03/TS502 -1-TS-Essentials-Guidance-Issue-1.2-WHITE.pdf. Accessed March 31, 2018.

13. Generally interpreted to mean that all commercially practicable action should be taken, but only to the extent that such action is not to the detriment of the obligor's commercial interests, and with no assumption of a requirement to divert resources from elsewhere within the business [Jolley v. Carmel Ltd [2000] 2 EGLR 154].

14. Generally interpreted to mean leaving no stone unturned [Sheffield District Railway Company v. Great Central Railway Company (1911) 27 TLR451] within the limits of a prudent board of directors acting properly in the interests of their company [Terrell v. Mabie Todd & Co Limited (1952) 69 RPC 234] and that would not be detrimental to the financial interests of the company nor would it undermine commercial standing or goodwill [Rackham v. Peek Foods Limited (1990) BCLC 895].

15. Health and Safety Executive, "Historical Picture." http://www.hse.gov.uk/Statistics/history/index.htm. Accessed August 22, 2016.

16. Sacha Brostoff and Angela Sasse, "Safe and Sound: 'A safety-critical approach to security,'" *NSPW'01*, September 10–13th, 2002, Cloudcroft, New Mexico, p. 43.

BIBLIOGRAPHY

BCS and OII. "The Societal Impact of the Internet of Things." *BCS-OII Forum Report*, March 2013. https://www.bcs.org/upload/pdf/societal-impact-report-feb13.pdf. Accessed March 31, 2018.

Bradgate, Robert. "Consumer Rights in Digital Products: A Research Report Prepared for the UK Department for Business, Innovation and Skills." September 2010. https://www.gov.uk/government/uploads/system/uploads/attachment_data/file/31837/10-1125-consumer-rights-in-digital-products.pdf. Accessed March 31, 2018.

Brewster, Thomas. "It's Depressingly Easy to Spy on Vulnerable Baby Monitors Using Just a Browser." *Forbes*, September 2, 2015. http://www.forbes.com/sites/thomasbrewster/2015/09/02/baby-surveillance-with-a-browser/#1b81d4cf7056. Accessed March 31, 2018.

British Standards Institution. "Software Trustworthiness—Governance and Management—Specification." PAS 754:2014 (May 2014).

Brostoff, Sacha, and Angela Sasse. "Safe and Sound: 'A Safety-Critical Approach to Security.'" New Security Paradigms Workshop 01 (*NSPW'01*), Cloudcroft, New Mexico, USA, September 10–13, 2002.

Cities2050. "Securing the Future in a Connected World." *Cities2050 Roundtable Event report, London, May 19–20, 2015*. Aquan Limited, 2015.

Consumers International. "Connection and Protection in the Digital Age—The Internet of Things and Challenges to Consumer Protection." April 2016, p. 4. https://www.consumersinternational.org/media/1292/connection-and-protection-the-internet-of-things-and-challenges-for-consumer-protection.pdf. Accessed March 31, 2018.

Dresner, Daniel and Neira Jones. "The Three Laws of Cyber and Information Security, 2014." First published in *Cybertalk* 6 (Autumn 2014). http://www.softbox.co.uk/cybertalk-issuesix. Accessed March 31, 2018.

The Guardian. "Consumer Reports Urges Tesla to Disable Autopilot after Driver's Death." July 14, 2016. https://www.theguardian.com/technology/2016/jul/14/consumer-reports-tesla-autopilot-death. Accessed March 31, 2018.

Health and Safety Executive. "Essential Principles." http://www.hse.gov.uk/leadership/essentialprinciples.htm. Accessed March 31, 2018.

Health and Safety Executive. "Historical Picture." http://www.hse.gov.uk/Statistics/history/index.htm. Accessed March 31, 2018.

Health and Safety Executive. "Regulating and Enforcing Health and Safety." http://www.hse.gov.uk/enforce/index.htm. Accessed March 31, 2018.

Hewlett Packard Enterprise. "Awareness Is Only the First Step: A Framework for Progressive Engagement of Staff in Cyber Security." White Paper, 2015. http://www.riscs.org.uk/wp-content/uploads/2015/12/Awareness-is-Only-the-First-Step.pdf. Accessed March 31, 2018.

IoT Security Foundation. "Establishing Principles for Internet of Things Security." https://iotsecurityfoundation.org/establishing-principles-for-internet-of-things-security/. Accessed March 31 2018.

Jacobs, Jane. *Systems of Survival*. New York: Random House, 1994.

Microsoft. "The OSI Model's Seven Layers Defined and Function Explained." 2014. https://support.microsoft.com/en-us/kb/103884. Accessed March 31, 2018.

Netherlands Ministry of Justice. "The Table of Eleven: A Versatile Tool." November 2004.

OWASP. "Internet of Things Project." https://www.owasp.org/index.php/OWASP_Internet_of_Things_Project. Accessed March 31, 2018.

OWASP. "IoT Security Guidance." https://www.owasp.org/index.php/IoT_Security_Guidance. Accessed March 31, 2018.

Probst, Laurent; Monfardini, Erica; Frideres, Laurent and Cedola, Daniela. "Smart Living, Smart Construction and Processes, Case Study 17." Business Innovation Observatory, European Commission, February 2014.

Royal Academy of Engineering & Engineering Council. "Statement of Ethical Principles." https://www.engc.org.uk/media/2334/ethical-statement-2017.pdf. Accessed March 31, 2018.

Salim, Hamid, and Stuart Madnick. "Cyber Safety: A Systems Thinking and Systems Theory Approach to Managing Cyber Security Risks." Composite Information Systems Laboratory Working Paper CISL# 2014-12. MIT, September 2014.

Sommerville, I. *Software Engineering*, 9th ed. Boston: Pearson, 2011.

Speed, Barbara. "Kettles Are Leaking Wi-Fi Passwords (and other failures of the Internet of Things)." *New Statesman*, October 22, 2015. http://www.newstatesman.com/science-tech/future-proof/2015/10/kettles-are-leaking-wifi-passwords-and-other-failures-internet. Accessed March 31, 2018.

Thomson, Iain. "25,000 Malware-Riddled CCTV Cameras form Network-Crashing Botnet." *The Register*, June 28, 2016. http://www.theregister.co.uk/2016/06/28/25000_compromised_cctv_cameras/. Accessed March 31, 2018.

Trustworthy Software Foundation. "Trustworthy Software Essentials." Issue 1.2, February 2016. http://tsfdn.org/wp-content/uploads/2016/03/TS502-1-TS-Essentials-Guidance-Issue-1.2-WHITE.pdf. Accessed March 31, 2018.

UK Department of Business Innovation and Skills. "Consumer Rights Act: Digital Content—Guidance for Business." September 2015. https://www.busi

nesscompanion.info/sites/default/files/CRA-Digital-Content-Guidance
-for-Business-Sep-2015.pdf. Accessed March 31, 2018

UK Government. Consumer Rights Act 2015. http://www.legislation.gov.uk
/ukpga/2015/15/contents/enacted. Accessed March 31, 2018.

UK Health and Safety at Work etc. Act 1974. http://www.legislation.gov.uk
/ukpga/1974/37/contents. Accessed March 31, 2018.

University of Cambridge. "Soft Systems Methodology." http://www.ifm.eng.cam
.ac.uk/research/dstools/soft-systems-methodology/. Accessed March 31,
2018.

CHAPTER 5

Disruption: Big Data, Artificial Intelligence, and Quantum Computing

Jack Caravelli and Nigel Jones

Humans are not good at predicting the future. Think about recent financial crises, elections, or referenda. Even while we are living in a period of huge computing power and sophisticated models and data, accurate predictions about big events and turns in history are elusive. On being briefed at the London School of Economics on the "credit crunch" of 2008, Queen Elizabeth asked simply, "Why did nobody notice it?" When it comes to technology, it is tempting to think that disruption always happens quickly and noticeably, such that predictions focus on single products, services, or devices. While we can witness moments, such as the launches of the iTunes store and iPhone, it is more difficult to understand what they mean or to where they might lead. Noticing when we are in the middle of a revolution and its implications can be equally difficult. Nevertheless, this is what we have set out to tackle in this chapter.

I wager (figuratively speaking, given the Las Vegas context discussed below) when thinking of big data, artificial intelligence (AI), and the processing power of quantum computing, the reader will have a sense of revolution or disruption. We can see it changing our relationships and our ways of living, working, and learning today. Where they are leading is hard to predict. This uncertainty affects markets driven by the prospect of opportunity, and also anxiety about what might be lost. To fully understand their implications, we need to consider them together. While we might be guilty of downplaying the upside of such a revolution, our focus is on the downside. That is, we are going to explore the issues more from a harm perspective, with a view not only to harm reduction but also to enable the realization of the upside. We start by examining big data, before we move to AI, and then quantum computing. We finish with a discussion on ethics, trust, and technology.

DATA ANALYTICS AND BIG DATA

Every day, thousands of customers stream into casinos around the world—Las Vegas, Atlantic City, Macau, and London—in hopes of striking it rich or at least paying for their travel expenses or a good meal. That most fail to do so is a direct reflection of how casinos understand and harness the importance of data. Skilled blackjack players, for instance, approach casino tables knowing their odds of winning any particular hand are close to but not quite 50 percent.

The small advantage belongs to the house. That small advantage also assumes, over a series of perhaps 20 to 30 hands, that the players make no mistakes in strategy. Of course, if they do so, the casino's odds increase substantially. Still, those who enjoy gambling are easily tempted by odds that place them, even continuously, at only a slight disadvantage. The casinos are quietly pleased by those with that attitude and take many steps to incentivize them to play, using various "comps," including free dinners, show tickets, and so forth.

As our (hopefully) lucky player sits at one table, probably surrounded by other players, the casino operates dozens of other active tables, with hundreds of other players. Many play other games, often with odds that are not as good as those "enjoyed" by our blackjack player. In short, every hand that has been dealt to every player in every gambling establishment for decades has favored the casino, sometimes slightly and sometimes a bit more. But small advantages on any one hand add up to huge profits, given that thousands of games are played every day. The casinos win because they have known for years the importance of understanding what we now call big data—that from small, individual advantages at every gaming table, multiplied over and over, can spring profits that create billionaires of casino owners.

If this rather mercenary and relatively unsophisticated use of big data is measured in financial terms in Atlantic City or London, the advantages of big data are apparent in many other ways for many other industries. For our discussion, we will, as a first step, define "big data" as exceptionally large volumes of data that exist from various sources. Data can be defined as existing, such as statistics on the number of automobile drivers stopped for various infractions of highway-safety rules. Other forms of data can be new, accumulated from many sources, such as sensors, social media, or other types of video, audio, and text. The data can be interesting in themselves, such as knowing where in a city drivers are most likely to be stopped for traffic infractions. But the real value of big data is that old and new data alike can, with computer assistance, be mined, analyzed, and used. Collected data may be further characterized as structured or unstructured. Structured data may be existing data, such as an individual's driving record for a selected period of time. Unstructured data may come from a myriad of sources, such as social media or Web sites. This entire process is referred to as big-data analytics, while the data being captured may be characterized as high variety, high velocity, and high value. Through this process, patterns and trends can be identified.

For some, big-data analytics present a holy grail or business nirvana. There is an underlying assumption, treated almost as axiomatic by some writers, academics, and business executives, that if big data is harvested and analyzed properly, it will yield to the user various business insights and efficiencies and, ultimately, profits. This is not an illusion or misplaced assumption. Many industries and businesses are doing exactly that, exploiting the promise and potential of big data in countless ways.

One of the most dramatic examples is seen in America's billion-dollar professional sports franchises. Baseball lovers, for example, revel in statistics. How many home runs have a player or team hit? What is a pitcher's earned-run average, and how does it compare to his competition's? What is a star player's batting average? How many errors does a team's infield make? These traditional and often beloved measures of skill, efficiency, and effectiveness have been part of the sport for more than a century. In the digital age, a new and much more complex world of sports analytics has emerged, and it is driven by data that couldn't be accessed as recently as the turn of this century. Today, when one player is substituted for another, he is assessed by how much he does or does not contribute to WAR (wins above replacement).

How sweeping is the impact of big data on professional sports? We have identified the following examples. Big data can tell a baseball manager when the starting pitcher is likely to tire and needs to be removed, drawing upon numerous other occasions when that pitcher, and many others like him, begins to wear down and is replaced. In 2017, Washington's professional baseball team, the Nationals, replaced a highly experienced and successful "old school" manager who shunned the predictive analytics of big data in favor of a younger manager who embraced that type of data. In-game decisions by professional and even college managers and coaches are increasingly driven by the insights provided by big data.

Big data also has considerable applicability to gleaning insights into fan preferences for seating or the scheduling of game times. Moreover, as a major entertainment business where most franchise owners are billionaires, contract negotiations for players and managers, many of whom are wealthy too, hinge increasingly on statistics used by agents to make the case that their player or manager merits a substantial raise or needs to be replaced.

These examples are sure to be overtaken or at least augmented by even more sophisticated future uses of big data. In the not-so-distant future, athletic clothing will be equipped with sensors to record virtually every second of athletes' performance, from how hard they run to how fast an outfielder can throw a ball to an infielder, to the trajectories of balls they hit while at bat.

Within the highly popular National Football League, which, compared to baseball, has been somewhat slower to accept the value of big data, there is now a chief information officer working in the league office, and many of the teams now have one or two full-time staff members who trace performance statistics.

The impact of big data on sports is certainly not limited to the United States, and, instead, is becoming a global phenomenon. By one estimate, the global sports market easily reaches into the hundreds of billions of dollars annually. Big data is fueling big business. Teams, players, and owners across the globe are learning the value of big data along with their U.S. counterparts. Moreover, both within the U.S. and overseas, big data is transforming not only the obvious parts of professional sports—the players, managers, and so forth—but also the less visible parts such as fans, fan clubs, sponsors, and supporting businesses. Various software approaches, such as IBM's "Fan Insight," are already used to forecast fan-based dynamics.

Far larger than even professional sports is the U.S. health care industry. Health care accounts for a prodigious amount of the U.S. economy, taking about one of every six dollars spent annually. Health care costs have been and remain a major financial drain for countless citizens, leading health care companies to seek ways to enhance efficiencies in an environment where high cost is driven in many ways by high-technology solutions, which are siren songs for millions. Big data and the analytics surrounding them are making major contributions in areas such as cutting costs and wasteful overhead, predicting epidemics, reducing medical errors, limiting data fraud, and improving quality of life and patient outcome for tens of thousands, including through apps that assist in lifestyle changes.

Here are two of many examples that point to what we might call the existing and increasingly antiquated practice of homogenized medicine. In our first example, statistics show that the top ten medicines given to Medicaid patients only benefit 21 percent of them. That leaves a staggering 79 percent of those patients who fail to benefit from the most-prescribed medicines. What explains these disappointing results? Can big data shed insight into this apparent shortfall in modern medicine's support to an aging population?

We have also looked at breast-cancer statistics. The common wisdom among health care consumers and many physicians alike (and actively promoted) is that mammography screening for women in their 50s is a desirable way to test for this dreaded disease. The statistics don't bear this out. Of 10,000 women in that age group who have mammogram screening for the disease for a decade, only five will avoid a breast-cancer death. Does that paltry result justify the effort and expenditures of time and money? Moreover, of those 10,000 tested patients, over 5,000 will receive false positive results with all the attendant emotional worry. These are among the many indications that standard treatments applied uniformly fall far short of their goals.

Big data and big-data analytics can serve medicine and medical practice enormously. While this sounds highly desirable and is a positive and even revolutionary development, the challenges in reaching this type of positive outcomes are daunting. For example, the data generated by and for just one patient is considerable. There are doctor notes, personal medical history, discussions with nurses, laboratory tests, medical imaging, and insurance information that cover even the simplest and briefest hospital stays. Traditionally, much of this data was stored in hard copy, often in various locations. In the era of big data and data analytics, this information can be brought together as a powerful tool and an aid to decision-making, leading to better and, ideally, less-expensive health outcomes. At the same time, the volume of this information, when digitized, can overwhelm even sophisticated hardware and software capabilities, requiring new expenditures to manage the available information.

At the Information Assurance Advisory Council's 2017 Annual Symposium, Professor Dave Robertson for the University of Edinburgh, examining the security of data in a health context, asked the audience to imagine the British health system in 10 years' time. He said that people often think it will simply be more of the same, but busier. However, he argued that a revolution was under way through targeted treatments based on an individual's genome. Therapy was now starting to treat everyone's cancer as *their* cancer—a rare cancer—the one that you have based on your genes. It has the potential to be much more effective, with less trial and error and unnecessary side effects. He went on to argue that if every cancer were rare, it would be necessary to share genomic data across the research community to make sure that medical practitioners are confident in the efficaciousness of any one combination of treatments. In fact, if every cancer were rare, the population of genomes required for effective research would likely be bigger than the UK population. It would need international sharing of genomic data. Are nations and individuals ready to do this? What are the security and privacy protocols?

The technology giant Google is finding the lure of becoming a major force in the health care industry irresistible. It is touting expanding partnerships with major health care organizations associated with the University of Chicago and Stanford University. Google researchers point out that every year in America, upward of 100,000 patients will die from hospital-associated infections. Another 770,000 will die in the hospital or require unplanned admissions.

In short, an almost endless number of potential applications for analytics in the health care industry could revolutionize it. Nonetheless, the picture is not completely rosy. There also are a series of underlying reasons why the benefits of big data have yet to be fully exploited by the health care industry. Some hospitals may invest substantial, if limited, funds in new technology but may not be prepared to invest heavily in big data. Other data that could be gleaned from the use of personal devices such as heart monitors for patients is not being fully exploited. On a larger scale, questions of information governance, interoperability, and standardization need to be addressed.

The impact of big data on consumer and commercial enterprises is no less compelling. Let's take just two disparate examples. The fast-food and fashion industries are notoriously competitive. For example, for years, major restaurant chains, such as McDonald's or Burger King, could track overall sales at their stores and know precisely how many hamburgers or chicken sandwiches were sold at each outlet. That process is similar in retail. Whether at a high-end Neiman Marcus boutique or a more pedestrian Target or Walmart store, there have long been streams of data reporting on store performance along with a more granular performance of each department, such as shoe or perfume sales.

Businesses want to grow their sales and profits and are expected to do so by their shareholders and boards of directors. What happens when McDonald's or Target want to expand the business base within existing markets or attempt to break into new ones? Much of the answer for those decisions is supported by big data. Consumer behavior is driven to a significant extent by convenience. The most profitable location of a new store or restaurant or advertising campaign can be ascertained through big data—in our example by combining demographic, road, and transport data.

Beyond those examples, marketers and advertising agencies are increasingly cognizant of the power of big data. We went back and looked at a business survey conducted in 2013. At that time, 85 percent of surveyed companies acknowledged that big data provided over half of their marketing initiatives. In addition, a large percentage used the Web to collect consumer data. There is every reason to believe those numbers would be even higher today.

Big data serves business and perhaps the overall quality of life in one community in another way. In Charleston, South Carolina, a low-lying, coastal area prone to seasonal flooding, a local realty company Xebec is searching for land to build warehouses. Quite reasonably, it seeks to avoid choosing a location that may become flooded as sea levels rise. As described in a *New York Times* article, in one respect, there is ample weather data to help Xebec in its decision-making. However, on close inspection, the data is lacking in key elements such as how rising sea levels could worsen already flood-prone parts of the area.

As a result, Xebec turned to an emerging Silicon Valley company Jupiter, which offers "to analyze local weather and hydrological data and combine it with climate model projections to assess the potential climate risks Xebec might face in Charleston over the next few decades from things like heavier rainfall, sea level rise or increased storm surge."[1] To deliver on its promises, Jupiter will have to harness the power of big data, copious amounts of information gleaned from disparate sources. In so doing, Jupiter may be able to provide Charleston insight on its coming meteorological future.

There is also a less appealing side to the story. In a previous chapter, we have seen how social media is being used in some nations to further democracy by, for example, allowing citizens to coordinate times and places for political rallies and demonstrations. At the same time, big data allows authoritarian or dictatorial regimes such as those in Russia and China to crack down on dissidents or those deemed in opposition, through such means as facial recognition, cyber monitoring, and data mining. Technology and politics are more intertwined than ever.

In the course of their daily operations, a handful of U.S. tech companies, led by Google, Amazon, and Facebook, is amassing extraordinary amounts of data. In simplest terms, as Rikky Hasan, a senior London financial analyst, says, "Data has value." In fact, data realizes its value when it is put to use. Today, there is much discussion about the intangible assets of a company. Unlike its physical assets, intangible assets such as data and research and development are not included on its balance sheet. Yet in the United States and the United Kingdom, investment in intangibles is outstripping investment in tangibles. In the industrial age, the value of a company was close to the value of its assets, whereas now we can see that it is much higher. Consequently, the market value of Uber and Airbnb is much higher than any cars or buildings they own. The value of data put to use has been well-demonstrated by our discussions of big data in professional sports and health care. For a growing number, the question is becoming how that data can and should be used—and how it should be protected.

Much of our book has centered on two themes; the first is the vast network of opportunities created by the Internet, and the second are the myriad of challenges from those who would abuse the Internet's vulnerabilities for profit or political gain. The third emerging theme looks more sharply at the tech giants that have shaped so much of our contemporary world. As we have seen, Google, Facebook, and Amazon have created a

revolution whose impact and involvement in the daily lives of governments, businesses, and consumer affairs will be hard to reverse. The question is, will that direction be, on balance, more positive than negative?

We have seen the positive developments arising from big data and predictive analytics in various applications. The leaders in that field—again,
Google, Facebook, and Amazon—have reached legendary business status
and amassed fortunes for their owners and investors. Amazon is run by
Jeff Bezos, assessed as being the world's wealthiest man. The negative cod-
icils to this are being discussed more openly than ever. In a dinner speech
at the 2018 World Economic Forum meeting in Davos, billionaire investor
George Soros described his concerns about the big data companies. Soros's
remarks painted a disturbing picture of how the big data companies operate and what the future holds for them.

It is only a matter of time before the global dominance of the U.S. IT monopolies is
broken…they are an obstacle to innovation…they are a near-monopoly distributor
of information…this makes them a public utility and they should be then open to
more regulations.

Perhaps above all, Soros worries that "they might be willing to compete
for the attention of authoritarian regimes like China." That combination
"could be an alliance between authoritarian states and large, data rich IT
monopolies that would bring together nascent systems of corporate surveillance with an already developed system of state sponsored surveillance." If Soros's worst fears play out, individual freedoms everywhere
would be under assault.

Soros looked like a prophet when, in late March 2018, it was revealed
that a Cambridge University psychologist, Aleksandr Kogan, had created
an app that accessed the personal data of 50 million Facebook users. Under
what was Facebook policy at the time, Kogan also collected data such as
names, residential locations, and religious affiliations of the "friends" of
those who downloaded the app. The data was shared with Cambridge
Analytica, a data-science and data-mining company that was assembling
data on American voters.

The revelations created a political and financial firestorm; in two days
in late March, Facebook lost $50 million in value. Facebook founder Mark
Zuckerberg acknowledged that there had been a "breach of trust" by Facebook's compromise of its users' data and pledged to "do the right thing."
He said Facebook would conduct a full forensic audit and ban any company that did not cooperate with it.

Legislators and regulators might not be able to reverse the revolution,
but perhaps there are ways in which privacy, rights, and our democratic
ways of life might be safeguarded. Before discussing this, however, we
must discuss AI and quantum computing.

ARTIFICIAL INTELLIGENCE AND MACHINE LEARNING

How much data could you analyze effectively before you would find some form of automation helpful? Perhaps a machine that finds relationships between words in unstructured text and recognizes the difference between a barrel of beer and the barrel of a rifle in context would be helpful. Maybe the automation could connect events to times and places for the purposes of investigation or crime reduction. Maybe, when trying to find the quickest route between two points in an unfamiliar city, you could have a machine weigh up the options, provide alternatives to select from, and provide information about the likely journey time of each route, taking into account traffic and time of the day. Maybe we could teach a machine to know how to best manage energy in a house or city. As with the examples explored earlier in the chapter, data analytics and some form of automation go hand in hand. It's here today, and we are in the middle of a revolution where it is hard to determine fact from fiction or hype from potential.

Automation is our starting point. Artificial intelligence (AI) is defined as "the mimicking of human thought and cognitive processes to solve complex problems automatically."[2] "'Machine learning' (ML) refers to the ability of computers to automatically acquire new knowledge, learning from, for example, past cases or experience, from the computer's own experiences, or from exploration."[3] Automation is at the heart of both AI and ML concepts, though they are different. It is best to think of AI as the broader concept that encompasses all forms of automation that mimic human decision-making. For example, a robot might perform a task as if it were human but not learn as it goes. ML, on the other hand, is a more specific concept involving the processes by which computers learn. Having some regard to the distinction is important if one wishes to speak to the right expert, conduct one's own research, or simply manage expectations about products. Take, for example, a driverless vehicle that is given the task to go from A to B, using its sensors to judge its speed, location, and direction and a set of rules that define what is safe. It can mimic a human driver by following the rules and making decisions based on the data acquired through its sensors. More often than not—indeed, a lot more often than not—it reaches its destination safely. This vehicle, making decisions according to the rules, is displaying AI. If, through the course of its driving, it learned to become a better driver, that would be machine learning. Data from all autonomous vehicles on the road can be fed to another machine that learns how to improve driving in all the contexts in which vehicles are deployed.

Melissa Buaman at RAND Corporation makes an interesting argument in which she explores the case for "why waiting for perfect autonomous vehicles (AV) may cost lives" and provides a calculator to allow the reader to weigh a number of variables. The reader can select when and how much safer an AV will be compared to a human driver. The calculator compares this to the number of deaths under these conditions to the projected number of deaths on U.S. roads without AVs. For example, let's suppose that AVs are introduced widely in 2020 when they are, for argument's sake, a little safer than human drivers. In 30 years' time, let's say they make up 80 percent of vehicles, and, at that point, they are twice as safe as human drivers. In these circumstances it is estimated that 690,000 lives would be saved over the next 50 years. If AVs are almost perfect compared to humans in thirty years' time, 1.2 million lives would be saved over the next 50 years. The article explores the case that even small advances in safety could save many lives over time.

The ethical dimension of vehicle decision-making is explored by some at a micro level. For example, what should a vehicle do when it is confronted with ethical choices relating to avoiding dogs, adults, children, or something else? How does it hand back control and decision-making to the human operator, and how quickly? At the time of writing, an investigation was underway into how a prototype Uber autonomous vehicle came to kill a person pushing a bicycle across the road, even with a supervising "driver" at the wheel while the vehicle was in automatic mode. How these micro and macro cases are weighed against other things that could go wrong, perhaps through the widespread loss of services through cyber attack, is something that all of us will have to try to untangle.

Machine learning and artificial learning techniques may be combined in the analysis of data or the modeling of systems. An online search shows many examples of machines automatically classifying photographic images. For example, the machine, with or without human assistance, may recognize for itself when a camel is in the picture. To date, this has not been a trivial exercise, though it is getting better by the day, given how similar a camel is to a horse from the perspective of a computer. We are also witnessing advances in the manipulation of video and animation so that a person's facial expressions might be communicated through an animated emoji. It is now possible to manipulate video so that the expression and mouth movements of one person can be replicated on a third party.[4]

The implications for understanding what is fake and what is real have become particularly heightened and politicized in recent times. Naturally, disinformation does not rely on AI. However, AI and ML can enhance disinformation and deception by selecting and targeting people in large populations and representing information in ways that appear authentic. The morality of this will also need to be untangled.

AUTOMATON IN CYBER SECURITY

The application of automation in cyber security is a growth industry. One U.S. orientated market report valued AI in security at USD 2.99 billion in 2016, rising to USD 34.81 billion by 2025.[5] Much of the interest in AI and ML in cyber security is based on many of the same drivers outlined above. With so much data passing through, being captured, and generated on enterprise and social networks, it has become impossible for a security analyst to monitor and respond effectively to incidents and attacks without automation.

Many technology companies are offering products based on "advanced AI," but it is not always clear how much AI and in what form is being used in practice. It is a truth of the current cyber security market that it is difficult for customers to interpret security hyperbole, including the words "advanced," "most secure," "predictive," and so forth. Nevertheless, in broad terms, a number of approaches are being offered or are in development to help augment or replace the human expertise of the security analyst. For example, some systems rely on anomaly spotting. The logic of this is that if one can assess what "normal" looks like on a network, events that lie outside of normal can be flagged for further investigation. This is meant to provide a way of addressing some of the shortcomings of, for example, "signature-based" antivirus systems, which alert about problems when they spot the "signature" of the malicious software delivered to or activated on a network. Consequently, attackers have been adept at making small changes to signatures in order to get through the antivirus systems. This measure and countermeasure dynamic can also be seen in an adversary's attempts to undermine anomaly-based detection systems by trying to make an attack appear normal. Sometimes this is through what might be described as a slow-onset attack, where small steps are taken over time so as to not attract suspicion. This to date has been associated with state-level advanced persistent threats (APT), but, increasingly, nonstate actors are developing capability in this area. As it is common practice for enterprises to delete their logs after a few months, the system in effect is continually reset to normal, and the attack continues. As a result, there is a desire for enterprises to keep evermore data and analyze it with a view to finding the weak signals of an attack: a slightly different needle from other needles in a haystack.

There is also an attempt to try to find other ways of recognizing the threat. One way is to try to build forward from events to try to create plausible scenarios about what might be going on in the network. Other ways involve the modeling of attacks against systems to find vulnerabilities and attacks vectors before the adversary finds them. This might be through the development, for example, of automated "penetration-testing" services. There is a huge amount of investment in research in this area, with highly innovative ideas being explored. This includes AI that can write better, more secure software and ML that manages self-healing networks. A persistent theme of research is how to stop false positives and negatives while continuing to automate as much as possible so that the analyst can attend to the highest priority events.

Of course, there is also the possibility that adversaries will use AI and ML methods in their attacks. Labeled by some as AI wars, this heralds the development of another countermove in the cyber arms race. This might mean that AI injects events into a network to make it appear normal or even attacks the defender's ML algorithm to skew the lessons being learned. AI assists the adversary and not just the defender in scanning ports, networks, and applications for vulnerabilities before automating the appropriate attack. One thing is certain. With this incremental technological development, there is little chance of getting far enough ahead of the innovative attacker to break the measure-and-countermeasure dynamic. Perhaps only something more revolutionary can do it, as we turn to quantum computing.

QUANTUM COMPUTING

The United Kingdom has a national strategy for quantum technologies. It looks ahead to a set of emerging quantum technologies that build on top of the "naturally occurring quantum effects" of quantum physics "that has given us the electronics that control the fabric of our world, including telecommunications and media, computing, and the control systems that underpin our infrastructure and transport systems." The UK Engineering and Physical Science Council (EPSRC) states that quantum technologies have "underpinned the emergence of the 'information age' in the same manner that technologies based on classical physics underpinned the Industrial Revolution of the eighteenth and nineteenth centuries."

At the quantum level, the classical laws of physics that guided the Industrial Revolution do not explain the behavior of atoms, particles, and light. Quantum technologies exploit quantum mechanics, including notions of entanglement and superposition, to develop practical applications in, for example, lasers, sensors, and computing. The following definitions are taken from a 2017 UK Parliament note on quantum technologies:

Superposition: A particle can exist in a combination of different states at once. For example, it can behave as if it is spinning both clockwise and anticlockwise at the same time. Once it is measured or interacts with its environment, it settles into a single state, randomly adopting either a clockwise or an anticlockwise spin.

Entanglement: Two (or more) particles can become intrinsically related, or entangled, so that they can no longer be described as separate entities. This means that a measurement made on one particle will determine the outcome of a similar measurement made on the other particle, even over great distances.

These definitions are important when we come to talk about the application of quantum computing in cyber security. However, there are many fields in which these technologies are being developed. See Table 5.1

Table 5.1

Research Area	Relevant Grants	Proportional Value
Artificial Intelligence Technologies	1	£250,233
Cold Atoms and Molecules	2	£1,614,066
Complexity Science	1	£84,126
Condensed Matter: Electronic Structure	5	£1,567,387
Light Matter Interaction and Optical Phenomena	2	£1,976,911
Optical Communications	3	£2,290,034
Optical Devices and Subsystems	4	£4,868,816
Optoelectronic Devices and Circuits	2	£756,469
Photonic Materials	2	£389,432
Quantum Devices, Components, and Systems	116	£182,172,255
Quantum Optics and Information	7	£7,080,317
Superconductivity	2	£1,178,233
Theoretical Computer Science	3	£2,318,321
Total		£206,546,600

for an overview of a wide field of applications for EPSRC research and investment in quantum technologies as of March 2018.

Both the UK Parliamentary note and Quantum Technologies Plan provide a variety of examples of specific applications, including navigation systems that can operate without GPS, by measuring small changes based on the starting position. They describe network timekeeping through atomic clocks and highly accurate synchronization and give an overview of quantum gravity sensors that can detect objects at 10 times the depth possible today. However, of particular interest to us is quantum computing.

A "bit" in classical computing is either a "1" or a "0." Because of entanglement and superposition, a "qubit" in quantum computing can be both a "0" and a "1" at the same time.

As Gabriel Popkin states:

Qubits outmuscle classical computer bits thanks to two uniquely quantum effects: superposition and entanglement. Superposition allows a qubit to have a value of not just 0 or 1, but both states at the same time, enabling simultaneous computation. Entanglement enables one qubit to share its state with others separated in space, creating a sort of super-superposition, whereby processing capability doubles with every qubit. An algorithm using, say, five entangled qubits can effectively do 25, or 32, computations at once, whereas a classical computer would have to do those 32 computations in succession. As few as 300 fully entangled qubits could, theoretically, sustain more parallel computations than there are atoms in the universe.

In November 2017, *Forbes* reported that IBM has already built functioning 16- and 17-qubit computers, while Google's quantum AI lab claims to have built a working 20-qubit computer. Google announced in March 2018 that it was testing a computer with 72 qubits. Quantum computing promises to deliver more processing power and better analytics, modeling, and simulation at a time of ever-increasing amounts of data and demand for insight. However, for a number of cyber security commentators, it presages a world without encryption.

Currently, encryption is secure to the extent that classical approaches to computing would require hundreds or thousands of years to crack the key, whereas quantum computing may be able to do this in minutes. Jeff Koyen, writing in Forbes, gives hope that quantum-key distribution may offer an approach to encryption before the full benefits of quantum computing come online. Key distribution is at the heart of encryption because one needs the receiver of, for example, a message to be able to open it with a key. Quantum key distribution involves information sent in a quantum state, usually with entangled photons (light particles) down a fiber-optic cable. As the photons are entangled, any attempt to intercept the communication changes the state of the photons and, therefore, the key. This means that the message remains encrypted, and we are alerted to attempts to eavesdrop. The key is discarded and replaced. Quantum computing, it would appear, does not in itself offer an end to the cyber arms race.

ON TRUST, ETHICS, AND TECHNOLOGY

The convergence of big data, AI, and processing power has emergent properties. We have discussed many benefits but also highlighted the challenges they may bring. How should we navigate the trust and ethical issues that technology bring? Perhaps the first thing is to take a lesson from the RAND discussion above, which examines the economics of safety and lives saved, even if imperfect autonomous vehicles are deployed. That is, we can't assess the risks associated with the downside without fully understanding our assumptions and the attractiveness and economics behind the upside. Of course, the fact that there is an upside should not mean we should be blind to the costs of the downside. Rather, like our discussion in chapter 4 on the Internet of things, we should allow ourselves some agency to make a difference.

We are going to frame this in terms of trust and ethics. This is because many of the problems raised in this topic have a trust or ethical dimension.

We commented on the use of analytics to target people for political purposes. It's important that people understand their audiences so that they can communicate effectively. This is not the same thing as manipulation or simply reinforcing prejudices in order to generate a short-term behavior. Using data to analyze audiences is not unethical in itself, but allegations of covert manipulation, data breaches, and improper information sharing damage public confidence, not only in elections, but also in the services we use. Likewise, we mentioned the benefits of sharing the most personal of information, the human genome—again, not unethical in itself, and arguably highly ethical for the purposes of better cancer treatment. However, what if there are insufficient controls or permissions? What if your genome is eventually used to decide on your level of health insurance or whether you should be given an employment contract? With big data, perhaps you wouldn't even need to disclose your genome; one might infer your health from images, Internet searches, and family history, all potentially available online in one form or another and perhaps self-disclosed.

We also examined the degree to which systems would make decisions about us. How do we know that the suggestions AI makes to us are accurate, in our best interests, or in the interests of someone else with a commercial or nefarious motive? Perhaps at a fundamental level, there are two main concerns about why we should trust automation at all or how our society inadvertently creates vulnerabilities to cyber attack because of evermore interdependency.

As was mentioned earlier in the chapter, the tradeoffs need to be untangled, but it's not a one-time shot. Systems evolve, and our relationships with them have to be monitored on an ongoing basis. It means taking trust and ethics into account when we consciously make decisions and are alert to them, even when we think fast in an unconscious way. Let's first start with trust before turning to ethics. This discussion is, in part, informed by research conducted by the Information Assurance Advisory Council (IAAC) on the future of trust and the development of the cyber security profession.

The *Oxford English Dictionary* defines trust as:

Trust. Noun: Firm belief in the reliability, truth, or ability of someone or something. Verb **(with object):** Trust someone with: allow someone to have, use, or look after (someone or something of importance or value) with confidence. Trust someone/thing to: commit someone or something to the safekeeping of.

This definition risks reinforcing a binary view of trust (trust or not trust), which is often much more nuanced than that in a social setting. For example, throughout the course of a long relationship with someone, trust will perhaps grow or fall, and sometimes in respect of certain aspects of life, be it money, work, or family. One can trust a little or trust a lot—and it can change from time to time.

Dr. Robert Hoffman from the Florida Institute for Human Machine Cognition argues that trust is a dynamic process best understood as "trusting." In a workshop for IAAC, he argued:

Trusting is a process of active exploration and evaluation of trustworthiness and reliability, within the envelope of the ever-changing work and ever-changing work system.

Consequently, people are engaged in an ongoing complex set of judgments concerning what to trust, when to trust, and why. It's complex because they also have to learn swiftly what, why, and when to distrust. Dr. Hoffman has developed a taxonomy of trust, including distrust and mistrust, and recognition that trusting is often judged quickly (swiftly) and intuitively, which may be justified or unjustified.

We often hear that there must be transparency concerning algorithms and how they work. However, Dr. Hoffman critiques this view by arguing that:

General recommendations for the creation of trustworthy automation are not very actionable; for example, "use simplified interfaces," or "make the automation transparent."

Feedback and understandability as ideas are not sufficient for trusting, as they can result in simplistic (reductive) understandings of what is involved in providing feedback and the ability of technology to be understandable. Trusting will be based on expectations within a given context. For example, expectations will be different depending on the criticality of the decision being made. The context for trusting a service to give accurate information about the state of, say, a cloud-based government program, and not to share it with a foreign intelligence agency is different from trusting a music-streaming site to make good recommendations about other top tunes.

The notion of a risk-based approach to algorithms is supported in Mateos-Garcia's NESTA 2017 blog post, "To err is algorithm." He takes an economist's view of the value of algorithms informed by the probability of its decisions being correct and the trade-off between the reward for a correct decision and the penalty for a wrong one. This risk view also informs the degree to which they should be supervised—for example, where there is risk that they are inaccurate but the requirement for accuracy is high. There is clearly a cost to this. Likewise, if the algorithm and computation make mistakes, this should limit the scale to which that output informs other algorithms. He argues that a human should always be kept in the loop from an algorithm-performance perspective.

In fact, the European Union General Data Protection Regulation (GDPR), to be launched in May 2018, provides legal direction on automated decision-making and profiling of EU customers and citizens. An example of a best-practice approach is given in the following official guidance on the UK Information Commissioner's Web site:

To comply with the GDPR...

- We have a lawful basis to carry out profiling and/or automated decision-making and document this in our data-protection policy.

- We send individuals a link to our privacy statement when we have obtained their personal data indirectly.
- We explain how people can access details of the information we used to create their profile.
- We tell people who provide us with their personal data how they can object to profiling, including profiling for marketing purposes.
- We have procedures for customers to access the personal data input into the profiles so they can review and edit for any accuracy issues.
- We have additional checks in place for our profiling/automated decision-making systems to protect any vulnerable groups (including children).
- We only collect the minimum amount of data needed and have a clear retention policy for the profiles we create.

As a model of best practice...

- We carry out a DPIA to consider and address the risks before we start any new automated decision-making or profiling.
- We tell our customers about the profiling and automated decision-making we carry out, what information we use to create the profiles, and where we get this information from.
- We use anonymized data in our profiling activities.

This represents a systematic approach, based on regulation, to build trust and guarantee protection from improper use of data and erroneous decision-making. However, at the moment of using a machine, Dr. Hoffman recommends that workers should be enabled to "discover indicators to mitigate the impacts and risks of unwarranted reliance, or unwarranted rejection of recommendations." It should also enable workers to "adjust their reliance to the task and situation" and "to understand and anticipate circumstances in which the machine's recommendations will not be trustworthy." There may even be times when the worker needs to "understand and anticipate circumstances in which the software should not be trusted even if it is working as it should, and perhaps especially if it is working as it should." These requirements remain a research challenge for many system and interface designers. Perhaps this is where social-media reporting and the crowd may be security virtues.

Bruce Schneier acknowledges the complexity of trust in systems in our interconnected world. He gives an example of restaurant dining, where we are required to trust a long chain of people and organizations, including the servers, cooks, food suppliers, and processing plants. He believes that much of society only works because we choose to trust. This is assisted through a combination of institutional structures, social norms, regulation, and security technology. It means that, for the most part, we can "trust" that things are mostly going to work. After all, Schneider argues, the ATM system works well around the world. It would seem that Dr. Hoffman's notion of swift trust, often justified, is in operation. Schneier is right in pointing out the necessity of the combination of social norms, institutions, and laws as control mechanisms. In these, ethical behaviors have to be lived.

ETHICS IN QUESTION

As each phase of technology has arrived, new ethical considerations have emerged. Standalone machines of 1950s to 1960s raised the issue of database privacy. The connected machines of the period from the 1970s to 1980s brought issues of software piracy and intellectual-property theft. The Internet in the 1990s brought free speech and censorship into focus. Today we are grappling with the decision-making of machines and the ethics of bio informatics. In these circumstances, what shapes behavior toward ethical positions? Some argue that it is the presence of stick or threat, without which no ethical code can be effective.

It is normal for organizations to produce ethics statements. The UK Engineering Council and the Royal Academy of Engineering have these top-level headings for ethical principles:

1. Honesty and integrity
2. Respect for life, law, the environment, and public good
3. Accuracy and rigor
4. Leadership and communication

The Sans Institute provides a long list of what professional behavior looks like. At a top level, they are:

1. I will strive to know myself and be honest about my capability,
2. I will conduct my business in a manner that assures the IT profession is considered one of integrity and professionalism.
3. I respect privacy and confidentiality.

However, people do not need these statements to act ethically. In an IAAC workshop facilitated by Reverend Philip McCormack, then a British Army chaplain and ethicist, argued that with or without the code, most people want to act ethically. When they do not act ethically, it is the result of a number of factors.

One of the factors is "ethical blindness." This is where people fail to see their activities as being a matter involving ethics. For example, producing an algorithm to connect data is simply a software-writing activity, seen by a company in terms of cool functionality and finance rather than a matter of ethics. In our day-to-day activities, we often see them as simply functional and administrative. This dynamic may be a result of people feeling remote from the consequences of their action. Stanley Milgram showed in his experiments in the 1960s how people could subordinate themselves to an authority, therefore distancing themselves from the consequences of their actions. This was the "only following orders" defense. Milgram called this the "agentic state" where it became someone else's job to think about ethics. McCormack points out:

It could be argued that this risk is greater where it appears to relate to a product—in this case, information technology—rather than to people, even though it is people who will be potentially the victims as much as the beneficiaries.

McCormack argues the case for "virtue ethics" and the idea that ethics are lived rather than written in lists or the law. To avoid ethical blindness and the impact of agentic state, he proposes several actions:

1. People have to be encouraged to reflect on their work and encouraged to think about its ethical dimension.
2. Doing small things well creates good habits that build good character.
3. This only happens if good character, reflection, and habits are lived within the social group or organization.
4. People have to see others around them behaving well; this is likely be the result of *effective leadership*.

If one thinks of a large tech company that does not appear to value people as much as the value to be earned from their data, it will not be surprising if a supply chain emerges to help them act without thought for ethics.

The emergence of big data, AI, and quantum computing is changing the world and the basis on which companies are valued. The economic, environmental, and social opportunities are huge, even as the way we work and live changes. However, we will be worse off if we live in an agentic state, thinking that the ethics of technology are someone else's business. With this is understanding the intent behind any innovation. Social-media analytics is not unethical in itself. Sharing genomic or citizen data is not unethical in itself. It is in how it is done and for what purpose that the arguments of ethics become important. If we are to avoid sleepwalking into crises, effective leadership by example will be as important as the brilliant innovation of any businessperson, engineer, or designer.

NOTES

1. Brad Plumer, "What Land Will Be Underwater in 20 Years? Figuring It Out Could Be Lucrative." *The New York Times*, February 23, 2018. https://www

.nytimes.com/2018/02/23/climate/mapping-future-climate-risk.html. Accessed November 4, 2018.

2. Stottler Henke, "Artificial Intelligence Glossary." https://www.stottlerhenke .com/artificial-intelligence/glossary/. Accessed March 30, 2018.

3. Ibid.

4. See Matthias Niessner, "Face2Face: Realtime Face Capture and Re-Enactment of RGB Videos," YouTube, March 17, 2016. https://www.youtube.com/watch ?time_continue=8&v=ohmajJTcpNk. Accessed March 30, 2018.

5. Marketsandmarkets, "Artificial Intelligence in Security Market by Technology Machine Learning, Context Awareness—2025." https://www.marketsandmarkets .com/Market-Reports/artificial-intelligence-security-market-220634996.html ?gclid=EAIaIQobChMI6eODhvGT2gIVLrftCh0fGg4uEAAYAiAAEgIejfD_BwE. Accessed March 31, 2018.

BIBLIOGRAPHY

Adamson, Doug. "Big Data in Healthcare Made Simple." https://www.health catalyst.com/big-data-in-healthcare-made-simple. March 14, 2016.

Ayers, Ryan. "How Big Data Is Revolutionizing Sports." https://dataconomy .com/2018/01/big-data-revolutionizing-favorite-sports-teams/January24, 2018.

Bauman, Melissa. "Why Waiting for Perfect Autonomous Vehicles May Cost Lives." RAND Corporation, November 2017. https://www.rand.org /blog/articles/2017/11/why-waiting-for-perfect-autonomous-vehicles -may-cost-lives.html. Accessed March 31, 2018.

Bezobrazov, S., A. Sachenko, M. Komar, and V. Rubanau. "The Methods of Artificial Intelligence for Malicious Applications Detection in Android OS." International Journal of Computing 15, no. 3 (2016): 184–190. http:// computingonline.net/computing/article/viewFile/851/764. Accessed March 31, 2018.

Blaut, Mary. "True Emoji Is an AI App That Uses Your Expressions to Create Animated Emojis." The AI Center, November 21, 2017. http://theaicenter .com/true-emoji-ai-emotion-app/. Accessed March 31, 2018.

Bond, S. "Artificial Intelligence and Quantum Computing Aid Cyber Crime Fight." Financial Times, May 25, 2017. https://www.ft.com/content/1b9bdc4c -2422-11e7-a34a-538b4cb30025. Accessed March 31, 2018.

Bostrom, Nick. Superintelligence: Paths, Dangers, Strategies. Oxford: Oxford University Press, 2015.

Cassidy, John. "How George Soros Upstaged Donald Trump at Davos." The New Yorker, January 25, 2018.

Dietterich, Thomas G., and Eric J. Horvitz. "Rise of Concerns about AI Reflections and Directions." Microsoft, October 2015. https://www.microsoft.com /en-us/research/wp-content/uploads/2016/11/CACM_Oct_2015-VP .pdf. Accessed March 31, 2018.

Engineering Council. "Statement of Ethical Principles." https://www.engc.org .uk/media/2334/ethical-statement-2017.pdf. Accessed March 31, 2018.

EPSRC. "Quantum Technologies." https://www.epsrc.ac.uk/research/ourport folio/themes/quantumtech/. Accessed March 31, 2018.

Gibney, E. "The Scientist Who Spots Fake Videos." Nature News, October 6, 2017. http://www.nature.com/news/the-scientist-who-spots-fake-videos -1.22784. Accessed March 31, 2018.

Greenfield, Adam. *Radical Technologies: The Design of Everyday Life*. London: Verso Publishing, 2017.

Haskel, J., and S. Westlake. *Capitalism without Capital: The Rise of the Intangible Economy*. Princeton, NJ: Princeton University Press, 2017.

Hay, Newman L. "Quantum Computers versus Hackers, Round One, Fight!" *Wired*, January 27, 2017. https://www.wired.com/2017/01/quantum -computers-versus-hackers-round-one-fight/. Accessed March 31, 2018.

Herman, Tavani T. *Ethics and Technology: Controversies, Questions and Strategies for Ethical Computing*, 3rd ed. Hoboken, NJ: Wiley, 2014.

Hoffman, R. R. *Emergent Trusting in the Human–Machine Relationship. Cognitive Systems Engineering: The Future of a Changing World*. Boca Raton, FL: CRC Press, 2017.

Jones, N., and L. J. O'Neill. *The Profession: Understanding Careers and Professionalism in Cyber Security*. IAAC Publication, 2017. https://www.iaac.org.uk/wp -content/uploads/2018/02/2017-03-06-IAAC-cyber-profession-FINAL -Feb18-amend-1.pdf. Accessed March 31, 2018.

Jones, N., and N. Price. *The Future of Trust*. IAAC Publication, 2017. https://www .iaac.org.uk/wp-content/uploads/2018/01/20171229-Future-of-Trust -Final.pdf. Accessed March 31, 2018.

Kitchin, Rob. *The Data Revolution: Big Data, Open Data, Data Infrastructures and Their Consequences*. London: Sage Publications, 2014.

Koyen, Jeff. "Voice: Cybersecurity in the Age of Quantum Computing." *Forbes*, November 1, 2017. https://www.forbes.com/sites/juniper/2017/11/01 /cybersecurity-in-the-age-of-quantum-computing/#63069940423c. Accessed October 16, 2018.

Lohr, Steve. "The Age of Big Data." *The New York Times*, February 11, 2016.

Makhani, Santosh. "Who Can You Trust? Fake News in a Post-Truth Era." Network Research. https://www.networkresearch.co.uk/our-view/who-can-you-trust -fake-news-in-a-post-truth-era/. Accessed March 31, 2018.

Marketsandmarkets. "Artificial Intelligence in Security Market by Technology Machine Learning, Context Awareness—2025." MarketsandMarkets. https://www.marketsandmarkets.com/Market-Reports/artificial-intelligence -security-market-220634996.html?gclid=EAIaIQobChMI6eODhvGT2gIVL rftCh0fGg4uEAAYAiAAEgIejfD_BwE. Accessed March 31, 2018.

Marr, Bernard. "What Is the Difference between Artificial Intelligence and Machine Learning?" *Forbes*, December 6, 2016. https://www.forbes.com/sites/ber nardmarr/2016/12/06/what-is-the-difference-between-artificial-intellig ence-and-machine-learning/. Accessed March 31, 2018.

Marshall, Aarian. "Uber's Self-Driving Car Just Killed Somebody in Arizona. Now What?" *Wired*, March 19, 2018. https://www.wired.com/story/uber-self -driving-car-crash-arizona-pedestrian/. Accessed March 31, 2018.

Mateos-Garcia, Jose. "To Err Is Algorithm: Algorithmic Fallibility and Economic Organization." Nesta, May 10, 2017. http://www.nesta.org.uk/blog /err-algorithm-algorithmic-fallibility-and-economic-organisation. Accessed March 31, 2018.

Milgram, S. *Obedience to Authority: An Experimental View*. New York: Harper-Collins, 1974.

Mozur, Paul. "With Cameras and A.I., China Closes Its Grip." *The New York Times*, July 9, 2018.

National Quantum Technologies Programme. "National Strategies for Quantum Technologies Strategy, 2015." https://www.gov.uk/government/uploads/system/uploads/attachment_data/file/414788/Strategy_QuantumTechnology_T15-080_final.pdf. Accessed March 31, 2018.

Niessner, Matthias. "Face2Face: Real-time Face Capture and Reenactment of RGB Videos." (CVPR 2016 Oral). https://www.youtube.com/watch?time_continue=8&v=ohmajJTcpNk. Accessed March 31, 2018.

Palazzo, G., F. Krings, and U. Hoffrage. "Ethical Blindness." *Journal of Business Ethics* 109 (2012): 323–338. https://www.researchgate.net/profile/Ulrich_Hoffrage/publication/256046104_Ethical_Blindness/links/5a01d78b0f7e9bfd7460554a/Ethical-Blindness.pdf. Accessed March 31, 2018.

Pierce, Andrew. "The Queen Asks Why No One Saw the Credit Crunch Coming." *The Telegraph*, November 5, 2008. https://www.telegraph.co.uk/news/uknews/theroyalfamily/3386353/The-Queen-asks-why-no-one-saw-the-credit-crunch-coming.html. Accessed March 31, 2018.

Plumer, Brad. "What Land Will Be Underwater in 20 Years? Figuring It Out Could Be Lucrative." *The New York Times*, February 23, 2018. https://www.nytimes.com/2018/02/23/climate/mapping-future-climate-risk.html. Accessed November 4, 2018.

Polyakov, Alexander. "The Truth about Machine Learning in Cybersecurity: Defense." *Forbes*, November 30, 2017. https://www.forbes.com/sites/forbestechcouncil/2017/11/30/the-truth-about-machine-learning-in-cybersecurity-defense/#460cc6b26949. Accessed March 31, 2018.

Popkin, Gabriel. "Scientists Are Close to Building a Quantum Computer That Can Beat a Conventional One." *Science*, December 1, 2016. http://www.sciencemag.org/news/2016/12/scientists-are-close-building-quantum-computer-can-beat-conventional-one. Accessed March 31, 2018.

Rajab, T. "Quantum Technology and Cyber Security." Tech UK, February 13, 2017. https://www.techuk.org/insights/meeting-notes/item/10226-quantum-technology-and-cyber-security. Accessed March 31, 2018.

Raphael, Marty. "AI and Machine Learning in Cyber Security." Towards Data Science, January 1, 2018. https://towardsdatascience.com/ai-and-machine-learning-in-cyber-security-d6fbee480af0. Accessed March 31, 2018.

Ross, James, and Cynthia Beath. "You May Not Need Big Data After All." *Harvard Business Review*, December, 2013.

Salinas, Sara. "George Soros: It's Only a Matter of Time before Dominance of Facebook and Google Is Broken." CNBC, January 25, 2018.

Samenow, Jason. Climate Change Could Put Businesses Underwater. Start Up from Jupiter Aims to Come to the Rescue." *The Washington Post*, February 12, 2018.

SANS Institute. "SANS—IT Code of Ethics." https://www.sans.org/security-resources/ethics. Accessed March 31, 2018.

SANS Institute. "Straddling the Next Frontier Part 2: How Quantum Computing Has Already Begun Impacting the Cyber Security Landscape." September 2015. https://www.sans.org/reading-room/whitepapers/securitytrends /straddling-frontier-2-quantum-computing-begun-impacting-cyber-se -35395. Accessed October 16, 2018.

Schneier, B. *Liars and Outliers: Enabling the Trust That Society Needs to Thrive.* Wiley, Indianapolis, 2012.

Schneier, B. "Liars and Outliers: Enabling the Trust That Society Needs to Thrive." RSA Conference, March 5, 2012. https://www.youtube.com/watch?v=hgE QfDV6NnQ&feature=youtu.be. Accessed March 31, 2018.

Smyth, Daniel. "8 Ways Big Data and Analytics Will Change Sports." https:// bigdata-madesimple.com/8-ways-big-data-and-analytics-will-change -sports/ March 13, 2014.

Stottler, Henke. "Artificial Intelligence Glossary." https://www.stottlerhenke .com/artificial-intelligence/glossary/. Accessed March 30, 2018.

Sutton, David. *Cyber Security: A Practitioner's Guide.* Swindon, England: BCS Learning Ltd., 2017.

UK Information Commissioner. "Rights Related to Automated Decision Making Including Profiling." https://ico.org.uk/for-organisations/guide-to-the -general-data-protection-regulation-gdpr/individual-rights/rights-related -to-automated-decision-making-including-profiling/. Accessed March 31, 2018.

Wester, Luke. "Big Data in Sports." *Boss Magazine,* July 2018.

CHAPTER 6

Can We Find Solutions to the Challenges of Cyber Security?

The PC has impacted the world in just about every avenue you can think of. Amazing developments in communication, collaboration, and efficiency. New kinds of entertainment and social media. Access to information and the ability to give a voice to people who would never be heard of.

—Bill Gates

Through much of this book, we have laid bare the myriad problems and challenges of using the PC and accessing the Internet in a way that brings to life Gates's extraordinary vision, much of which has come true. The free and open element of cyber space remains a central and most desirable element of the Internet, but there are clearly forces at work that would take us in a much less desirable direction. For this reason, while we fully acknowledge and respect all that has been achieved in cyber space, with this technological marvel, our goal is also to provide a roadmap of the problems and possible solutions to enhancing cyber security. To this end, this chapter focuses on how countless individuals (and the programs they represent) who lack Gates's extraordinary skills shape the Internet for better and worse.

This is far from an academic exercise. Cyber security is a battle that is not just about control of hardware and software. It is every bit as much about the human factor behind the tools that make up cyber space. In particular, there is an enormous body of evidence showing that human error can lead to successful hacking attacks and data breaches. The attendant costs, no matter how they are measured, are almost incalculable.

We know what our cyber adversaries seek to accomplish and have cataloged their activities in considerable detail. Still, when we look at how just one adversary, Russia, has used and defined information warfare to include the four key elements of it—electronic warfare, intelligence, hacked warfare, and psychological warfare—we can appreciate the extent and diversity of challenges to cyber security and why the human factor takes on such importance.

For Vladimir Putin, the use of cyber is nothing less than a major political weapon against the West. Similarly, China's Xi Jinping, now ensconced as de facto president for life, has supported his government's aggressive use of cyber to steal Western secrets and commit countless acts of cyber espionage. For both Russia and China, cyber vulnerabilities are to be exploited ruthlessly in support of broader foreign policy goals. As we have seen, cyber war and cyber attacks, unlike traditional warfare in most cases, can occur at any time. This implies that constant vigilance is a prerequisite for government and business to defend their interests (and data). It also implies that all elements of cyber security, including—and perhaps most importantly—human factors, require appropriate focus.

Even the simplest acts of human error in the cyber domain—intended or not—can bring devastating results. For example, one of the many tactics used to disrupt legitimate computer operations is known as a "candy drop." Here's how it worked in one real-world example. In 2008, a foreign intelligence service—rumored, but never confirmed, to be linked to Russia—deliberately left a flash drive in the dirt near a U.S. military base in the Middle East. As the hostile foreign service hoped, a careless soldier found the flash drive, brought it onto the base, and plugged it into the military's Central Command network. The drive uploaded a worm that scanned computers for data and created back doors. The result evolved into Buckshot Yankee, a major cyber breach that required the Pentagon to spend 14 months and countless hours to resolve.

For the attacker, the results were spectacular, although there has been no official U.S. military accounting of how much data was stolen or compromised. Nonetheless, the resulting chaos and time spent by the U.S. military in its lengthy and intense forensic investigation was far in excess of the initial modest effort required to leave a flash drive near a military installation. In many ways, the offense has not only the initiative but also the opportunity for payoffs that are far out of proportion to the level of effort required to initiate an attack. That is the cost when one individual doesn't practice what we may call good cyber hygiene.

Under these circumstances, and as we assess human factors in cyber security, a new reality has appeared on the horizon. In the West, there is a tendency to think of warfare as an on/off dynamic. We either enjoy peace or are involved in conflict across the globe. The new reality for both government and business is that we are in a constant state of conflict among nations and with various subnational groups. Among many other factors, this mind-set implies human factors will take on even greater importance in cyber security in the coming years.

In the West, we often act as though there are rational solutions to problems, which we can solve with enough effort. In a different, and perhaps better, world, the international community, through mechanisms such as the United Nations, would be capable of reaching agreement on a code of conduct or rules of the road that would support enhanced cyber security for all. Ideally, we would reach a global consensus that cyber threats present a unique challenge and, therefore, require a unique approach. Criminals would be stifled in trying to use the Internet for financial gain, while aggressive cyber nations would refrain from disruptive conduct.

We don't live in that world. The best case scenario is probably years, if not decades, of debate over what constitutes acceptable cyber behavior. Different nations have different cyber priorities. Major nations, such as Russia and China, for example, derive considerable value in their aggressive cyber activities and often pay little diplomatic or financial price for them. Beyond that, criminal organizations continue to exploit cyber vulnerabilities for enormous profit. Western democracies are beginning to fight back with much greater awareness of the various manifestations of cyber threats. This is a positive and desirable development but does not begin to compensate for the continuing loss by government and business of sensitive data or equally significant financial losses. If our institutions cannot protect our secrets, we must develop other means of self-defense. Our view is that while it is fine, and even admirable, to think globally, governments and business need to act locally, shaping the environments in which they operate. This leads us right to the importance of the human factors in cyber security.

This also is a good place to dispel the naïve and profoundly wrong-headed notion some experts advocate that cyber security can be enhanced if we literally pull the plug and create an air gap. At first blush, creating a physical separation between the Internet and critical local systems may seem a tempting idea. This practice has been used by energy companies, for example, to protect critical infrastructure.

The problem is that turning back the clock in an attempt to "inoculate" a system from possible external attack is unrealistic. We live in an interconnected world and derive great value from that. In the case of trying to use air gaps—a desperate measure the Iranians sought to employ as the Stuxnet virus raged at the Natanz uranium enrichment facility—the practical reality is that old data needs to come out, and new instructions need to go in. Systems need to be patched and maintained on an ongoing basis. There may be exceptional circumstances that call for isolating a system from the Internet, but, in general, efficiency and effectiveness are also compromised by trying to isolate a system from the Internet. Employing an air gap as a security strategy is the technological equivalent of touting the benefits of vacuum tubes for use in today's computers.

Within both government and business, there is a growing, but far from comprehensive recognition of human factors in cyber security, especially in organizational settings. Academic and corporate interest in these dynamics is increasing and should be encouraged. This is not to say this is a universal trend. Japanese colleagues, for example, claim most of their corporate colleagues remain fixed on the concept of cyber security that revolves around technical factors. We can't corroborate this or say whether there are cultural factors at work but remain strong advocates for recognition of the human factors in cyber security. From time to time, many yearn for a simpler world. On the cyber front, that world can't be recreated by isolating machines from the Internet.

By way of introduction, two brief anecdotes illustrate the importance people play in cyber security. The first took place on a rainy night in April, 2015. One of the authors (Caravelli) had been asked to speak at Villanova University, which is located in a Philadelphia suburb. There was a large crowd of about 110 MBA students. Almost all were also in the early stages of their professional careers. As the presentation ensued, the students were asked how many believed there was an appropriate level of C-suite support—CEO, COO, CIO, and so forth—within their own organizations for developing and implementing sound cyber security policies. Albeit unscientific, the response was fully disappointing, but perhaps not shocking, with only about 10 percent answering in the affirmative.

Our second anecdote also brings us back to Villanova, one year later. At that time, the author joined the regional president of Lockton Insurance, a large independent writer of cyber security policies, in a class for MBA students on cyber security. During that discussion, the insurance executive was asked to describe how cyber security insurance programs are written, and what triggers a valid claim. He told the class that as many as 50 percent of claims were the result of inadvertent or deliberate human error or were caused by junior or low-ranking employees. We have heard stories and read studies where other insurance companies confirm these figures or claim that the percentages are even higher. One way or the other, a sizable problem looms at the heart of our efforts to enhance cyber security.

This all points to the need for continual focus on human factors and how to ensure best practices and adherence to corporate and governmental security practices are being implemented as fully as possible. How do we best achieve that standard? Humans can, and have, proven to be weak points in the management of any cyber security program, but, despite this recognition, how do we best maximize their commitment to good cyber security practices? Before delving into specifics, we have been impressed by some innovative research conducted by British researchers.

The first was a study conducted by University of London researchers Anne Adams and Martha Angela Strasse, who argue that users—those pesky, unpredictable, vulnerable humans—are not the enemy. We take the well-documented position that users at all levels of the government and corporate worlds often have enormous (and demonstrated) capacity to badly undermine cyber security goals within their organizations. Nonetheless, the Adams and Strasse research suggests several underlying reasons for these vulnerabilities, which often escape notice of executives and security officers alike, but which can be addressed.

As the researchers note, it is well-understood what the optimal approaches to password security are for government and corporate employees. Those include the size of a character set that incorporates alphanumeric as well as letter characters and short password lifetimes that increase individual accountability. Yet those most basic of standards are far from routinely followed. Is it because employees are careless or indifferent?

In their study, Adams and Strasse set out to test that assumption. They looked at the behavior of two organizations and how they interact with their employees in securing passwords. One of the emerging findings was that organizations that ask their users to have multiple passwords in an attempt to protect vital data often trigger, perhaps counterintuitively, new problems. This is sometimes because users are often tempted to create passwords that were related to one another to enhance memorability or, in worst case examples, users simply wrote down their passwords.

The negative aspects of this situation were compounded when looking at the attitudes of security departments at these organizations as they interacted with their employees. There was frequently an attitude that employees were "inherently unsafe." As a result, security departments often erred, albeit inadvertently, by minimizing information they shared with employees, a corporate version of many government's "need to know" application of security practices. The result, the authors claim, is that many employees did not perceive the full importance of the security practices. The authors conclude by recommending a series of common-sense steps:

- System security needs to be visible and seen to be taken seriously by the organization. Security officers should be seen to be in action around the organization.
- Employees need to be kept informed about existing and potential threats to the organization's systems and the sensitivity of information contained in them. Awareness of threats and potential losses to the organization are the raisons d'être for security mechanisms; without them, users are likely to perceive security mechanisms as tedious motions they have to go through.
- The role of passwords should be made explicit to all members of the organization. Those of us who have worked in government jobs that involve routine access to extremely sensitive information rarely, if ever, received any training in such basic practices.

- Users' awareness of the importance of security and threats to it need to be maintained over time.
- All information is not equally sensitive, but users should be expected to maintain proper security for all the information they access.

The second study was conducted in 2017 by another British researcher, Lee Hadlington. Hadlington's study picks up where Adams and Strasse left off, examining if, and how, personality traits affect attitudes and behavior toward cyber security. Hadlington posed a series of questions to 515 employees of several British firms. The results showed Internet addiction can be one factor in explaining risky cyber behavior, such as indifference to password security.

Hadlington also probed deeper, learning that employees' attitudes toward cyber security were negatively correlated to the frequency with which they engaged in risky cyber security behavior, leading to the conclusion that "pockets of individuals appear to be disengaged or ill-equipped to act appropriately."

Adding to these troubling insights, Hadlington claims a staggering 98 percent of respondents devolved responsibility for cyber security to management. This is exactly the attitude that needs to be swept away. Another 58 percent of respondents said they did not know they could protect their companies from cyber crime. If those attitudes are widely shared in corporate Britain or in the United States, which would not be surprising, a considerable amount of training needs to be accomplished to reach our view that cyber security is a shared responsibility across all governmental and business entities.

If senior executives are not paying attention to the roles they need to play in this area—and all the attendant financial and reputational risks that failing to do so bring—and if other lower ranking-employees are not paying attention to their individual duties to protect against cyber intrusions, is it so hard to understand why corporate Britain—and presumably counterparts in other nations—are encountering so many cyber incidents?

We hasten to add that those in government offer few better approaches or performance, as shown by the U.S. government's staggeringly inept OPM debacle, described in an earlier chapter, and the government-wide directive from the Department of Homeland Security to ban all Kaspersky Laboratory products across the federal government, after years of usage. Factoring in the extensive damage caused to U.S. national security by Edward Snowden, discussed in an earlier chapter, it is apparent that government has much to do to make its own operations meet our CIA standard.

None of these shortfalls and problems should come as a surprise to experts on the front lines, the staff of IT departments around the world. Perhaps more than any group, their experience and observations help define the current state of play regarding how the good and bad practices of individuals, both executives and staff members, shape cyber security and Internet environment. We draw upon our exchanges with them, as well as a growing body of literature on their perceptions, as well as those of other industry professionals.

Let's start at the top. Across the leading American companies and industries, age remains a strong predictor of those who are corporate leaders. Mark Zuckerberg, yet to reach age 35 at this writing, is an outlier, but even a cursory look at the top 100 or 500 corporations in America reveals leadership who, in the main, are 50-65 years in age. Most are highly competent but, at the same time, began their careers in an era when meeting the demands of cyber security was not at the top of reasons their careers advanced.

Put differently, America's current generation of corporate leaders seldom made their careers by being cyber leaders or innovators in their formative years. Such career trajectories held little promise for being a path to the top of any corporate ladder. An understanding of marketing, finance, or manufacturing have been the predominant skill sets that boosted the careers of almost all corporate leaders. None of this is surprising. Does this possible discomfort or lack of personal engagement with cyber issues even partially explain the large number of MBA students at Villanova, all at the start of their careers, who were concerned that their leadership was not well-informed or active in promoting cyber security issues?

This generalization may be unfair to some of corporate American (or European) leaders, but there is ample evidence that challenges—and, to put it more bluntly, problems—remain at the top of the corporate world in leading new thinking on cyber security. In a changing business environment where cyber threats are at, or near the top, of corporate challenges, leadership from the C-suite is not a luxury—it's a necessity. It is no longer acceptable for these C-suite executives to go to a board of directors or shareholders and confess to lack of preparation or weak response to a major cyber attack that may have imposed significant financial, data, or reputational losses.

Responsibility starts at the top, but it does not end there. Thus, we also cannot ignore the activities of the rank and file, beginning with the need for a new generation of IT specialists who are prepared to deal with a fast-paced and often hostile IT environment. The first conclusion we draw is deeply troubling. Setting aside skill sets or commitment to the job, in the coming years, the IT industry, according to several reports, requires hundreds of thousands or more or new IT employees to populate government and large and smaller businesses. "There is a chronic shortage of qualified staff," according to Steve Morgan, founder of Cyber Security Ventures, a consulting firm. He adds, "It's an absolute epidemic." Others take a similar posture, with one claim that as many as 3.5 million job openings will exist by 2021. In essence, in the IT field across the United States, there is, for all practical terms, 0 percent unemployment. Across Europe there are similar demands.

As the U.S. private sector strained to find a large cadre of trained IT specialists to meet future demands, the Russian government took a different tack. Inspired by an idea from President Vladimir Putin, whose ideas usually garner special attention in his nation, Russia created the Sirius Center for Gifted Education. Located in Sochi, site of the 2014 Winter Olympics, Russian officials tout the Sirius Center as a mechanism to bring together talented Russian youth for training in various career areas, including math, science, and the arts. Students live comfortably in a former four-star hotel and are given access to top-of-the-line laboratories and equipment, depending on their courses of study. Particular emphasis is placed, according to school director Elena Shmeleva, on new technologies. She added that Putin monitors the school's developments and progress almost every month.

His support has done nothing but bolster the school's fortunes, including its finances. In the authoritarian twist on public-private partnerships, wealthy Russians from around the country have rushed to provide their own funding in support of their powerful president. Putin claims to want the school to inspire the creation of other such schools around Russia, something that has yet to materialize.

Within the United States, the demand for expanded IT talent does not sound all bad for young job hunters, but is it possible to find even a substantial portion of the expertise required over the next five to 10 years? The average starting salary for a U.S. IT worker is a hefty $116,000 according to a McKinsey report, almost three times the average of other starting jobs in corporate America. That is presumably an inducement in itself. Because problems in recruitment persist but are deepening, we wanted to push further into this issue.

What we found is a modicum of good news, beginning with attempts to not only recognize, but to address, the problem. For example, a National Cyber Security Workforce Alliance has been formed to assist in finding and developing new cyber security talent. That's an excellent starting point.

What about programs and policies to enhance the skills of current IT staff as others work through ways to recruit and retain a new generation of IT specialists? We would include the following for consideration in any "to-do" list for those seeking to retain as well as recruit IT specialists:

- Ensure that all Internet users are regularly certified in cyber security best practices and policies.
- "Recruiting" can have more than one meaning. Americans are, by nature, trusting in their relationships. That goodwill can provide the backdrop for illicit recruitment efforts against junior or even senior

officials with access to valuable information. This is an unpleasant reality for those in and out of government, but the importance of even a modicum of counterintelligence training cannot be overstated.

- Maximize brand exposure. Prestigious corporate names such as Microsoft or Oracle probably have greater appeal to those in search of IT jobs than less-known corporations. Not every company can be Microsoft in its appeal or reputation, but promoting a good corporate identity has multiple appeals to corporate leaders, staff, and would-be recruits.

- Provide training and certification opportunities. In a fast-paced job environment, many IT workers understand that in a job-friendly environment, competitive value is derived from companies that offer a strong training environment. Some corporate executives may, in a rather short-sighted way, believe that providing the training will pave the way for staff departures. Those concerns may be true to some extent, but that is the price of business. There is considerable movement within the IT field. Nonetheless, companies and governments have a duty to serve the developmental needs of both their staff personnel and, ultimately, their organizational interests by providing state-of-the-art training opportunities.

- Create partnerships with universities. America remains a global gold standard of higher education with Harvard, Stanford, Yale, Princeton, MIT, and Georgetown, among numerous firs-rate sources of higher education. While a small number of universities, under the guise of political correctness, shun the idea of free speech as a compelling core value, many others are pushing the frontiers of learning. Those entering the job market should be encouraged by their employers to remain academically active to the fullest extent possible. Investing in the future is never a bad idea.

- Make cyber security an integral part of a company's business strategy and practice. For too long, the demands of cyber security were viewed as "something apart" from most corporations' business strategies. This is short-sighted and a tactical blunder. The best-run companies will have at their core rigorous commitment to sound cyber practices and will promote those values constantly.

- Run red-team programs—the major defense contractor Lockheed Martin is a good example—to test the attentiveness of employees to simulated cyber attacks.[1]

- Major corporations inevitably rely on a supply chain that is comprised of numerous large and small vendors. The competence and reliability of the personnel in those companies represents either a strength or vulnerability in securing vital data. Corporations, as with governmental organizations, need to form alliances and relationships that build maximum confidence that vendors are hewing to the highest possible security standards.

These approaches have merit but still fall short of fully answering our questions about how to best train and motivate new and experienced staff members to support and implement effective cyber security practices. A staff member who is indifferent or sloppy with protecting a password can be the cause of significant financial, data, and reputational loss for corporations. The same applies to the tens of thousands of those working in government.

The unpleasant experiences we have detailed that have befallen OPM, Equifax, Sony, the U.S. intelligence community, Aramco, and many others underscore the importance of the most robust approaches to cyber security. We can reduce threats, but, under current technical conditions and capabilities, no one can guarantee the free and safe operations of the Internet that were envisioned by its "founding fathers." However, we need not despair; we have options that go beyond the value of training programs. In this regard, we are drawn to the importance of building resilience into the daily operations of government and business.

Resilience is a concept used in many fields and for different purposes. Perhaps it is most memorably exemplified to many by the undaunted courage of the British in May 1940 when a then new Prime Minister, Winston Churchill, refused to bow in the face of what looked to be inevitable Nazi triumph. Churchill's courage and that of wartime Britain may exceed our requirements for resilience in defending cyber space, but the concept is not wholly out of place.

For our purposes, we would define resilience as the ability to adapt to unfavorable conditions and recover. Resilience preserves the functions of an organization or government department. We must assume that intrusions and various forms of cyber attacks will be ongoing problems. As described in a Brookings Institution study, "In cyber security, we should think about resilience in terms of systems and organizations." Thus, we are now stretching our focus from individuals to corporate and government settings, where "Plan B" programs are developed and, if necessary, implemented, in the case of a major cyber attack. The Brookings authors conclude that resilience has three main elements. The first is development of an intentional capacity to work under degraded conditions. The second is that resilient systems must recover quickly, and, finally, lessons must be learned and shared to deal effectively with future threats. These can serve as useful guidelines for any organization that is willing to invest the time in making resilience a focus of corporate cyber security strategy.

Much of our chapter's focus has been on human factors, such as meeting the need for a new generation of cyber experts, the importance of leadership on cyber security issues, inculcating best practices in a workforce, and ways to build resilience into the daily operations across various enterprises. As we proceed, and because our book aspires to be forward-looking, with attention to key emerging trends, our focus shifts to three macro cyber security issues. Those are the political and military U.S. cyber policies being adopted by the Trump administration, the shifting sands of the concept of privacy and the protection of data and personal information, and the battle for technical dominance in a rapidly changing technological environment. How these issues are shaped will determine many aspects of the way we live and work in coming years.

For example, we can begin by looking at the intersection of geopolitics and technology that reflects the changing face of cyber security. A *New York Times* report in May 2018 described the personnel consequences for a Chinese firm, ZTE, of political decisions made by the U.S. government.

ZTE announced that it had ceased "major operating activities" as a result of a decision by the Trump administration to ban the company from accessing or using U.S. technology in the company's telecommunications products. The halt in manufacturing brought ZTE work to a widespread standstill, including at a main plant in Shenzhen, idling thousands of workers, who were ordered into perfunctory training activities when they were not pursuing leisure activities in a nearby dormitory.

ZTE, which began business in 1985 and is nearly half owned by two Chinese state entities, had been a highly successful firm prior to the U.S. government's decision, generating nearly $17 billion in annual revenue and employing 75,000 people. In what the *Times* described as a death sentence, ZTE faced a collapse of its shares, largely as a result of the U.S. Commerce Department blocking the company's access to U.S. technology until 2025. This measure was taken, according to a Commerce Department spokesman, as a result of ZTE employees, "who violated trade controls against Iran and North Korea."

The administration's original decision is on solid substantive ground; for years, China has been a flagrant violator of many international norms regarding its cyber activities. In the ZTE case, the company had courted popular U.S. entertainment outlets, such as the National Basketball Association's popular Cleveland Cavaliers, to show the company's support of the United States and demonstrate its lack of predatory practices. That strategy seems to have failed. ZTE's punishment, as proposed by Commerce, is significant in its duration and scope. The company had used its access to U.S. technology, including microchips and optical equipment for its optical fiber networks, to provide products not only in North America, but also in Africa and Asia.

What started out as a toughened U.S. stance—the United States had previously fined ZTE $1.2 billion, and, in April, the Commerce Department slapped ZTE with a denial of export privileges—reverberated across China, not only in terms of jobs that might be lost, at least temporarily, by companies such as ZTE, but also for the broader implications of how the world's two largest economies will cooperate or compete in the high-technology arena in coming years. China's initial reaction to the Commerce

Department announcement was one of defiance, in which President Xi Jinping, among others, sought to portray the decision as part of larger trade cold war with the United States. He may be right, and the loss of tens of thousands of jobs at ZTE underscores that, in coming years, cyber politics will also be a factor shaping global economic trends in a way few might have predicted a decade ago.

As these elements played out in May 2018, the Trump administration, led by a president epically capable of foreign policy zigzags, hinted at a new approach in the middle of the month. As the self-proclaimed king of the deal, the president sent tweets that he was open to the Commerce Department providing some unspecified form of relief for ZTE that would allow it to keep operating. Trump hinted that, in exchange for this largesse, he would seek concessions from China on other trade issues, including moves that would open more markets for U.S. agricultural products. Cyber issues are now embedded into larger trade and policy discussions, and no one knows where this will lead.

As a consequence, the politics of cyber is taking on ever-more expansive meaning, domestically as well as overseas. In the wake of Trump's revision of initial U.S. policy toward ZTE, his Democratic Party opponents, including Senator and Minority Leader Chuck Schumer (D-NY) and Senator Ron Wyden (D-OR), expressed outrage in a letter to the president that "America's national security must not be used as a bargaining chip in trade negotiations." They added, "Offering to trade American sanctions enforcement to promote jobs in China is plainly a bad deal for American workers and for the security of all Americans. Bargaining away law enforcement power over bad actors such as ZTE undermines the historically sharp distinction between sanctions and exports control enforcement and routine trade decisions made by the U.S."

This was not the first instance in which Trump was drawn into the details of controversial deals with international overtones. In the past year, as reported by *The Economist*, "Hock Tan, the boss of Broadcom, a semiconductor firm based in Singapore on November 2, flatter[ed] the president. Mr. Trump hugged him and called Broadcom really great, but in March (2018) Broadcom's bid for Qualcomm, an all-American rival, was squelched on national security grounds." It is impossible to say if factors other than the mentioned "national security grounds" were on the president's mind.

Commercial issues also took on political overtones. One of the potentially most consequential and perhaps surprising developments in how people interact with cyber technology occurred in the wake of the debate that erupted on both sides of the Atlantic after revelations that data belonging to as many as 87 million Facebook users had been accessed without permission by Cambridge Analytica, a political (and now bankrupt) research firm that was working for the 2016 Trump presidential campaign. As we have discussed in detail elsewhere, this created enormous negative publicity for Facebook founder Mark Zuckerberg and his company, reflected in Zuckerberg's agreement to provide congressional testimony stretching over two grueling days of hearings, in which he fielded 600 questions from dozens of members of Congress.

Wearing a jacket and tie and with his short haircut short, he looked almost like a prep-school pupil. Zuckerberg used a phalanx of his company's media experts to prepare him. His answers were mostly forms of abject apologies with vague promises of the reform of Facebook's policies, not only on privacy but on its penchant for discriminating against those espousing conservative views. One Zucerkberg comment summarizes his entire approach to the unwanted glare of media scrutiny, "We didn't do enough to prevent these tools from being used for harm."

Zuckerberg's problems continued on the other side of the Atlantic. British and European Union lawmakers promised their own investigation into the issues. Zuckerberg continued his apology tour in late May with an appearance before members of the European Parliament. He took a line of defense that was similar to what he did several weeks earlier before the U.S. Congress, admitting whether in fake news, foreign interference in elections, or the misuse of private information, Facebook did not do enough. The irony is that the European members of parliament spent most of their time with Zucerkberg speaking in broad generalities about Facebook and barely pressed him for details of his plans to reform the company. The Europeans were said to have been self-satisfied with their hearing. In conjunction with their CEO's promises in American and Europe, Facebook began running full-page advertisements in major U.S. newspapers, promising to be more transparent. It was unclear how convincing any of this was to those who had watched Facebook's performance in recent years.

While the congressional and European hearings in which Zuckerberg was the "star" witness received extensive media coverage (and deservedly so), it is the aftermath of the hearings that have largely escaped media notice but are perhaps even more important. Since its founding, Facebook and other social-media platforms have profited in every sense from the mantra-like chant that they are "connecting the world." Implied in this "enlightened" phrase was that Facebook was doing important and laudable social good, that its technology was a force for good, and that those using it and other social media, by definition, were in the vanguard of technological progress. Accountability was hardly in the vocabulary of any U.S. social-media giants.

These glossy "can do no wrong" and "see no evil" perceptions, fed in large measure by a fawning media, changed swiftly and radically after the Cambridge Analytica revelations, which, in July 2018 resulted in Facebook being fined by the British Information Commission a paltry $663,000, the most allowed under British law. The company is worth about $590 billion. While Facebook was doing a broad series of mea culpa advertisements and promotions in various mass and social media to show how and why it was changing and was more committed than ever to protecting the personal data of its users, there were indications that Facebook's attempt to "reboot" was far from an unmitigated success. Facebook customers were coming to their own conclusions. After the Zuckerberg revelations, the hashtag #deletefacebook appeared more than 10,000 times on Twitter in a two-hour period in early May. Albeit reluctantly in many cases, Facebook was confronted by the first crisis in its history, and one that shows no signs of relenting.

Zuckerberg and Facebook have been darlings of Silicon Valley for years. Even that privileged position of trust among the other tech giants as well as the general public has begun to erode. Perhaps most interesting has been the criticism heaped on Facebook by insiders and those who grew wealthy because of Facebook. One notable example is reflected in the evolving thoughts of Brian Acton, widely regarded through the years as a major supporter of social media. He became a billionaire in founding WhatsApp, and then selling it to Facebook for $19 billion in 2014. Acton sent a message in support of #deletefacebook that, according to the *New York Times*, was retweeted 10,000 times.

Similarly, Justin Rosenstein, who created the Facebook "like" button, went public with his commitment to delete the product from his phone and speak out against what he called the industry's use of psychologically manipulative advertising. A Facebook operations manager, Sandy Parakilas, said, "Zuckerberg must be held accountable for the negligence of his company."

The *Times* also surveyed rank-and-file social-media users who were closing or modifying their social-media accounts. Among their reasons for doing so are the following:

- Richard Perry, a filmmaker, said, "I suspected this stuff [about Cambridge Analytica] was going on, but this is the first time it is plainly exposed."
- "It seems so malicious, and Facebook seems so complicit, all the way up and down like it doesn't care about its users."[2]
- Dan Clark, a retired Navy veteran, said, "Facebook was the main platform I used to keep in touch with them [his family], and it was a difficult decision to give it up. But you have to stand for something, so I just put my foot down and said enough is enough. There are just so many ways nowadays to stay in contact: phones, e-mail, instant message. Facebook is more obsolete than people would think."
- Alexandra Kleeman, a writer in New York, said, "I don't have a great feeling when I log in," in reference to exposure to fake news accounts on Facebook, adding, "The idea that my data could be used for purposes that I expressly don't want freaks me out."

Box 6.1 Are We the Problem?

One of the most troubling social-media trends has been the proliferation of "fake news" stories. Many of them, such as those on Twitter, are often viewed—usually for good reason—as the product of partisan zealots or Russian hackers. That's a major concern. At the same time, there may be a deeper truth that touches on human nature. According to a study published in 2018 by Massachusetts Institute of Technology researchers and covering the years 2006–2017, false news "travels faster, farther and deeper" through social media than true news. The researchers claim that the finding applies to every subject they surveyed, from politics to business to science and technology.

As reported by *The New York Times*, some 126,000 stories were tracked by the MIT group, and "false claims were 70 percent more likely than the truth to be shared on Twitter. True stories were rarely retweeted by more than 1,000 people, but the top 1 percent of false stories were routinely shared by 1,000 to 100,000 people. It also took true stories six times as long to reach 1500 people." One of the study leaders, MIT professor Sinan Aral, said, "It's sort of disheartening at first to realize how much we humans are responsible. It's not really the robots who are to blame."

Other and smaller studies had reached similar conclusions, but the MIT study was the most comprehensive to date because of its use of Twitter data covering more than a decade. The study team did not identify one easily implemented "fix" for the findings they presented but left little doubt that the human fixation with the extraordinary, novel, or sometimes bizarre holds a fascination for many, a finding that probably could be applied with equal validity over the course of human history.

Our story would be incomplete without mention of how groups working in large organizations were operating to enhance the nation's cyber security while—deliberately or not—redefining the phrase "right to privacy." In the aftermath of the 9/11 attacks, America underwent a radical transformation in many ways. One of the most obvious manifestations of this came with passage of the Patriot Act.

A *New York Times* report from early May 2018 noted that in 2017, the National Security Agency in Fort Meade, Maryland, had collected more than 534 million records of phone calls and text messages from American service providers, such as AT&T, Verizon, and T-Mobile. That was a staggering three times as many records as were collected in 2016. At the same time, the *Times* report claims intelligence analysts are collecting massive amounts of data from call-detail records, information on who individuals are speaking to.

There is no clear explanation for the surge in data collection, although senior NSA officials claim they have not changed their collection practices. What is apparent is that NSA continues to access to enormous volumes of information on the everyday lives of thousands of American citizens. What concerns senior legislators and right-to-privacy advocates such as Senator Rand Paul (R-KY) about these developments is the breadth of NSA's capabilities against U.S. citizens. For example, almost 1,400 Americans were targeted through court-approved searches in 2017, a slight decrease in numbers compared to about 1,600 targeted in 2016. At the same time, NSA's warrantless surveillance program in 2017 targeted nearly 130,000 non-Americans. As we will see, it isn't only the U.S. government that carries out activities that call into question how much privacy Americans can expect in the digital age.

Our chapter on people has looked at individuals as well as activities and attitudes within groups that have shaped both the past and current state of cyber security. We believe that many of these trends are likely to persist. On the foreign front, we assess that Russia and China, for example, are likely to continue using aggressive cyber tactics in many forms to roil Western governments and business. Simply put, despite some responses that signal displeasure from Western governments, Russia and China still appear to have little incentive to restrain their hostile cyber activities.

Beyond this rather obvious conclusion, there are a series of critical emerging trends that will affect all of us. The first centers on the competition for cyber dominance. We believe, for example, that governments and business will continue to develop policies and programs to mitigate hostile cyber activities and, through experience and collaborative efforts, may well become more sophisticated and effective. This is an encouraging development that needs to be taken much further. At the same time, the offense, as represented by aggressive governments and organized-crime groups, will also continue to develop increasingly diverse and sophisticated means of attack, continuing to challenge the West. There is a vast amount of "hackster" talent available for hire to the highest bidder. Governments, including Russia's, terrorist groups, and organized-crime groups, have used those talents. Again, with little incentive to change those practices, hackers will almost certainly continue to find numerous lucrative outlets for their skills.

But there are much larger stakes in play. The battle for cyber space and technological dominance is likely to be fought for years to come, probably with the United States and China as the main rivals. Russia likely will not be far behind. The outcome may have both global and local implications for those who seek to use the promise of the Internet to the fullest extent. For example, we have entered an era where Artificial Intelligence and quantum computing are in their infancy but are sure to mature. The implications of these developments are enormous.

Let's illustrate the challenges and opportunities by focusing on quantum computing. Quantum computing has the potential to change how we live and work. That's a bold statement, but let's dig deeper. Today's computers are often described as classical computers. They encode information in bits of 1 and 0, and this drives computer functions. On the other hand, quantum computing is based on qubits and is derived from the complexities (and sometimes mysteries) of quantum physics. There are two guiding principles. In quantum computing, one of those principles is superposition by which—and unlike traditional computing a qubit can represent a 1 and a 0 at the same time. The other principle is entanglement, which means that quibits can be correlated with each other. The result is enormous computing power that is far in excess of even today's fastest and most-powerful classical computers.

The practical results can be extraordinary. New medicines and approaches to health care may be developed. Sophisticated financial models may be created, and the complexity of global risk factors may be much-better understood. This is just the start. In these emerging and increasingly sophisticated interlocking technological developments, protecting intellectual property and reviewing prospective overseas deals takes on ever greater importance, especially in the West, which has been repeatedly victimized in these areas.

The harsh reality is there are no simple answers and none that don't entail trade-offs. In the United States, the Committee on Foreign Investment (Cifus), a little known interagency body led by the U.S. Treasury Department, is playing a central role. Cifus is looking at prospective deals involving the new 5G wireless technology and, among others, has blocked a prospective deal involving the U.S. firm MoneyGram and China's Ant Financial on the grounds that China could access large amounts of personal and corporate U.S. financial data. The authority of Cifus may expand under Trump administration thinking and is already being applauded by many in America. At the same time, protecting American secrets could bring a high price, as China may retaliate by limiting, as it does routinely, access to its market for American companies. Major corporate entities such as IBM are raising this issue, with no immediate compromise on the horizon.

Because our book aspires to be forward-looking in areas where there is uncertainty about the direction of cyber change, we have identified a second area of significant "cyber unknowns." In this context, we are most intrigued by the approach the Trump administration will take to the development of U.S. policy on cyber security. We have seen how President Trump, moving in a different direction than his own Cifus, may be prepared to forgive almost any "cyber sin," as he is proposing to overturn his own administration's actions against China's ZTE. But this is not to say that his evolving version of the cyber art of the deal reflects or will become declared U.S. policy in this area.

We have seen through the Stuxnet attack—now a decade old—the power of U.S. offensive cyber capabilities. Would Trump support the development of Stuxnet 2.0, assuming such a capability beyond what was demonstrated by the Stuxnet attack already has not been developed? Would he support the development of a national cyber security policy that places much greater emphasis than past U.S. policy on offensive cyber operations? How far is the president willing to go to convey U.S. determination that it will respond in response to attempts at political manipulation; cyber espionage; and the endless theft of vital industrial, trade, and financial secrets that constitute much of the current cyber environment?

To date, the Trump administration, bogged down with numerous political and policy challenges, has not taken this issue to the American public or to Congress. It does not seem inclined to do so any time soon, implying that the current U.S. policy of absorb an attack and then respond diplomatically, if at all, may stay in place for the foreseeable future.

One hint of its future emphasis on cyber policy may have been provided in spring 2018 by then new national security adviser, John Bolton. Bolton is a highly experienced and deeply substantive national-security expert, who also has been in countless bureaucratic battles over his long career. He understands what moves programs forward, and what bogs them down. As the president's principle national-security adviser, Bolton also directs the president's entire White House national-security establishment, the National Security Council.

Under Barack Obama, the NSC had become bloated and lost much of its luster as the preeminent foreign-policy body in the U.S. government, due to the hiring of poorly vetted junior staff and some self-aggrandizing individuals who never learned to follow before being asked to lead. Bolton recognized these deficiencies and has been moving to consolidate overlapping functions within the NSC and establish clear lines of authority. In the cyber case, Bolton has asked White House cyber security coordinator Rob Joyce to return to the National Security Agency. Bolton has decided he will not fill that position but will, instead, rely on more junior White House staff to continue monitoring and coordinating U.S. cyber interests and policies. It is too soon to know how this organizational shift will unfold within the Washington bureaucracy, but there is little doubt that Bolton—who has spoken powerfully about the importance of the United States maintaining a strong cyber security capability—will be watching unfolding events closely, given the broad implications for national-security policy.

Similar issues attend the future direction of the U.S. military's use of cyber in a crisis or conflict. Would the U.S. military continue to build on its successes in using cyber against terrorist groups in the Middle East, such as ISIS, into a broader doctrine of cyber use—similar to how Russia incorporates cyber in its military thinking? The Pentagon has been assessing these questions for at least a decade, but uncertainties remain in its thinking. Near the end of the Obama administration, then secretary of defense Ash Carter pushed to begin partnering with Silicon Valley in exploring new technologies with military applications. Google, for example, has begun working on a Pentagon contract to enhance the U.S. military's use of artificial intelligence. How far is the Pentagon, under the new leadership of the highly respected James Mattis, prepared to extend this area of cooperation?

The Department of Defense continues to stress its cyber capabilities are oriented toward defending DOD computer networks, defending the U.S. homeland and national cyber interests and providing cyber capabilities in support of military operational and contingency plans. These are broad objectives and do not fully explain—perhaps deliberately—how hard decisions will be made involving cyber attacks against the United States or how the United States might respond, for example, to a massive cyber attack.

One answer might be embedded in the Pentagon's recently published Nuclear Posture Review. Traditionally, the triggers for a U.S. nuclear attack could include a nuclear attack launched against vital U.S. assets or population centers, U.S. allies, and U.S. military forces. As in so many other areas, the world of defense planning is changing. A close reading of the new Pentagon thinking on the use of nuclear weapons expands the traditional "triggering" elements to include the possible use of nuclear weapons in the event of a major cyber attack. Would a cyber attack against a major U.S. infrastructure target, such as the electrical power grid on the east coast, result in a presidential order for a nuclear strike? Planning and working through these issues is desirable, but we hasten to add that in a crisis situation, the choices made by a president would be driven by many factors. Aides, experts, the media, and allies would all have views, but, ultimately, only the president can make what may rightly be described as the most momentous and loneliest decision on the world.

The third critical future issue is the extent and ways in which Americans and Europeans can have expectations of privacy from corporations. We have already examined how the U.S. government is (literally) rewriting how and when it can collect information on Americans. The closely related issue is how corporations, especially those representing social media, will approach those same issues. In one respect, the problems that surfaced in the wake of the Facebook-Cambridge Analytica scandal performed a service by revealing the depths to which privacy issues have been conveniently overlooked or buried by powerful corporations.

Beyond whatever pious or reassuring approaches Zuckerberg and Facebook may share, fundamental questions remain of what the U.S.

Supreme Court said many years ago was the right of all Americans "to be left alone." In the digital age, that phrase begins to look hollow. The good news is that these issues are being debated in both Europe and America. The tangible result in Europe has been the development of, and, beginning in late May 2018, implementation of, General Data Protection Regulation (GDPR). This is a complex set of regulations that will affect nearly every individual and corporation in Europe as well as those corporations operating in Europe from America, the Middle East, and Asia.

GDPR provides for heavy financial fines for corporations that do not protect the data entrusted to them or report data breaches in a timely manner. It is intended, in theory, to give individuals greater control over their personal data. That sounds fine on the surface. Underlying this approach is the usual European reliance on sweeping measures—a one-size-fits-all strategy befitting the heavy-handed approach of many sweeping regulatory directives coming from Brussels, the E.U. headquarters.

Beyond its reliance on financial penalties, GDPR builds on the concept of "data subjects," introduced in Europe in the 1980s. A data subject is defined as a "natural person" inside or outside the European Union whose personal data is used by a "controller (a company) or processor." As such, individuals become subjects of the data. While we can physically be in only one place at one time, our data can be, and most likely is, in multiple locations. GDPR tries to blunt the power of international and mostly U.S. based companies, like Facebook and Google, by forcing them to operate by European Union rules.

Can this approach be applied in an American context? We quote at length the views of Professor Alison Cool of the University of Colorado in a *New York Times* op-ed:

No one understands GDPR...The law is staggeringly complex...What are often framed as legal and technical questions are also questions of values. The European Union's 28 member states have different historical experiences and, as a result, different contemporary attitudes about data collection. Germans, recalling the Nazis' deadly efficient use of information, are suspicious of government or corporate collection of personal data; people in Nordic countries, on the other hand, link the collection and organization of data to the functioning of strong social welfare systems. Thus, the regulation is intentionally ambiguous, representing a series of compromises. It skirts over possible differences between current and future technologies by using broad principles...What the regulation really means is likely to be decided in European courts, which is sure to be a drawn out and confusing process.

That's hardly an encouraging assessment, but Professor Cool makes some compelling points. The GDPR may force Europeans into new ways of thinking and acting on data-protection issues, but it is far from perfect and probably of little utility for adoption in America. Columbia University law professor Tim Wu advocated for a different approach, the adoption of the concept of fiduciary duty—which governs the activities of doctors, lawyers, and accountants to look after their clients' interests and information—to technology companies. For example, search engines, such as Google, and social-media platforms, like Facebook, would be held liable in state courts (as there are few federal laws on this) if accused of violating their responsibility for protecting the data of individuals and corporations.

This is not to say that the Europeans don't deserve credit for trying to work through a series of complex questions on data protection. Their approach is probably faster and clearer than what is being proposed by Professor Wu. That places them ahead of America in some ways. What we can conclude, nonetheless, for both Europe and America—perhaps ironically after nearly 250 years as a nation that treasures individual freedoms—is that in the digital age, we are still in the early phases of finding solutions to questions of personal privacy. In that regard, our thinking on these political and social issues is not further advanced than our understanding of the implications of artificial intelligence, quantum computing, or the Internet of things.

Finally, we have already explored the pace and scope of hacking by Russia and its attempts to influence the 2016 U.S. presidential election as well as subsequent elections in Western Europe. Here we share one final insight. Efforts to sway elections around the globe have a long pedigree, and, in this regard, the United States has its share of culpability. At the same time, we have come to view our elections as sacrosanct, a moment where people are expected to have the ultimate privacy.

Given this run of hacking efforts in 2016 to 2017 against the West, we conclude our chapter by asking if, in elections to come, we will see a repeat of those efforts to influence outcomes. We have assessed that Russia probably has little incentive to refrain from future efforts to disrupt elections in the West. Supporting this view is that the FBI warned Americans in late spring 2018 to reset their routers out of concern that the Russians were hacking hundreds of thousands of routers with malware. The penalties imposed by the Obama and Trump administrations against Russian personnel operating in the United States, while not inconsiderable, also are not highly punitive or crippling. We would also note that U.S. operations in Russia were equally punished by the Russian government in retribution.

What we have to focus on here is the extent to which our election system remains vulnerable to outside interference. In this regard, there is both good and bad news. The good news is that America is a large nation with over 3,000 counties—the U.S. electoral system is run by the 50 states—administering the balloting process. In theory, this should make it difficult for any outside entity to attack the voting infrastructure, but the details are important. Some counties in Illinois, for example, may have had their machines accessed by hackers, but no apparent tampering of actual vote totals was found.

The bad news is that most experts, according to a late May 2018 *Washington Post* survey, conclude that, despite the warning signs, such as the Illinois hacking, resulting from the 2016 events, the states are not fully prepared to defend against future cyber attacks. In March 2018, the U.S. Congress approved $380 million to be spent by the 50 states and five territories to secure their election systems against future attacks. That's an impressive figure on the surface, but it may be inadequate for the coming tasks at hand, according to Representative Jim Langevin (D-RI) who cochairs the Congressional Cyber Security Caucus.

There are obvious vulnerabilities in the system. For example, as the *Post* reported, "millions of Americans will vote this year on old, hack-prone digital machines that produce no paper trail. Without a paper record, it is nearly impossible to audit the final vote tally. Federal officials and experts recommend scrapping such machines in favor of paper ballots."

Leadership from the Trump administration has been less than auspicious. Department of Homeland Security Secretary Kirstjen Nielsen, whose department, along with the FBI, has a major role in protecting against cyber attacks, told reporters in late May that she was unfamiliar with a key finding from the U.S. intelligence community that concluded that the Russian government was behind the 2016 attempts at hacking and disinformation.

It is unknown why she would acknowledge being poorly informed, but it not heartening that a senior official with direct responsibility for safeguarding the integrity of one of the most important citizenship acts performed by millions of Americans appears to be out of touch with her duties. Some had speculated that little in her professional background, including staff work in the Trump White House, prepared her for the demands of running a large department with direct responsibility for many national security issues. Adding to what is often contradictory views and statements from administration officials on foreign-policy issues, Secretary of State Mike Pompeo, in testimony to the House Foreign Affairs Committee, one day after Nielsen's remarks, stated that the administration would not tolerate Russian meddling in future U.S. elections. This brings us back to questions of dedication and competence and how the U.S. bureaucracy coordinates its activities, beginning at the highest levels.

At the same time, we can't refrain from sharing an anecdote that sums up how people are and will interact with technology.

We began our chapter with a quotation from an extraordinary businessperson and philanthropist, Bill Gates. We close with a quote from Senator John McCain (R-AR), who, in spring 2018, was battling a highly aggressive form of brain cancer. At a cursory glance, McCain's words quoted here may have little apparent link to our book's themes on cyber security. Nonetheless, we want to step back to contemplate the broad message behind his words in his memoir, *The Restless Wave*:

To fear the world we have organized and led for three quarters of a century, to abandon the ideals we have advanced around the globe, to refuse the obligations of international leadership for the sake of some half-baked, spurious nationalism cooked up by people who would rather find scapegoats than solve problems is unpatriotic.

NOTES

1. Major U.S. corporations are heavily engaged in various forms of cyber work. Among the most prominent is Lockheed Martin, which operates a Cyber Center of Excellence.

2. *The Guardian* ran a series of articles on Cambridge Analytica, titled "The Cambridge Analytica Files."

BIBLIOGRAPHY

Cool, Alison. "Don't Follow Europe on Privacy." *The Washington Post*, May 16, 2018.

Department of Defense. "Nuclear Posture Review." January 2018. www.mediade fense.gov. Accessed April 6, 2018.

Hadlington, Lee. *Cybercognition: Brain, Behavior and the Digital World*. London: Sage Publications, 2017.

Hughes, Siobhan, and Kate O'Keefe. "Senate Rejects Trump Deal, Votes to Reinstate Ban Against ZTE." *The Wall Street Journal*, June 18, 2018.

Ingram, David. "Factbox: Who Is Cambridge Analytica and What Did It Do?" *Reuters*, March 19, 2018. www.reuters.com.

Kosoff, Maya. "Things Go from Bad to Worse for the Corpse of Cambridge Analytica." *Wired*, June 6, 2018. www.wired.com.

Lapowsky, Issie. "Former Cambridge Analytica CEO Faces His Ghosts in Parliament." *Wired*, June 6, 2018. www.wired.com.

Leonard, Jenny. "US Allows ZTE to Resume Some Business Activities Temporarily." *Bloomberg Businessweek*, July 3, 2018. www.bloomberg.com.

Leyden, John. "Hack of Saudi Arabia Hit 30,000 Workstations, Oil Firm Admits." *The Register*, August 29, 2012. www.theregister.co.uk.

Lucas, Louise. "Washington's Moves on China's ZTE May Just Be a Warm Up Act." *Financial Times*, July 10, 2018. www.ft.com.Martin, Anthony. "How Trump Consultants Exploited the Facebook Data of Millions." *The New York Times*, March 17, 2018.

McCain, John, and Mark Salter. *The Restless Wave: Good Times, Just Causes, Great Fights, and other Appreciations*. New York: Simon & Schuster, 2018.

Meredith, Sam. "Here's Everything You Need to Know about the Cambridge Analytica Scandal." *CNBC*, March 21, 2018. www.cnbc.com.

New York Metro InfraGard. "Overview of the Cybersecurity Workforce Alliance."
     https://www.nym-infragard.us/presentations/2016-06-29/CWA%20
     iQ4%20InfraGard%20NYC%20June%2026.pdf.
Singer, P. W., and Allen Friedman. *Cybersecurity and Cyberwar: What Everyone
     Needs to Know*. Oxford: Oxford University Press, 2014.
Soldatov, Andrei. "How Vladimir Putin Mastered the Cyber Disinformation War."
     Financial Times, February 18, 2018. www.ft.com.
Usas, Alan. "The Quantum Computing Cyber Storm Is Coming." *CISCO*, July 9,
     2018. www.ciscoonline.com.

CHAPTER 7

Innovation as a Driver of Cyber Security

Nigel Jones

When we started thinking about the title for this book, we initially considered *The Cyber Arms Race*. We wanted to position cyber security as a contest between the defender and attacker. This relationship, in which the notion of complete security is impossible, is characterized by move and countermove. Rather cyber security continues to be an enduring effort, a dynamic that needs constant attention. Central to it is the ongoing motivation and adaptive processes of actors trying to maintain control of their assets while others are trying to deny, degrade, disrupt, destroy, and steal. Incidentally, we chose not to use that book title because we concluded that it remained too associated with great power games and that there were many other policy and strategic factors that needed to be addressed outside of this oppositional construct. Nevertheless, we still believe that understanding cyber space as a contested space has utility, particularly when it comes to exploring the function of innovation as a driver of cyber security technology, products, and services. In doing so, we have to examine the conditions that inspire innovation, including security and business drivers in an ecosystem of innovation initiatives. We start by defining innovation and providing a theoretical structure for the analysis of innovation. We then explore innovation in the cyber contest, followed by the business of cyber security. We examine ways to enhance innovation and the strategies and interventions employed today. A key conclusion is that innovation is essential in cyber security, and it needs planned assistance.

INNOVATION

One view of innovation is that it takes an idea from one area and applies it in another. This is seen as being distinct from invention because invention is about creating something new. Others see a relationship between invention and innovation that is based on taking a good idea (invention) and turning it into reality (innovation). Steve Jobs at Apple is often cited as an innovator, as described in Grasty's 2012 blog entry. He notes that the iPod wasn't the first music player, nor could the Mac computer have been realized without the ideas derived from others regarding microchips and personal computers. In these instances, innovation added value to pre-existing ideas. In its 2008 publication, "Innovation Nation," the UK government defines innovation as:

the successful exploitation of new ideas, which can mean new to a company, organization industry or sector. It applies to products, services, business processes and models, marketing and enabling technologies.[1]

This broad, but helpful, definition captures the idea of the exploitation of new ideas, and not just in terms of products, but also across other activities, such as processes and services. "Successful exploitation" can perhaps be given more meaning by adopting Greg Satell's definition of innovation as "a novel solution to an important problem," quoted in his 2017 book, *Mapping Innovation: A Playbook for Navigating a Disruptive Age*. He recognizes that what is important depends on the perspective of the beholder. The UK's National Data Guardian for Health and Care describes a case of a simple innovation at the Bank of England, which placed a reporting button in Outlook for staff who spot suspicious phishing e-mails. It combines a technical solution that addresses a more effective process, which could also alleviate people's anxiety when they are unsure of what to do. Not all innovation has to be seen in truly disruptive terms, but it may be incremental and improving. Satell makes room for different types of innovation and provides a structure in his book for our discussion of innovation in cyber security.

Satell identifies four types of innovation, based on two key questions, namely how well the problem to be addressed is defined, and how well the domain in which it sits is defined. Basic research is akin to fundamental research, where time horizons may naturally be a little longer. People may be working on basic ideas or solutions to problems that might not yet exist. They may be addressing emerging problems that are not yet well understood. Satell argues that companies often seek to form partnerships with universities, develop their own research divisions if sufficiently resourced, and take interest in journals and conferences and the output from other researchers. He argues that companies that are seen as participants, rather than just observers, are more likely to gain access to good research. In other words, they need to be seen to be engaging in the problem, and this may be sufficient to gain access to research, even without a formal partnership with a university.

Breakthrough research is where a problem is well-defined but the domain is not. Take, for example, the problem of authentication in cyber security. The problem is understood, but the domains involved may include electronic sensors, biometrics, social science, patterns of behavior, biology, and many other possibilities. Consequently, a breakthrough solution may be characterized as the most "impactful discoveries" coming from "combining deep expertise in closely related fields with just a smidgen of knowledge from some unlikely place." The answers lie in the combination of ideas with different people, often from outside narrow domains of knowledge. As much of this might be exploratory, Satell believes that many companies do not invest in this type of research. This may be compounded by companies that don't venture outside their well-understood domains, highlighting the need for interventions that give companies a reason to do so. This provides the basis for many of the government innovations that are mentioned later.

Satell describes "sustaining innovation" as constituting incrementalism and improvement. This means that it is sometimes seen as not being as "cool" as other forms of innovation, yet he insists that it is where there is much value to be had, particularly as it can be delivered early upon existing ways of working and the problems of today. Satell is right in pointing this out, and, in truth, much of the available innovation information regarding cyber security, business, and national strategy, is not focused on this kind of work. As we will see, the economic aspirations relating to cyber security strategy is mostly couched in terms of developing a sector of vibrant companies that have markets at home and abroad. This means that we will be mostly looking at breakthrough and disruptive innovation.

Disruptive innovation is based on the ideas of Professor Howard Christensen. It is characterized by Satell as sometimes being about "solutions looking for problems" in markets or business models that do not yet exist. It is not always about a radically new technology. For example, Uber and AirBnB use well-established technologies for completely new business models. We have also seen how smartphones change the way people listen to music, access the Internet, conduct banking, or take photographs. Amazon is disrupting the high street.

Satell argues that we should understand the nature of the problems we are trying to solve, before developing our own "playbook" about how to address them, and create a mix of innovation interventions set against the innovation types. For example, take how the domain of Internet of things technology might be defined. Many devices are deployed, and their purpose, software, hardware, and networked features are well-enough understood that they are sold and functioning. However, when we examine how the community at large is trying to address IoT security, we run into questions about where security happens, who is responsible, what the nature of the solution is, and so forth. The problem to be addressed can be well-defined in terms of a security control placed on a network boundary, or it might be difficult to define when one looks at vulnerabilities at a system-of-systems level. One can therefore see how national attempts to address IoT security require a multistranded approach, each working in its own timeline, with varying degrees of problem and domain definition. Satell also addresses the timeline issue by defining a 70-20-10 model, incorporating three time horizons. The nearest horizon constitutes 70 percent of innovation. It sustains innovation that is directed at existing markets that are currently served and capabilities that are already deployed. He argues that the next horizon constitutes 20 percent of innovation, characterized by disruptive and breakthrough innovation. This is aimed at existing markets that are not currently served and existing capabilities that have not yet been deployed. The furthest horizon is 10 percent of innovation and is basic research and breakthrough innovation. This is aimed at new markets and new capabilities.

The first horizon is usually seen as today's core business, with the second horizon understood as adjacent markets and capabilities. The third horizon is seen as what Satell calls "long-term bets." There are clear issues in the investment choices of companies and the degree to which they invest in future capability and markets. There may need to be interventions by government to ensure that the challenges of the future are addressed. In fact, Satell charts the rise of the "grand-challenge" approach to innovation and strategy. Due to the complexity of challenges faced and the need for multidisciplinary solutions with diverse stakeholders, government innovation interventions may, for example, stimulate the formation of consortia of groups that would not have otherwise collaborated. The United Kingdom has produced a strategy outlining four grand challenges facing the United Kingdom: artificial intelligence and data, Aging, clean growth, and the future of mobility. Each of these has a stated mission with associated funding. The artificial intelligence and data mission is to use data, artificial intelligence, and innovation to transform the prevention, early diagnosis, and treatment of chronic diseases by 2030. It builds upon £220 million worth of funding that was already announced under a challenge fund.

CYBER SECURITY CONTEST, TECHNOLOGY, AND BUSINESS

Turning to cyber security specifically, it is worth examining some of the companies, products, and services that have recently come to the market that are considered to be good examples of innovation. This gives us a way of referencing Satell's four types of innovation to understand the issues that are currently being addressed by companies in the near-term.

One area to look at in understanding industry trends is that of awards and prizes for technology. Technology claims do not always receive independent testing, and award nominees are often self-nominated. Nevertheless, they are a useful guide of the trends and the evolution of challenges that technology and services seek to address. *SC Magazine* is an example of a highly respected cyber security publisher that holds awards competitions in the United States and Europe. Table 7.1 indicates that the 'Trust" award categories in the U.S. awards are relatively stable, although there are some notable trends in the period from 2013 to 2018.

Table 7.1

TRUST Award Categories *SC Magazine* U.S. Awards 2013–2018

Award	2013	2014	2015	2016	2017	2018
Best Anti-Malware gateway	Yes	No	No	No	No	No
Best Enterprise Firewall	Yes	No	No	No	No	No
Best Intrusion Detection System/ Intrusion Prevention System (IDS/ IPS) Product	Yes	No	No	No	No	No
Best IPsec/SSL VPN	Yes	No	No	No	No	No
Best Mobile/Portable Device Security Best Multifactor Product	Yes	No	No	No	No	No
Best Mobile Security Solution	No	Yes	Yes	Yes	Yes	Yes
Best Multifactor Solution	No	Yes	Yes	Yes	Yes	No
Best Policy Management Solution	Yes	No	No	No	No	No
Best Risk/Policy Management Solution	No	Yes	Yes	Yes	Yes	Yes
Best Cloud Computing Security/ Solution	Yes	Yes	Yes	Yes	Yes	Yes
Best Computer Forensic Tool/ Solution	Yes	Yes	Yes	Yes	Yes	Yes
Best Data Leakage (Loss 2017) Prevention (DLP)	Yes	Yes	Yes	Yes	Yes	Yes
Best Database Security Solution	Yes	Yes	Yes	Yes	Yes	Yes
Best E-mail Security Solution	Yes	Yes	Yes	Yes	Yes	Yes
Best Identity Management Application/Solution	Yes	Yes	Yes	Yes	Yes	Yes

(continued)

Table 7.1

TRUST Award Categories *SC Magazine* **U.S. Awards 2013–2018**   (*continued*)

Award	2013	2014	2015	2016	2017	2018
Best-Managed Security Service	Yes	Yes	Yes	Yes	Yes	Yes
Best NAC (Network Access Control) product/Solution	Yes	Yes	Yes	Yes	Yes	Yes
Best Security Information/Event Management (SIEM) Appliance/ Best SIEM Solution	Yes	Yes	Yes	Yes	Yes	Yes
Best UTM (Unified Threat Management) Security/Solution	Yes	Yes	Yes	Yes	Yes	Yes
Best Vulnerability Management Tool/Solution	Yes	Yes	Yes	Yes	Yes	Yes
Best Web Application Firewall/ Solution	Yes	Yes	Yes	Yes	Yes	Yes
Best Web Content Management Product	Yes	Yes	Yes	No	No	No
Best Fraud Prevention Solution	Yes	Yes	Yes	Yes	No	No
Best Advanced Persistent Threat Protection	No	Yes	Yes	Yes	Yes	Yes
Best Behavior Analytics/Enterprise Threat Detection	No	No	No	Yes	Yes	No
Best Authentication Solution	No	No	No	No	No	Yes
Best Deception Technology	No	No	No	No	No	Yes
Best Threat Detection Technology	No	No	No	No	No	Yes
Best Threat Intelligence Technology	No	No	No	No	No	Yes

Source: Source data from and analysis of *SC Magazine* U.S. Awards 2013–2018

One can detect a shift in the naming of the awards from "tool" or "appliance" to "solution," indicating a trend toward addressing problems with combinations of techniques. This is also reflected in the move away from signature-based approaches of detecting threats, typical of antivirus/malware approaches that relied on spotting the signature of a known threat as it passed a gateway or was executed in a program. This is typified by the 2013 awards categories of best antimalware gateway and best enterprise firewall, categories that did not appear from 2014 onward. Instead, we see the rise of advanced persistent-threat and "non-signature-based" approaches, and, in 2018, the creation of new categories involving machine learning and artificial intelligence for "threat detection" and "intelligence." Deception technology also makes an entry in 2018. "Best advanced persistent threat protection" made its debut in 2014, with the

first winner being Websense by Triton Enterprises. A number of charac-
teristics are promoted in describing this category winner. It analyzes Web
and e-mail traffic—an example of a "solution" addressing more than one
threat vectors. Data at rest and in motion are also described, highlighting
the need to protect data not just when it is being communicated, but also
when it is stored. It uses the term "signature-less" threat identification,
through "real-time" analysis using "10,000-plus analytics and composite
risk" scoring. It states that "TRITON Enterprise differs significantly with
advanced malware protection. It protects against malicious scripts and
zero-day threats that circumvent anti-virus products."

It is no surprise that APT appears as a category in the 2014 Awards,
given that Fireeye brought APT1, a Chinese operation, to world attention
in 2013, showing a multiyear attack , with slow-onset incremental properties, designed to avoid traditional methods of detection. Fireeye released
over 3,000 indicators that could help "bolster defenses against APT1 operations." The 2014 description of the Triton product outlines the protection
of data at rest and in motion. This aspect of security also came to the fore in
2013, with the release of the "Snowden papers," where it became clear that
data had been compromised while in transit between servers and not simply as a result of a hack into where it was stored. What is also clear from
the product description is the use of computational power to address the
threat in cyber space. This is indicated both in the use of "real-time" analytics and the number of processes undertaken to triangulate risk factors
in determining a threat. We, therefore, have in this description of a 2014
product, a technology that is positioned to address the challenges highlighted very publicly in 2013 through APT1 and Snowden. We also see a
technology that is responding to the move and countermove dynamic of
the cyber contest. Signature-based antimalware approaches make technological progress but are then subverted by attacks that avoid using their
signatures. For example, hackers found that making small variations in
malware avoided signature-based detection or that small changes, made
over long periods of time, were not picked up.

The consequence of these trends is the demand for more computational
power, increasing automation and situational awareness for defenders, who have to handle more and more data and face multiple attacks
from different actors, even while they need to continue to operate. This
is evident in the category winners in 2018. The best SEIM solution was
Securonix, which won in the context that:

Infosec professionals understand that there really can be too much of a good thing.
Too much data. Too many tools. Too many threat alerts, too many of which are
false positives…Securonix and its Next Gen SIEM product relieves the burden of
"too much," offering customers a single enterprise solution that churns through
high volumes of data, using signature-less, behavior-based analyses to detect and

prioritize the true threats to an organization. In so doing, Securonix reduces the number of security alerts by up to 95 percent, which saves time and resources because Infosec professionals can respond to the highest risk events, not false alarms.

This product description highlights the new language of cyber security threat detection, which is presented in terms of advanced analytics and supervised and unsupervised machine learning. Return-on-investment considerations are highlighted in scalability of deployment, "number of digital assets leaked or shared, better educated employees, and time savings due to automation." The efficiency and economic aspects of this product are important marketing messages, in a context where an increasing number of companies offer "advanced analytics." It means that tech companies must show that they are not simply technically good, but that they meet the investment criteria of companies whose security staff have to bid for budget and justify expenditure.

The machine-learning theme is carried through into the winner of the 2018 category "Best Threat Detection Technology," Aruba Introspect. It claims to notice:

tiny anomalies and deviations in network activity that more conventional technologies might miss. IntroSpect uses machine learning-based analytics to automate the detection of attacks, exploits and breaches by keying in on suspicious behavior that strays from established normal baselines—even if the malicious actions are subtle or take place in incremental steps.

This description fits the emerging threats embodied in the notion that traditional defenses are inadequate; that weak signals of an attack matter; and that the extended timeline of an attack, not just a single event, are hard to detect. Aruba, like the other products mentioned, also leverages computational power, in this instance to continually make risk assessments with "over 100 AI-based models." It also provides estimates of money and time saved in investigations.

The 2018 "Best Threat Intelligence Technology" extends the analysis of data beyond a company's own system to search "hacker dump sites, underground markets, hacktivists forums, file-sharing portals, threat actors libraries, botnet exfiltrations, data leaks, malware logs, lists of compromised credentials and various IOCs [indicators of compromise]." It even "scans third-party partner and vendor sites for flaws." This description highlights two further trends. The first is the need to go beyond the firewall of one's own company to try to get early warning of attack. This allows defenses to be configured before an attack happens when working in real-time isn't enough. It also indicates the increasing web of interdependency with third parties and partners, where one's own security may depend on the security of others. This is what patrolling in cyber space looks like, beyond one's immediate defenses.

Three further awards, two from 2018 and one from 2017, are worth mentioning here. The first is the winner of "Best Deception Technology," a category introduced in 2018. Illusive Network's solution is described as follows:

Users of this deception technology already assume malicious hackers are going to get inside the network. The key, however, is to keep attackers away from the organization's crown jewels by sidetracking them with convincing decoys that, once meddled with, trigger an "incident detection" alert and an active forensic collection. Built to be endpoint-based, rather than an extension of a centralized honeypot architecture, the machine learning-based solution is lightweight, agent-less, and highly scalable, serving large environments with as many as 300,000 nodes. Illusive Networks automatically designs, deploys, updates and manages tailored deceptions based its own interpretation of the business environment it's protecting, including how endpoints are used and any vulnerable attack vectors it foresees.

This product highlights automation and learning and the ability to "foresee" attack vectors, based on the activity of adversaries. The notion of "crown jewels" is also highlighted. This is the language of prioritization in the enterprise. One cannot protect everything to the same level with limited budgets, so focus on priorities. It highlights a further trending assumption in cyber security—if you are Internet facing, you are already compromised. This means that security solutions have to consider how we treat threat actors that are already on our networks. Honeypots and honeynets are "deception technologies" that have come to represent a technique whereby an attacker is diverted into, or attracted toward, fake assets, where their attack can be contained, understood, or impact-reduced. Illusive Network's offering claims to provide an alternative to a "central honeypot architecture," by deploying to the end points in its system. These end points would normally be devices, such as the mobile phones of users or sensor on a network. As such, Illusive Network argues that its product is "lightweight" which likely means it does not require a large computational burden on end points, which would get in the way of day-to-day users, and the capacity of end-point technology. This is interesting because it offers an alternative vision of products that rely on centralized computational power, likely to be seen as a market differentiator amongst other machine-learning offerings.

The second example is the 2017 Award for "Best Behavior Analytics/Enterprise Threat Detection," which went to Falcon, by Crowdstrike. This category was offered in 2016 and 2017, before presumably being replaced by a number of categories in 2018. Crowdstrike offers another alternative regarding how computational power is harnessed and is described as follows:

To analyze billions of events swiftly and accurately in real-time, machine learning models require a level of computational power and scalability that is only possible with a fully SaaS-based [security as a service] architecture. As Falcon collects more threat intelligence and identifies attacks, this information is turned into a new detection and learned by the algorithm, and deployed across its cloud network so all endpoints are protected—sending the bad actors back to the drawing board.

Here the computational power is framed in terms of billions of events, and a service model is offered. It, too, recognizes the importance of end-point security, rather than centralized information assets alone. Once again, machine learning and scalability are emphasized, as is timing, as bad actors are sent back to the drawing board, even as their attacks are in progress.

The third example is the 2018 award for "Best Authentication Technology." This was won by Jumio and its Netverify solution, a technology that prevents an attacker from using enlarged photographs of people, say from stolen ID cards or drivers' licenses, to circumvent facial-recognition technology. Within seconds, it recognizes the photograph as a duplicate of other documents. Jumio claims a dataset of over 80 million verifications, with a 95-percent detection rate of detectable fraudulent transactions, "allowing over 99.9 percent of valid customer transactions." This is an excellent example of having to counter a criminal's attempt to counter a biometric form of authentication.

It would be tempting to think that the quoted descriptions relating to products are simply marketing hype. They do reflect the emerging language and concerns of the community, and it is understandable that the marketing blurb would reflect that language. However, there is most certainly more going on, as the language of innovation used above reflects the extent to which the complexity and scale of the cyber challenge demands innovative and compelling responses. What is clear is how computing power, artificial intelligence, imaging, sensors, business processes, software engineering, data science, cyber security subject-matter expertise, behavioral analytics, intelligence, and many other factors producing indicators of attack have had to be assembled to rise to the challenge.

Returning to Satell's types of innovation, in regard to the SC Awards, we can see a clear preference for rewarding breakthrough and disruptive innovation for the emerging problems of too much data, complexity, timescale, and magnitude of attack activity. That many domains had to come together to provide solutions indicates that collaborative work has been a necessity. It is now becoming routine for those deploying automation, computer and data scientists, software engineers, and cyber defenders to have to combine their knowledge in a cross-domain way. Of course this may be seen as creating new domains of understanding, but it is that understanding this dynamic has been done as "building the ship whilst at sea, whilst under attack." According to SC Awards, the last six years has seen the transformation of castle-and-moat perimeter security into one that reaches beyond the perimeter to hacker communities and the end-point technologies of customers and partners. They have seen the rise of automation and machine learning that tries to behave dynamically, pre-dict, and pre-empt. They have seen the utilization of computational power to assess in real-time. All of this is a result of changes in the environment and the activity of companies, customers, and criminals, in a world where neither the problem nor the domain are always well understood. This is recognized within the way markets have responded to cyber security innovation—and sometimes in how solutions look for problems.

CNBC produced a list of 50 disruptor companies for the last six years from across sectors. According to CNBC, the 2018 list was selected from 981 nominated companies, using the following criteria:

- Nominated companies submitted key quantitative and qualitative information.
- "PitchBook" provided data on fundraising and implied valuations.
- CNBC used IBISWorld's database of industry reports to compare the companies, based on the industries they are attempting to disrupt.
- CNBC's Disruptor 50 Advisory Council of 52 experts ranked the quan-titative criteria by importance and ability to disrupt established indus-tries and public companies.
- CNBC editorial staff, along with members of the advisory council, read the submissions and assigned a holistic qualitative score to each com-pany. This score was combined with a composite quantitative score to determine each company's overall ranking.

Table 7.2 highlights the declared cyber security companies beside selected other companies for illustration.

Some companies on the CNBC Disruptor 50 list that are not in this table, worked in areas that were related to cyber security, such as IT recruit-ment. For example, HackerRank, was listed 30th in 2015 for its approach to gamifying recruitment of IT skills. Other companies were working in the adjacent areas of, for example, big data analytics. The companies listed in red in the table had "cyber security" noted as one of their sectors of disruption—except for Palantir Technologies, which was listed as disrupt-ing defense, enterprise technology, and software in 2014, but also included cyber security after that. Synack was specifically listed as working against penetration testing and automated tools.

Table 7.2

2014		2015		2016		2017		2018	
Rank		**Rank**		**Rank**		**Rank**		**Rank**	
1	SpaceX	1	Moderna Therapeutics	1	Uber	1	Airbnb	1	SpaceX
2	Warby Parker	2	Space X	2	Airbnb	2	Lyft	2	Uber
3	Etsy	3	Bloom Energy	3	Ezetap	3	WeWork	3	AirBnb
5	Palantir Technologies	7	Palantir Technologies	4	Palantir Technologies	8	Palantir Technologies	14	Survey Monkey
24	Dropbox	20	Synack	16	Snapchat	9	Cylance	27	Crowdstrike
32	Pinterest	31	Coinbase	20	Synack	11	Crowdstrike	33	Palantir Technologies
41	Airbnb	35	Pinterest	25	Spotify	32	Illumio	34	Darktrace
48	Snapchat	47	Spotify	38	Okta	36	Dropbox	36	Pinterest
49	Kickstarter	50	Snapchat	40	Cylance	38	Synack	44	Illumio

Source: Source data from an analysis of CNBC Disruptor 50

Five companies, Airbnb, Pinterest, Palantir, SpaceX, and Uber, have made the list in all six years of the project. One can observe a general trend towards more cyber security companies in disruption, though their ranking is also averaging downward. This might be explained by growth in cyber security markets, which brings in more companies but also creates a greater number of similar companies. Palantir Technologies, headquartered in California, was launched in 2004 and specializes in big-data analytics across multiple sectors. It pitches cyber security across governance and risk, intelligence, and data protection (GDPR), among others. It has attracted huge levels of funding: $896.2 million in 2014, $1 billion in 2015, $2.7 billion in 2016, $1.5 billion in 2017, and $2.8 billion in 2018. Its estimated valuation was $20.5 billion in 2018. Crowdstrike, mentioned above as an SC Award winner in 2017, is also headquartered in California and also appears on the CNBC list in 2017. In that year it attracted $156 million in funding and an estimated market valuation of $666.7 million. In 2018, it again appeared on the list, attracting another $281.2 million, with a market valuation of $1.1 billion. Darktrace is a UK company based in Cambridge. It launched in 2013 and attracted $179.5 million in funding, according to the 2018 list, with an estimated valuation of $1.25 billion. Markets have seen beyond the marketing hype.

CYBER SECURITY INNOVATION POLICY

It is unsurprising that the cyber security companies listed on the CNBC Disruptor 50 are from the United States and the United Kingdom. Cyber Security Ventures publishes an annual list of 500 of "the world's hottest and most innovative cyber security companies," which allows a geographical analysis of innovative companies. Companies are selected on the basis of a range of factors:

- Cyber security sector (market category)
- Problem(s) solved
- Customer base
- Feedback from CISOs and decision-makers
- Feedback from IT security evaluators and recommenders
- Feedback from Value Added Resellers (VARs), Systems integrators (SIs), and consultants
- Venture Capitalist (VC) Funding
- Company growth
- Published product reviews
- Demos and presentations at conferences
- Corporate marketing and branding
- Media coverage
- Notable implementations

Table 7.3

United States	358
Israel	41
United Kingdom	23
Canada	15
France	7
Sweden	7
Germany	6
Switzerland	6
China	6
Ireland	5
Other Asia-Pacific, including Australia	13 (with less than 5 in any one country)
Other Europe	13 (with less than 5 in any one country)

Source: Source data from Cyebsecurity Ventures

- Founder and management pedigree
- Interviews with senior management

Table 7.3 shows the number of companies in the listed 500 by country.

Companies based in the United States comprise nearly 72 percent of the 500 listed, with Israel second with just over 8 percent. One might expect this, due to the digital technological dominance of Silicon Valley. Within the United States, Silicon Valley accounts for 25 percent of companies on the list, and a further 24 percent are based between New England and Washington, D.C.. Interestingly, China has only six companies on the list, even as observers discuss its rise within the tech sector to compete with the United States. Part of this difference might be explained by issues of trust and technological provenance. Private-sector differences in doing security business with government might also explain this. Much of the innovation in Chinese cyber security remains in government hands. Perhaps it is an attribute of incentives through innovation programs. Undoubtedly, some of it is due to the historical legacy of Internet business development in the United States. Perhaps more interesting is why Israel is second on the list. Why is it that these geographical differences exist?

In terms of Israel, Gil Press, writing in *Forbes* in July 2017, stated that there are six factors why Israel has become a "cyber security powerhouse." First, the Israeli government plays a coordination role in developing an ecosystem that can deal with unpredictable threats. He characterizes this as a constantly evolving framework for collaboration between government, business, and universities. He sees the main function of the government as an adviser. Some businesses are reluctant to work too closely with government, as they have an international market. This has meant that the government tries to address cyber security of the nation, while keeping a distance from business decision-making and their databases. The second factor is government as a business catalyst, constructing a strategy with a mission to be in the top-five leading nations in the area. Cyber security was an area where the government could see economic growth. Third, it made the military a "start-up incubator and accelerator." Given the geo-strategic dynamics of the region, cyber security was seen as a key area for defense attention. One important aspect of innovation was creating a start-up-like culture within cyber-related military units. In this way, national service for young people was seen as being broadly beneficial in terms of skills and development. The fourth factor was investment in "human capital" through a focus on skills, experience, and ambitions. Gil Press describes a dynamic culture of innovation and initiative. Development of skills in this area has spanned schools and universities, including the development of research centers that specialize in cyber security.

Press argues that the fifth factor is interdisciplinarity and diversity. While cyber security has a technological base, many of the problems are not technical. Therefore, having diverse teams is a key ingredient in innovation. This is consistent with the breakthrough innovation noted by Satell. This approach is enhanced in Israel by diversity in disciplines, as well as the diversity displayed in the Israeli workforce—Press cites that in 2014, 25 percent are immigrants, and 35 percent children of immigrants.

The final factor Press describes is "rethinking the [cyber] box." He claims that Israel made a strategic pivot, which changed old thinking from who might attack Israel to what threats might Israel face. This resulted in a strategy on three levels—robustness, resilience, and defense. These levels have an increasing contribution from government. There is an expectation that organizations will work to be robust, perhaps with some advice from government. Government will contribute to resilience and have responsibility at the defense level for attribution and response to attacks in major events. Press sees this strategy as effective in bringing private sectors and government together in areas where responsibility is defined and in which cross-pollination of ideas is encouraged.

The United States and Israel have established closer cooperation on R&D in cyber security, supported by the United States–Israel Cyber Security Cooperation Enhancement Act, introduced in January 2017. The United States has also created a Cyber Security Division (CSD) in the Department of Homeland Security to lead the federal government's efforts in funding cyber security R&D. Key to its mission is getting practitioners involved so that ideas can be developed quickly into deployable solutions. The diagram in Figure 7.1 is taken from the CSD Web page and illustrates their R&D lifecycle in which there is continuous "customer" engagement.

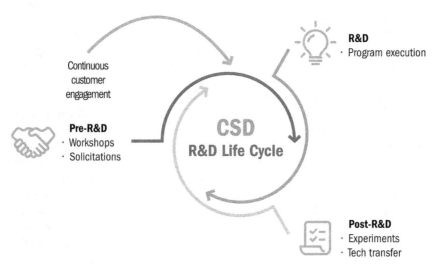

Figure 7.1

Department of Homeland Security Cyber Security Division

CSD provides a number of examples in which partnerships work to address real-world problems. They take a challenge format. For example, the "Anonymous Networks and Currencies" project is described as follows:

Law enforcement (LE) agencies face significant challenges investigating criminal activity involving the use of anonymous networks and cryptocurrencies. Anonymous networks are intentionally configured to keep browsing and personally identifiable information—such as IP addresses—anonymous. Though there are many legitimate uses for this technology, it also has broad appeal with criminals seeking to evade law enforcement. This project seeks to develop cost-effective and novel solutions to aid LE agencies in their investigations into criminal activity in these areas.

In partnership with LE agencies, DHS is, for example, developing tools "to enable LE to perform forensic analysis of cryptocurrency transactions and facilitate the tracing of currencies involved in illicit transactions."

Another example is work being conducted on data privacy, which works with customers to identify "needs that cannot be met with current technologies." CSD lists two current projects running with Northeastern University and Raytheon respectively. The first is on auditing and controlling the leakage of personal information from mobile devices, browsers, and IoT devices. The second is examining cryptographic approaches that preserve privacy while searching and sharing.

CSDS list other R&D programs, including:

- Application of network measurement science
- Critical infrastructure design and adaptive resilient systems
- Cyber-risk economics (CYRIE)
- Cyber physical-systems security (CPSSEC)
- Cyber security forensics
- Cyber security competitions
- Cyber security for oil and gas systems (COGS)
- Distributed denial of service defense (DDoSD)
- Federated security
- Experimental research testbed (DETER)
- Homeland open security technology (HOST)
- Identity management
- Information marketplace for policy and analysis of cyber risk and trust (IMPACT)
- Insider threat
- Mobile-application security
- Mobile-device security
- Next generation cyber infrastructure apex
- Smart cities
- Software assurance marketplace (SWAMP)
- Software quality assurance
- Static analysis tools modernization project (STAMP)
- Transition to practice (TTP)

The approaches described for Israel and the United States are consistent with Satell's discussion regarding types of innovation where government provides opportunities and a reason for various stakeholders to come together to address cyber security challenges when the market is failing or being slow to address them. The United Kingdom has adopted a similar approach.

The United Kingdom published an interim Cyber Security Science and Technology (S&T) Strategy in November 2017, which came in the context of multiple initiatives that had already been running for some time, guided by the broader National Cyber Security Strategies, as discussed in chapter 9. Nevertheless, it stated the formal goals for the United Kingdom regarding science and technology in cyber security. These are to ensure that:

- the country has the cyber security science and technology capability and expertise needed to meet our security needs and inform policy-making
- the United Kingdom has a single authoritative voice that can assess the sufficiency of our national cyber security science-and-technology

capability and identify significant cyber security science-and-technology developments that require a policy response

- the United Kingdom is applying independent expert assurance so that we have confidence in our ability to identify and respond to significant science and technological developments and that policy-making is sufficiently informed by scientific understanding
- the United Kingdom has the right relationship with the cyber security and wider science and technology community in academia, industry, and internationally to support the above and drive continuous improvements in our efforts.

In brief, the government's declared roles are to ensure capability against needs, expert assurance of capability, assessment of its sufficiency, and the sustainment of relationships in the S&T community.

Part one of the strategy identifies emerging trends and technologies that are most likely to affect the cyber security of the country. This echoes the threat-based approach taken by Israel, discussed above. Five areas are briefly described. The first is Internet of things and smart cities, in which security in devices and networks, by default, is essential. End-point security is also identified, along with maintaining security of rapidly changing networks, ID management, and authentication of end points and dealing with legacy systems. The second area relates to security of data and information. This reflected much of the discussion above, in that it was concerned with data volume and big-data analytics. The third area is automaton, machine learning, and AI. The fourth area is "human computer interaction." This involves the need to develop visual and speech interfaces as well as presentation of data for decision-making and people's interaction with the environment. The fifth area is a catch-all category regarding smart building, quantum technologies, and others that have already been discussed in this book.

A key element of delivery of the strategy is a cyber security research plan, which is yet to be published. However, it will aim to work across government, industry, and academic partners through the UK research councils, Government Chief Scientific Advisors, and academic centers of excellence (as briefly described in chapter 9). The interim strategy explicitly states that it has to look beyond existing or identified technology and ensure that it keeps "emerging technology and human factors challenges under regular review."

The National Cyber Security Strategy made a commitment to open two innovation centers, one in Cheltenham, and one in London. The innovation centers are run by the private sector in association with government. The first, run by Wayra, was launched in January 2017. Its second cohort of companies has embarked on a nine-month program, with £25k worth of funding. The second innovation centre will be launched in London in the summer of 2018, run by Plexal. It has called for a range of organizations and people to get involved:

- Start-ups that can address real-world cyber challenges
- Large companies that are seeking to address cyber challenges and engage with start-ups
- Investors and funders
- Cyber academics, innovation centers, start-up clusters, and research institutes
- Cyber security professionals

Other initiatives run throughout the United Kingdom, including a series of activities overseen by Innovate United Kingdom, the government's "innovation agency." It is focused on businesses, to help support them in their innovation. It has funded over £1.8 billion on innovation since 2007. It established a network of "catapult: centers around the United Kingdom, including one for digital, based in London and Northern Ireland. They are independent organizations that use Innovate United Kingdom's core funding to provide "access to expertise, equipment, and facilities that may not be available to the market."

Other accelerators are operated by the private sector. Two of note are Cylon and Cyber39. Cylon today claims that 53 companies have been accelerated since its launch in 2015, utilizing a network of 350 mentors and 150 investors, from which the start-ups learn and to whom they pitch their ideas and connect on challenges. Cyber39 is part of the Level39 initiative, based in Canary Wharf London and owned by Canary Wharf Group. Level39 aims to support the growth of tech companies through mentoring and access to customers, talent, and infrastructure. It claims the United Kingdom's largest collection of cyber security companies that are "contactable alone, or in combination, to respond to critical requirements."

DISCUSSION

This chapter has provided a definition of innovation and a model provided by Satell that breaks innovation into four types. These include basic research, breakthrough innovation, disruptive innovation, and sustaining innovations. Satell also described three time horizons, the closest being akin to core business for a company or today's problem. The second is slightly further out and looks at innovations that address issues not yet served. The distant horizon is one of new capabilities and new markets. Satell believes that companies may find it most difficult to visualise and invest in the horizons further from today and in ideas that are not yet well understood. We have seen through the review of awards and features of innovative companies that there is considerable innovation and growth already in the market. Yet the activities of the United States, Israel, and the United Kingdom show that the market is failing in some areas or not yet addressing those areas that could be of national interest in terms of security and economy. Consequently, government initiatives are aimed at having businesses and universities join them in addressing challenges in breakthrough and disruptive innovation. They also promote basic research in academia. It is clear that innovation from a national perspective requires planned assistance.

Yet, look at the levels of funding attracted by innovative companies, such as Palantir and Crowdstrike, companies that also benefit from having government as customers. Governments want to find the secret to producing more companies like these. They hope that start-ups, with some assistance, can follow in their footsteps. We can see from the geographical distribution of innovative cyber security companies that whether through strategic interests, culture, capacity, investment, or government interventions, only a few countries lead the way in cyber security innovation to date. To try to maintain, or to gain, position, no doubt a national strategy, utilizing some of the interventions described in the innovation ecosystem in this chapter, is essential. However, if you are a business, where do you go next? We said at the beginning of the chapter that Satell recommended the development of a playbook based on one's understanding of the innovation problem to be addressed. He recommends six principles, which we summarize now in the context of cyber security and as a conclusion to this chapter.

1. Actively seek out good problems. Satell argues that you don't need a brilliant idea, just a good problem—and there are plenty in cyber security. Domains and problems have expanded with more and more connectivity, requiring new ways of working, alternative insights, and blends of technology, packaged as solutions. The list of areas for awards and projects being undertaken in the interests of national security, privacy, e-commerce, and law enforcement means that there are not just many domains to be involved in a solution, but many domains in which a solution might be applied. Innovation is about an effective solution to an important problem.
2. Choose problems that suit your organization's capabilities, culture and strategy. There isn't one culture that works for innovation. IBM is different from Google is different from Microsoft. Start-ups are innovative and unlike corporate cultures. Certain problems will suit your organization and you more than others because of your talent, resources, and network. Cyber security is like every other area of business in this regard. However, there is plenty of diversity in cyber security because, as we have pointed out, many of the problems we face are not technical, even if much of the solution is. Israel is showing how multidisciplinarity and

diversity works for them. There is room for psychologists, economists, data scientists, software developers, and engineers to work together to make cyber security effective.

3. Ask the right questions to map the innovation space. For Satell, this is about understanding how well the problem and domains are defined. This then launches you into an approach, depending upon where you sit on the innovations matrix. The key here is whether your strategy addresses the problem. Do you need help from academia, a venture capitalist, or some support from outside your own speciality? Think about where you need to go for advice, and get it.

4. Leverage platforms to access ecosystems of talent, technology, and information. If you are in the United Kingdom, speak to Innovate UK, the Digital Catapult, Cylon, or your local enterprise partnership. Don't forget to look out for competitions that are run by the government around the challenges they face, and go to industry days. Find ways to collaborate. As Satell points out, open innovation and collaboration is needed for many aspects of today's complex and connected society.

5. Build a collaborative culture. To get teams to work together, often with different goals, requires a meeting of the minds around the problem to be solved. Single-minded you might be to get your business of the ground, but innovation usually works best when effective teams can be developed who get behind the project, where antagonism is minimized, and creativity flows.

6. Understand that innovation is a messy business. Many innovators meet with failure at some point along the way to success. Many of the interventions described in this chapter are designed to give innovation a chance, rather than to guarantee it. That a nation has an innovation strategy does not mean that all succeed. Rather, it is aimed at giving it the best chance, with the assurance that many will succeed. Cyber security is messy in itself. It is based on a context in which an adversary has a say in the future. Today's solutions may face the perfect countermeasure. Fixing a problem today is likely to need further innovation tomorrow.

NOTE

1. U.K. Department for Innovation, Universities. and Skills, "Innovation Nation," http://webarchive.nationalarchives.gov.uk/tna/+/http:/www.dius.gov.uk /publications/scienceinnovation.pdf/. Accessed June 22, 2018.

BIBLIOGRAPHY

ACT-IAC. "Strengthening Federal Cybersecurity: Results of the Cyber Ideations Initiative." 2015. https://www.actiac.org/system/files/cybersecurity-inno vation.pdf. Accessed June 22, 2018.

Avant, D., S. P. Campbell, E. Donahoe, K. Florini, M. Kahler, M. P. Lagon, T. Maurer et al. "Innovations in Global Governance: Peace-Building, Human Rights, Internet Governance and Cybersecurity, and Climate Change." Council on Foreign Relations, September 2017.

CNBC. "Meet the 2016 CNBC's Disruptor 50 Companies." 2016. https://www.cnbc.com/2016/06/07/2016-cnbcs-disruptor-50.html. Accessed June 22, 2018.

CNBC. "Meet the 2018 CNBC Disruptor 50 Companies." 2018. https://www.cnbc.com/2018/05/22/meet-the-2018-cnbc-disruptor-50-companies.html. Accessed June 22, 2018.

Corera, G. "Rapid Escalation of the Cyber-Arms Race." BBC News, April 29, 2015. http://www.bbc.co.uk/news/uk-32493516. Accessed June 22, 2018.

Craig, A., and B. Valeriano. "Conceptualizing the Cyber Arms Race." 2016 8th International Conference on Cyber Conflict Cyber Power. NATO CCD COE, 2016. http://orca.cf.ac.uk/91754/1/Conceptualising%20Cyber%20Arms%20Races.pdf. Accessed June 22, 2018.

Cybersecurity Ventures. Press Release. "Cybersecurity 500." 2018. https://cybersecurityventures.com/cybersecurity-500/. Accessed June 22, 2018.

CyLon. "Europe's First Cybersecurity Accelerator." 2018. https://cylonlab.com/. Accessed June 22, 2018.

Digital Catapult. "Future Networks." Digital Catapult. https://www.digicatapult.org.uk/technologies/future-networks. Accessed June 22, 2018.

Emmanuel, Z. "CyLon Continues to Drive Cyber Security Innovation with Next Accelerator Cohort." ComputerWeekly.com, April 19, 2018. https://www.computerweekly.com/news/252439317/CyLon-continues-to-drive-cyber-security-innovation-with-next-accelerator-cohort. Accessed June 22, 2018.

Fannin, R. "Watch for China's Silicon Valley to Dominate in 2018 and Beyond." Forbes, January 1, 2018. https://www.forbes.com/sites/rebeccafannin/2018/01/01/watch-for-chinas-silicon-valley-to-dominate-in-2018-and-beyond/. Accessed June 22, 2018.

Franceschi-Bicchierai, L. "Edward Snowden: The 10 Most Important Revelations from His Leaks." Mashable, June 5, 2014. https://mashable.com/2014/06/05/edward-snowden-revelations/. Accessed June 22, 2018.

Goździewicz, W., C. Gutkowski, L. Tabansky, and R. Siudak. "Security through Innovation. Cybersecurity Sector as a Driving Force in the National Economic Development." The Kosciuszko Institute, 2017. http://www.ik.org.pl/wp-content/themes/ik/report-img/security-through-innovation.pdf. Accessed June 22, 2018.

Grasty, T. "The Difference between 'Invention' and 'Innovation'." Huffington Post, April 3, 2012, updated December 6, 2017. https://www.huffingtonpost.com/tom-grasty/technological-inventions-and-innovation_b_1397085.html. Accessed June 22, 2018.

Greenwald, G. "NSA Collecting Phone Records of Millions of Verizon Customers Daily." The Guardian, June 6, 2013. http://www.theguardian.com/world/2013/jun/06/nsa-phone-records-verizon-court-order. Accessed June 22, 2018.

Ismail, N. "It's War: The Cyber Arms Race." *Information Age*, August 18, 2016. http://www.information-age.com/war-cyber-arms-race-123461885/. Accessed June 22, 2018.

KPMG. "The Changing Landscape of Disruptive Technologies." 2018. https://assets.kpmg.com/content/dam/kpmg/ca/pdf/2018/03/tech-hubs-forging-new-paths.pdf. Accessed June 22, 2018.

Maughan, D. "Government Cybersecurity R&D: Innovation, Transition, and Opportunities." DHS Presentation, May 17, 2017. https://www.nwo.nl/binaries/content/assets/bestanden/cybersecurity/17-csre-100b-csd---nl---17may2017---maughan---finala.pdf. Accessed June 22, 2018.

McWhorter, D. "Mandiant Exposes APT1—One of China's Cyber Espionage Units & Releases 3,000 Indicators." Fireeye, 2013. https://www.fireeye.com/blog/threat-research/2013/02/mandiant-exposes-apt1-chinas-cyber-espionage-units.html. Accessed June 22, 2018.

Morgan, S. "Cybersecurity 500 by the Numbers: Breakdown by Region." *Cybersecurity Magazine*, 2018. https://cybersecurityventures.com/cybersecurity-500-by-the-numbers-breakdown-by-region/. Accessed June 22, 2018.

Owens, B. K. "Air Force CISO Says Innovation Key to Future Cyber Defense." *Defense Systems*, August 16, 2017. https://defensesystems.com/articles/2017/08/16/air-force-cybersecurity.aspx. Accessed June 22, 2018.

Plexal. "What Is the London Cyber Innovation Centre?" *Plexal*, 2018. https://www.plexal.com/cybersecurity/. Accessed June 22, 2018.

Press, G. "6 Reasons Israel Became a Cybersecurity Powerhouse Leading the $82 Billion Industry." *Forbes*, July 18, 2017. https://www.forbes.com/sites/gilpress/2017/07/18/6-reasons-israel-became-a-cybersecurity-powerhouse-leading-the-82-billion-industry/#2665cefa420a. Accessed June 22, 2018.

Satell, G. "The 4 Types of Innovation and the Problems They Solve." *Harvard Business Review*, June 21, 2017. https://hbr.org/2017/06/the-4-types-of-innovation-and-the-problems-they-solve. Accessed June 22, 2018.

Satell, G. *Mapping Innovation: A Playbook for Navigating a Disruptive Age.* McGraw-Hill eBook.

SC Media US "2013 *SC Magazine* US Awards Finalists." 2013. https://www.scmagazine.com/awards/2013-sc-magazine-us-awards-finalists/article/543307/. Accessed June 22, 2018.

SC Media US "SC Awards 2014." 2014. https://media.scmagazine.com/documents/64/botn2014sm_15797.pdf. Accessed June 22, 2018.

SC Media US "SC Awards 2015." 2015. https://media.scmagazine.com/documents/118/botn2015sm_29485.pdf. Accessed June 22, 2018.

SC Media US "SC Awards 2016." 2016. https://media.scmagazine.com/documents/213/botn_final_53207.pdf. Accessed June 22, 2018.

SC Media US "SC Awards 2017." 2017. https://media.scmagazine.com/documents/286/botn2017_71287.pdf. Accessed June 22, 2018.

SC Media US "SC Awards 2018." 2018. https://media.scmagazine.com/documents/340/botn_2018_84754.pdf. Accessed June 22, 2018.

Schreiber, O., and I. Reznikov. "The State of Israel's Cybersecurity Market." *TechCrunch*, January 14, 2018. http://social.techcrunch.com/2018/01/14/the-state-of-israels-cybersecurity-market/. Accessed June 22, 2018.

Silver, J. "Growing the UK's Digital Economy." Innovate UK, August 10, 2016. https://innovateuk.blog.gov.uk/2016/08/10/growing-the-uks-digital-economy/. Accessed June 22, 2018.

UK Cabinet Office. "Interim Cybersecurity Science and Technology Strategy." 2017. https://assets.publishing.service.gov.uk/government/uploads/system/uploads/attachment_data/file/663181/Embargoed_National_Cyber_Science_and_Technology_Strategy_FINALpdf.pdf. Accessed June 22, 2018.

UK Department for Innovation, Universities and Skills. "Innovation Nation." 2008. http://webarchive.nationalarchives.gov.uk/tna/+/http:/www.dius.gov.uk/publications/scienceinnovation.pdf/. Accessed June 22, 2018.

UK DTI. "Cybersecurity Export Strategy." 2018. https://assets.publishing.service.gov.uk/government/uploads/system/uploads/attachment_data/file/693989/CCS151_CCS0118810124-1_Cyber_Security_Export_Strategy_Brochure_Web_Accessible.pdf. Accessed November 4, 2018.

UK Government. "The Grand Challenge Missions." 2018. https://www.gov.uk/government/publications/industrial-strategy-the-grand-challenges/missions. Accessed June 22, 2018.

UK Government. "Groundbreaking Partnership between Government and Tech Start-Ups to Develop World-Leading Cyber Security Technology." 2016. https://www.gov.uk/government/news/groundbreaking-partnership-between-government-and-tech-start-ups-to-develop-world-leading-cyber-security-technology. Accessed June 22, 2018.

UK Government. "World-Leading Cyber Centre to Be Developed in London's Olympic Park." UK government, April 10, 2018. https://www.gov.uk/government/news/world-leading-cyber-centre-to-be-developed-in-londons-olympic-park. Accessed October 16, 2018.

UK MOD-DCO. "Trends and Innovations in Defence and the Cyber Security Challenges that Come with Them." 2017. https://www.contracts.mod.uk/blog/trends-and-innovations-in-defence-and-the-cyber-security-challenges-that-come-with-them/. Accessed June 22, 2018.

UK Research and Innovation. https://www.ukri.org/. Accessed June 22, 2018.

U.S. Department of Commerce. "Cybersecurity, Innovation, and the Internet Economy." 2011. https://www.nist.gov/sites/default/files/documents/itl/Cybersecurity_Green-Paper_FinalVersion.pdf. Accessed June 22, 2018.

U.S. Department of Homeland Security. "CSD-Privacy." 2016. https://www.dhs.gov/science-and-technology/csd-privacy. Accessed June 22, 2018.

U.S. Department of Homeland Security. "CSD Projects." 2012. https://www.dhs.gov/science-and-technology/csd-projects. Accessed June 22, 2018.

CHAPTER 8

International Policy: Pitfalls and Possibilities

Nigel Jones

The triumph of economic globalization has inspired a wave of techno-savvy investigative activists who are as globally minded as the corporations they track.

—Naomi Klein, No Logo

It may seem odd to start a chapter on international policy with a quote that doesn't mention governments. It's a reminder that there are many actors in the international environment in which cyber attacks and cyber crime take place. Global corporations and globally minded tech-savvy activists are but two. Simply using the categories, state and nonstate actors, does not do the diversity of actors in each justice, whether they are rich and powerful or technologically complex—or not. Indeed, in cyber space the distinction between these categories might appear rather simplistic when one considers that government services may be delivered by private-sector companies or state actors using hacker groups as proxies. Arguably, each of us as individuals is an international actor through the use of a global cyber infrastructure. A network of private- and public-sector actors, operating in and across multiple jurisdictions, provide the services on which we have come to rely.

In this context, bringing order to our international cyber space is no easy task. Governments have to work with companies to allow trade and services to work effectively. Criminals have to be tackled across borders. Individuals may choose to exercise power as consumers rather than as citizens, or corporations can influence by contract rather than the law. Consequently, each of us as citizen, consumer, employee, or activist, plays a part in the shape and function of cyber space; how and on what basis is the fundamental question addressed by this chapter.

We will start with an examination of states in the international system. They remain the key stakeholders for the formal development and shaping of international policy. The chapter will then examine the policies and strategies of the United States, the European Union, the North Atlantic Treaty Organization (NATO), and the Gulf Cooperation Council (GCC). We have chosen these because they exhibit a network of relationships that range from the formal and obligatory to the collaborative and aspirational. Key facets are the boundaries between public and private sectors and the implications for both. The chapter will examine attempts to mitigate threats that emerge from abroad or have an international character. It will review current policies and guidance for public and private sectors that are conscious of the international foundation of cyber space as pitfalls and possibilities are identified.

INTERNATIONAL POLICY—WHY STATES RATHER THAN COMPANIES?

It is argued that the basis for international system goes back to the Treaties of Westphalia and Osnabruck in 1648. These treaties ended the Thirty Years' War, a largely religious war that left eight million dead in Europe. Subsequent treaties of Utrecht (1713), ending the Wars of Spanish Succession, and Paris (1814), ending the Napoleonic Wars, established the basis for the principles of the international system that are recognizable today, such as:

- The principle of "territorial integrity"
- The principle of the sovereignty of states and the right of political self-determination
- The principle of legal equality between states
- The principle of nonintervention of one state in the internal affairs of another state

The principles are also encoded in the in United Nations Charter, an institution formed after another deadly war. Such is the enduring nature of these principles that, for example, it is only since the Rwandan genocide and the civil wars in the Balkans that "duty to protect" (rather than stand by and watch a genocide) has gained international status as an exceptional reason for the intervention in the affairs of another state. Globalization through the 20th and 21st centuries has created markets and companies working across the globe, whose value rivals or exceeds many countries' Gross Domestic Products. The market capitalization of Apple on NASDAQ in January 2018 was approximately USD 890 billion, which is between the projected GDPs of Mexico and Turkey, ranked 16th and 17th of all countries in the world. Starbuck's market capitalization was USD 84 billion, comparable to Sri Lanka's or Slovak Republic's GDP. Efforts to promote and/or regulate global trade and economy have been made through the formation of institutions or agreements such as the World Bank, the International Monetary Fund, the Global Agreement on Tariffs and Trade, and World Trade Organization. The members of these institutions or signatories to the agreements are states that remain the representatives of citizens at the international level, through their governments. Less formal forums such as the G8 and G20, comprised of the top economies in the world, are again represented by national governments.

There is no global governance capable of creating and enforcing international law except through the agreement of states in bilateral or multilateral agreements and treaties. It is, therefore, through states that most formal international policy will come into being, either because they choose to agree or because they influence through diplomacy, economics, or force. However, one should not underestimate the power of markets, corporation, and consumers on the work of governments and behavior of citizens. Some of this influence is institutional, while some is a consequence of the emergent properties of the system of trade, markets, and the flow of wealth.

The World Economic Forum is an example of the tangible and institutional side. It exists to act as a network for public- and private-sector leaders and attempts to tackle issues by getting the right people in the room. Another highly relevant example is ICANN, an organization that champions what it calls a multistakeholder model in its management of the Domain Name System at the heart of the Internet. This model comprises of businesses, Internet service providers, third-sector organizations, and government representatives, working to manage the Internet because all have a stake in its success. Nevertheless, the Internet is often at the center of politically charged discussion concerning such issues as the interests of states, censorship, citizens' rights, safety, espionage, and net neutrality. We shall return to some of these as we explore the policies of the United States, European Union, NATO, and GCC states.

We first turn to the United States, which, at the time of writing had, under the Trump administration, brought the issue of net neutrality to the fore, along with what some fear would be a mercantile approach to national security.

THE UNITED STATES

National security strategies can often be criticized for being more political statements than instrumental frameworks for action and implementation. However, with caution, they can serve as guides for the broad assessment of how an administration views context, success, cause, and effect. The challenge for us in making an assessment of the Trump administration's cyber policy is two-fold. First, we are just over a year into the new administration. According to Feaver,[1] compared to other presidents, Trump has done well to have his team produce a strategy within his first year in December 2017. Consequently, it is a little early to assess if the strategy will cascade into a series of other plans and actions, marking a change in the plans laid down by the previous Obama administration. Second, it is still unclear, even with the national strategy, how Trump's "America First" premise will operate in practice. This lack of clarity exists for a number of reasons. Trump has been vocal in saying that many multilateral deals, such as those relating to North American and Trans-Atlantic trade, are bad deals. He has been equivocal on the utility of the North Atlantic Alliance and has announced withdrawal from a global agreement on global warming. The clear linkage made by his administration between aid and votes in the United Nations regarding the status of Jerusalem might be interpreted as a transactional view of influence. These actions are, by degrees, at odds with elements of the national strategy, yet also consistent with others. This dynamic needs to be taken into account in understanding how the United States will try to influence cyber space and address cyber threats.

In this section, we will start with the strategic position in the new national security strategy (NSS) regarding cyber. We can also draw on a number of other early Trump documents but will also have to examine plans and activities put in place under Obama.

The following statements, taken from the NSS, highlight the importance of cyber space and its relationship to business, security, wealth, and prosperity.

America's response to the challenges and opportunities of the cyber era will determine our future prosperity and security.

The flow of data and an open, interoperable Internet are inseparable from the success of the U.S. economy.

They demonstrate the idea that cyber security is good for prosperity. Yet it is also clear that the NSS proposes that a strong economy is good for national security. In other words, prosperity leads to better security. The strategy exemplifies this relationship by setting out four pillars in which cyber is a cross-cutting feature.

Pillar One: Protect the American People, the Homeland, and the American Way of Life

This pillar describes defense against threats to borders and territory, covering weapons of mass destruction, "biothreats" and pandemics, border

control, and immigration. It aims to pursue threats at their source, specifically jihadist terrorist and criminal organizations. It aims to keep America
safe in cyber space and promote U.S. resilience. In pillar one, cyber space
is seen as a domain on page 8, along with land, air, maritime, and space. It
relates to cyber crime in page 12, where priority actions are stated as using
'sophisticated investigative tools "to disrupt criminal activities including the use of online marketplaces, and cryptocurrencies." Page 12 then
frames cyber as an era in which to keep America safe. In the NSS, this
era is characterized by state and nonstate threat actors, who can conduct
"low cost and deniable" attacks against infrastructure, businesses, federal
networks, and the "tools and devices Americans use every day." Priority
actions include:

- To identify and prioritize risk across the sectors of national security,
  energy and power, banking and finance, health and safety, communications, and transportation.
- To build defensible government networks. In this, the adoption of commercial capabilities, shared services, and best practices for modernization of federal networks, are highlighted.
- To deter and disrupt malicious cyber actors. Here the federal government is charged with providing "the necessary authorities, information
  and capabilities" to prevent attacks to those accountable for security of
  critical infrastructure. International information sharing is highlighted,
  as is a commitment to "swift and costly" consequences to foreign governments and criminals who undertake malicious activities.
- Improve information sharing and sensing. This represents a commitment to work with critical infrastructure to assess and share information. This also includes being able to better attribute the course of
  attacks.
- To deploy layered defenses. This is with a view to "remediating attacks"
  at the "network level," acknowledging that attacks transit globally. It
  is proposed that this approach can defeat "bad activities" and prevent
  them from being passed on elsewhere in the network.

In terms of policy making, pillar one shows the difficulty in trying to tie
down cyber as a domain of competition, a set of enabling technologies,
and an era of change. The activities that emerge to give direction rely on
close collaboration with critical infrastructure that necessarily requires
public- and private-sector collaboration. While information sharing is
clearly important, so too are the tools and techniques to be able to trace
and defeat cyber attacks. Critically there is a call for critical infrastructure
providers to have the right authority to take action. An emerging trend,
both in the United States and the United Kingdom, as will be seen in the
next chapter, is the proposal for interventions that stop attacks closer to the
source, rather than letting them cascade through a network as far as users.

Pillar Two: Promote American Prosperity

This pillar lays out a rationale for economic policy that focuses on growth of the domestic economy and proposes "free, fair, and reciprocal economic relationships." It focuses on innovation and the technological capacity of the United States, including skills, and aims to achieve "dominance" in energy. Key principles that are evident in the prose include reducing government intrusion in the economy, creating tax policies that maintain jobs in the United States, reducing regulation, and curtailing intellectual property theft.

In relation to cyber, this pillar discusses the poor state of American infrastructure and notes that "protection from persistent cyber attack" is needed "to support America's future growth." It proposes a require-ment to reduce regulatory burdens that drive up costs for businesses and impede R&D. This has to be balanced against "adequate protection and oversight." What this balance looks like in practice, given the scope of pil-lar one is, of course, something that needs further exploration later. How-ever, we know that the intention is one that is fundamental, even including design and engineering:

Security was not a major consideration when the Internet was designed and launched. As it evolves, the government and private sector must design systems that incorporate prevention, protection, and resiliency from the start, not as an afterthought. We must do so in a way that respects free markets, private competi-tion, and the limited but important role of government in enforcing the rule of law.[2]

Also of relevance to cyber is the priority action to prepare the workforce for the science, technology, engineering, and mathematics (STEM) jobs of the future. This is directly linked to security in the extract below:

To maintain our competitive advantage, the United States will prioritize emerg-ing technologies critical to economic growth and security, such as data science, encryption, autonomous technologies, gene editing, new materials, nanotechnol-ogy, advanced computing technologies, and artificial intelligence.[3]

The infrastructural system that support this aim is referred to in the NSS as the U.S. National Security Innovation Base. Cyber Security plays an important role in protecting intellectual property and the data on its networks. The U.S. government is charged with "encouraging practices across companies and universities to defeat espionage and theft." By using the word "encouraging," a tacit acknowledgment is made of the weakness of the government in bringing about good cyber security, certainly in com-parison with the language used in relation to critical infrastructure, above, regarding the right authority and accountability. Nevertheless, the use of the term "U.S. National Security Innovation Base" is a useful way to con-vey the strategic importance of a network of businesses, organizations, and institutions that may not have the formal designation of critical national infrastructure and yet will be attractive for cyber attack and espionage by adversaries. Finally, in pillar two, cyber security of energy infrastructure is emphasized.

Pillar Three: Preserve Peace Through Strength

The NSS sees the contest for power as a "central continuity in history." As such, it posits that the United States has been weakened by a lack of investment in capability, while rivals have grown. It argues that there was misplaced belief in past administrations that peaceful collaboration could become the norm of international politics. Consequently, this pillar is about creating a stronger America that integrates political, diplomatic, informational, economic, and military power. It proposes capability investment in defense, including nuclear, space, cyber space, skills, and technology. The crux of this is captured in this extract from pillar three:

The United States will seek areas of cooperation with competitors from a position of strength, foremost by ensuring our military power is second to none and fully integrated with our allies and all of our instruments of power. A strong military ensures that our diplomats are able to operate from a position of strength. In this way, we can, together with our allies and partners, deter and, if necessary, defeat aggression against U.S. interests and increase the likelihood of managing competitions without violent conflict and preserving peace.[4]

The key to this will be the notion of maintaining "overmatch"—to be better armed, skilled, and prepared than any adversary. The need to work with allies and competitors is also important. Some ambiguity remains in interpretation here and because of some of the actions taken by the Trump administration to date. How does collaboration with competitors work in practice? Is the intended collaboration with Allies altogether consensual, and on whose terms? Certainly, the NSS "needs" allies to modernize, improve capability and readiness, expand their force size, and "affirm their political will to win."

Cyber in the NSS discussion is seen as offering a means of strategic attack, short of resorting to nuclear weapons, against the United States. It argues that deterrence has to be extended to cyber space, and indeed across all domains. This must be continuous, as the old boundaries of peace and war become blurred, and states and criminal gangs try to prosecute ongoing activities against the United States below a threshold of "traditional military conflict." Priority actions for cyber space include:

- The reaffirmation from pillar one of the need for improved attribution, together with accountability and response. Rapid response is highlighted.

- To enhance cyber tools and expertise.
- To improve integration and agility across the U.S. government so that operations against adversaries can be conducted. This needs the integration of authorities and procedures. The NSS alludes to challenges that need to be addressed with Congress, which currently get in the way of timely intelligence and information sharing, planning, and development of cyber tools.

This pillar also details action in respect to intelligence capability. Of note from a cyber perspective is the intent to prevent the compromise of U.S. capabilities before they are fielded. The military and law enforcement intelligence communities are noted for their strong international relationships, which allows cooperation with "allies and partners to protect against adversaries." Intelligence priority actions include prevention of the theft of information and "maintaining supply chain integrity." The NSS seeks to exploit an information-rich environment for intelligence and conduct counterintelligence activities against actors who threaten U.S. "democratic institutions." This includes, under "information statecraft," the ability to "expose adversary propaganda and disinformation."

Earlier, in February 2017, the Department of Defense's Defense Science Board published a report on cyber deterrence, which made a number of recommendations that would be included under this pillar. There is discussion in the report about developing technologies that aid in the attribution of cyber attacks. This is considered essential if appropriate sanctions are to be applied. There is also a discussion regarding the emerging norms for cyber attacks. The board considers the circumstances when implanting and prepositioning offensive malware on an adversary's critical infrastructure might be infrastructure. They concluded that it was becoming an established norm and that there was a risk that if an adversary were doing so to U.S. systems, then doing the same may have a deterrent effect—the threat of pulling the trigger. This was seen as potentially being part of a posture that could "hold at risk a range of assets that the adversary leadership is assessed to value." It is clear from the report that, in order to act strategically, the creation of a U.S. cyber "playbook" requires fundamental rethinking in terms of how cyber specialist and intelligence personnel interact with the procurement process and how the adversary is assessed, both in terms of capability and intent and also in terms of what they value.

Pillar Four: Advance American Influence

The global environment is framed as a contest for influence in which America seeks to support "aspiring partners" achieve better outcomes in multilateral forums and champion American values. A number of cyber-related priority actions are outlined. This involves the United States providing leadership and technology to maintain the freedom of common domains, such as air, space, and cyber space, "within the framework of international law." This includes the "protection of a free and open Internet," through protecting its interests by "active engagement in key organizations." ICANN, The Internet Governance Forum (IGF), the United Nations, and the International Telecommunication Union (ITU) are listed as examples.

The NSS's final section focuses on regional dynamics. Much of the NSS addresses challenges presented by China and Russia. However, the word "cyber" is only specifically mentioned three times in the regional sections: once in relation to the development of North Korean capability, once in relation to increased cooperation in cyber security in Europe, and once in relation to Iranian malicious cyber activity in the Middle East. Cyber is not specifically mentioned with regard to U.S. interests in South and Central Asia, Africa, and the "Western Hemisphere" (essentially the Americas), which may be a strategic oversight for a forward-looking strategy.

The NSS certainly represents a strategic political statement, and it, as yet, unclear how much is aspirational and how much will result in strategic action. Further clues to action can be found in Trump's Presidential Executive Order on Strengthening the Cyber Security of Federal Networks and Critical Infrastructure, published in May 2017. As the names suggests, it focuses on government and critical infrastructure, areas where orders can be given. This requires some specific actions, such as "effective immediately, each agency head shall use the Framework for Improving Critical Infrastructure Cyber Security (the Framework) developed by the National Institute of Standards and Technology, or any successor document, to manage the agency's cyber security risk." It calls for a series of reports and plans to be prepared, which, once again, hints at strategic priorities. These reports include, for example:

- Transitioning U.S. government agencies to shared services, including e-mail, cloud, and cyber security services
- Defense against botnets
- Assessment of electricity disruption
- Cyber risks to the defense industrial base
- Strategic options for deterrence against cyber attack.

Two reports were required in terms of international cooperation. The first, on international cyber security priorities, was to be completed in 45 days, to include "investigation, attribution, cyber threat information sharing, response, capacity building, and cooperation." The second, to be prepared within 90 days, was to document an engagement strategy for international cooperation in cyber security.

It is assumed that the national cyber strategy will follow in due course. Until then, we have a glimpse of the approach to be taken by the United States under the Trump administration. It is one in which the world is seen as a competitive environment and where one negotiates and collaborates from a position of strength. Trump's actions to date suggest a rather transactional view of international politics, where carrot and stick relate to specific American interests. For some commentators, this has been interpreted as more than a realist ideology, and one that echoes the mercantilism of Europe in the 15th to 18th centuries. Mercantilism arose during the expansion of global European trade and prior to the evolution of liberal economics. Ahmed and Bick (2017) note that it led nations to:

organize all instruments of state power to expand trade and industry, more effectively compete with foreign rivals, and enable their sovereigns to amass the resources required for war.[5]

Quoting the historian Jacob Viner, Ahmed and Bick point out that:

Power and plenty...were the twin goals of mercantile policy. Mercantilists "sought enough superiority of power to 'give the law' to other countries, to enable conquest of adjoining territory or overseas colonies, or to defeat their enemies in war."[6]

Cyber policies that are prosecuted today were largely set up under the Obama administration. Much of the Trump NSS is consistent with the themes developed in Obama's 2015 NSS. It, too, highlights security, prosperity, and values but differs in tone and the nature of the international collaborative effort. This is presented as much more consensual around common interests. The cyber security section in Obama's NSS is framed in terms of assured access to shared spaces. It draws on the "voluntary cyber security framework" for securing federal networks and working with the private sector, made compulsory by Trump, as pointed out above. It also seeks to help other countries develop laws to deal with cyber threats that come from their infrastructure, noting the need to have "norms of international behavior." "Long-standing" norms regarding intellectual priority, online freedom, and respect for civilian infrastructure are specifically mentioned.

The Obama administration had launched an "International Strategy for Cyber Space" in May 2011, which articulated the following goal:

The United States will work internationally to promote an *open, interoperable, secure, and reliable* information and communications infrastructure that supports international trade and commerce, strengthens international security, and fosters free expression and innovation. To achieve that goal, we will build and sustain an environment in which *norms of responsible behavior* guide states' actions, sustain partnerships, and support the rule of law in cyber space. [Emphasis original.]

The strategy represents a rounded list of diplomatic, defense, and development actions. It establishes the values that drive U.S. policy and aims to promote norms of behavior regarding cyber space in the international system. It advocates a multistranded approach, incorporating bilateral and multilateral working the creation of international standards in technology and security, the bolstering of collaboration with the private sector, capacity building, and support to international conventions, such as the Budapest Convention on cyber crime. At the heart is a multistakeholder approach that brings public, private, and third sector together. This approach is specifically included in a description of the norms sought in cyber space.

The strategy notes that the existing principles in international law that should support cyber space norms are:

- Upholding fundamental freedoms: States must respect fundamental freedoms of expression and association, online as well as off.
- Respect for property: States should, in their undertakings and through domestic laws, respect intellectual property rights, including patents, trade secrets, trademarks, and copyrights.
- Valuing privacy: Individuals should be protected from arbitrary or unlawful state interference with their privacy when they use the Internet.
- Protection from crime: States must identify and prosecute cybercriminals to ensure that laws and practices deny criminals safe havens and cooperate with international criminal investigations in a timely manner.
- Right of self-defense: Consistent with the United Nations Charter, states have an inherent right to self-defense that may be triggered by certain aggressive acts in cyber space.

The strategy then states that there are a number of essential emerging norms relevant to cyber space:

- Global interoperability: States should act within their authorities to help ensure the end-to-end interoperability of an Internet accessible to all.
- Network stability: States should respect the free flow of information in national network configurations, ensuring that they do not arbitrarily interfere with internationally interconnected infrastructure.
- Reliable access: States should not arbitrarily deprive or disrupt individuals' access to the Internet or other networked technologies.
- Multistakeholder governance: Internet governance efforts must not be limited to governments but should include all appropriate stakeholders.
- Cyber security due diligence: States should recognize and act on their responsibility to protect information infrastructures and secure national systems from damage or misuse.

One can track some of the activity advocated in the principles and strategy through pre-existing work done by organizations such as NIST, the U.S. National Institute for Standards and Technology, whose standards and principles have had an impact beyond the border of the United States. Likewise, corporate law, such as Sarbanes Oxley, continues to require that companies make provision for cyber security and insuring the quality of their data. However, in the years since the formulation of the strategy, the United States has acknowledged the challenges to building an international consensus on norms of behavior in cyber space.

Christopher Painter, the State Department's coordinator in cyber issues, provided evidence in May 2016 to a Senate foreign relations subcommittee in which he discussed the policy challenge of "alternative views of the Internet." Both China and Russia's motivations regarding the Internet are framed in terms of the priority they give to internal stability and content control. However, Painter also points toward progress. He argues that there has been general acceptance of the application of international law to cyber space. He describes progress in confidence-building measures in work with the Organization for Security and Cooperation in Europe (OSCE). These have enabled greater transparency and mechanisms for dialogue and handling cyber incidents as well as outlining measures for protection of critical infrastructure in private hands. He points to progress on agreement with China on non-use of cyber espionage for commercial gain.

Writing in 2014, Eichensehr agrees that the United States has had some success in ensuring that the multistakeholder approach came to the fore, but more work has yet to be done on forming international norms. This was after a period in which a number of countries favored an alternative approach to Internet governance, such as management of the Internet by the United Nations, in part spurred on by the Snowden revelations of 2013 concerning U.S./U.K. espionage. These revelations significantly undermined the diplomatic efforts of the United States (and the United Kingdom) to persuade others of their value-based approach to international norms. However, they did give impetus to the confidence-building measures described by Painter in his evidence above, essential in the process of international norm building from a position of low trust. Trust was affected by the Snowden revelations, even within countries of the European Union, to which we now turn.

THE EUROPEAN UNION

The EU is sometimes called a supra-national organization, as its 28 members agree to pool some sovereignty in bodies such as the European Court of Justice, the European Commission, and the European Parliament. The European Union envisages a European single market in which a set of rules established at the EU level governs the free movement of people, goods, services, and capital. Although championed by the Council of Europe (not the European Union), the European Convention on Human Rights also establishes a series of fundamental freedoms that are designed to protect the rights of citizens. The European Court of Justice attributes special significance to the convention, and EU treaties continue to uphold the notion of fundamental rights. It is this combination of fundamental rights and the integrity and performance of the European single market that are of interest to us regarding an EU view of cyber security. Essentially, the ability to create European law in respect of trade practices and human rights give teeth to cyber policy between states in the European Union in certain areas. In certain circumstances, it also affects countries outside the European Union who wish to trade with it.

In 2013, the European Commission published "Cyber Security Strategy of the European Union: An Open, Safe, and Secure Cyber Space." The context for this strategy was a move toward a digital single market that promised to boost the economy of the European Union by €500 billion. This required the trust and confident of citizens to use the Internet to its full potential. As with the U.S. strategies, the early paragraphs highlight values and principles for cyber security. These include:

- The European Union's core values apply as much in the digital world as in the physical
- Protecting fundamental rights, freedom of expression, personal data, and privacy
- Access for all
- Democratic and efficient multistakeholder governance
- A shared responsibility to ensure security (that is, involving public and private sector)

Consequently, the strategy has five priority areas:

1. Achieving cyber resilience
2. Drastically reducing cyber crime
3. Developing cyber defense policy and capabilities related to the Common Security and Defence Policy (CSDP)
4. Developing the industrial and technological resources for cyber security
5. Establishing a coherent international cyber space policy for the European Union and promoting core EU values

The Network and Information Security (NIS) Directive was introduced to achieve cyber resilience. It came into force in May 2018 as the first EU-wide legislation on cyber security. It is primarily aimed at critical infrastructure and mandates that member states develop a national strategy, appropriate computer security incident response teams, and a national NIS authority. It provides for strategic and operational mechanisms for information sharing and notification. It promotes a culture of cyber security across sectors such as energy, transport, water, banking, financial market infrastructures, health care, and digital infrastructure.

In attempting to drastically reduce cyber crime, the European Union "urges" member states to ratify the Budapest Convention on cyber crime. It also aims to help states identify gaps in their ability to investigate cyber crime and support the then recently created Europol, European Cyber crime Center.

In terms of defense policy, a series of assessment and collaborative activities were identified, in which NATO is specifically mentioned as an international partner as is the promotion of civil and military coordination in information exchange and good practice.

Central to the development of industrial and technological resources is the promotion of a single market for cyber security products. Technical guidance was to be produced in support of the adoption of standards. R&D investment in cyber security would be fostered.

A critical element of the development of cyber space policy was the aim to make cyber space a mainstream aspect of all policy. No new legal instruments would be required, as pre-existing core values and instruments are already applied in cyber space.

The European Commission issued another communication in 2017, in which it was stated that the 2013 strategy remained valid. However, in recognition of growing cyber crime, the development of Internet of things technology, and the increased risk of politically motivated attacks, the European Union had to be more proactive and less reactive in its cyber security posture. This would involve an enhanced intelligence capability, designed to improve the quality and timeliness of information sharing through Europol and the EU Intelligence and Situation Center. The European Union plans to enhance its approach to deterrence, improving investigation across member states, and early response. It also aims to strengthen the European Union Agency for Network and Information Security (ENISA). Plans are in place to expand the agency and to give it a more prominent role in, for example, coordination of certification frameworks across Europe. The communication argues that the digital single market in cyber security has been held back, and that its potential can be unlocked through this framework. This will initially be a voluntary framework, which will prompt work in three "priority areas." The first is critical and high-risk applications, where core components require rigorous security assessment. The second involve security of "widely-deployed digital products, networks, systems, and services used by private and public sector alike," such as e-mail encryption, firewalls, and virtual private networks. The third is "security by design" methods in low-cost mass consumer devices of the Internet of things. This work is based on the premise that 100-percent security does not exist, but getting design right early on can design-out many of the common problems that affect networks, systems, and products. The European Union also urges the inclusion of cyber security into trade and investment, taking account of, for example, foreign acquisition and standards in "critical technologies."

Two other regulations, with the status of law, are worthy of note, as their impact will be felt beyond the 28 member states of the European Union. The first is the General Data Protection Regulation (GDPR), which came into effect at the same time as the NIS directive in May 2018. This law aims to safeguard citizens' personal data. It imposes much higher fines for data breaches and critically applies to anyone who will process EU citizen data. It has privacy by design and by default and security of personal data, recognized as principles in the law. The other regulation which was due to come into force with GDPR is the E-privacy Directive. This is aimed at protecting citizens regarding their data that is generated through electronic communications and online services, including cookies and automated processing. It includes regulations regarding the generation and analysis of meta-data. Many commentators believe that this legislation may improve data security in general, though some argue it might only cause organizations to focus on personal data at the expense of effort in securing other forms of data.

The European Union also intends to deepen its relationship with NATO on cyber security and hybrid threats. This includes cooperation on research and innovation, as well as joint exercises. We look at NATO next.

THE NORTH ATLANTIC TREATY ORGANIZATION (NATO)

NATO came into being on April 4, 1949, as the Cold War was taking hold across Europe. Its membership rests on the 29 states that have signed the North Atlantic Treaty and taken on the obligation of collective defense, as mandated in article 5 of the treaty. This is where an attack on one member is considered as an attack on all. Over the years, the alliance has had to adapt to changing strategic environments and, most recently, take into account the defense of cyber space. At the NATO summit in the United Kingdom in 2014, the members agreed that international law applied in cyber space. The following declaration was made:

Cyber attacks can reach a threshold that threatens national and Euro-Atlantic prosperity, security, and stability. Their impact could be as harmful to modern societies as a conventional attack. We affirm, therefore, that cyber defence is part of NATO's core task of collective defence. A decision as to when a cyber attack would lead to the invocation of Article 5 would be taken by the North Atlantic Council on a case-by-case basis.[7]

The case-by-case clause at the end indicated that any cyber attack on the alliance might invoke article 5 (collective defense) of the treaty; however, this would not be automatic, as it would first have to be assessed as to whether it had met a threshold of severity. The declaration also made it clear that NATO's fundamental duty was to protect its own networks, and then to help members on the basis of solidarity. Nevertheless, the Warsaw summit of 2016 sought to strengthen this commitment to help members, though cyber defense in the first instance would remain the responsibility of national governments. This is also true of cyber offensive capability, where NATO policy remains entirely defensive in its posture. However, NATO heads of state and governments agreed the following as part of Cyber Defense Pledge in 2016:

We will:

    I. Develop the fullest range of capabilities to defend our national infrastructures and networks. This includes: addressing cyber defence at the highest strategic level within our defence related organisations, further integrating cyber defence into operations and extending coverage to deployable networks;

    II. Allocate adequate resources nationally to strengthen our cyber defence capabilities;

    III. Reinforce the interaction amongst our respective national cyber defence stakeholders to deepen co-operation and the exchange of best practices;

    IV. Improve our understanding of cyber threats, including the sharing of information and assessments;

    V. Enhance skills and awareness, among all defence stakeholders at national level, of fundamental cyber hygiene through to the most sophisticated and robust cyber defences;

    VI. Foster cyber education, training and exercising of our forces, and enhance our educational institutions, to build trust and knowledge across the Alliance;

    VII. Expedite implementation of agreed cyber defence commitments including for those national systems upon which NATO depends.

The year 2016 also saw a joint declaration between the European Union and NATO on cyber defense in the light of the Warsaw Summit. This declaration included:

- With immediate effect, the European Union and NATO will exchange concepts on the integration of cyber-defense aspects into planning and conduct of respective missions and operations to foster interoperability in cyber-defense requirements and standards.
- In order to strengthen cooperation on training, as of 2017, the European Union and NATO will harmonize training requirements, where

applicable, and open respective training courses for mutual staff participation.

- Foster cyber-defense research and technology innovation cooperation by further developing the linkages between the European Union, NATO, and the NATO Cooperative Cyber Defence Centre of Excellence to explore innovation in the area of cyber defense. Considering the dual use nature of cyber domain, the European Union and NATO will enhance interoperability in cyber-defense standards by involving industry where relevant.
- Strengthen cooperation in cyber exercises through reciprocal staff participation in respective exercises, including in particular Cyber Coalition and Cyber Europe.

NATO has set up a "center of excellence" in Tallinn, Estonia, dedicated to cyber defense. It is perhaps best known for the Tallinn Manual, which is regarded as the most comprehensive advice available on how international law relates to cyber space. Like all NATO centers of excellence, it exists to train, educate, and support concept development. Notably, Estonia has become synonymous with cyber space through its digital transformation and digital citizenship, prompted by severe cyber attacks that were denied by Russia in 2007.

Also of note are NATO efforts in coordinating defense of its own networks, through its Communications and Information Agency. It claims that 80 percent of its work is done through contracts with national industries. This sits beside an attempt by NATO to work closely with industry through an industry cyber partnership and a network of other organizations working on R&D and supply chain. The partnership has several stated objectives including:

- Improve cyber defense in NATO's defense supply chain;
- Facilitate participation of industry in multinational smart defence projects;
- Contribute to the alliance's efforts in cyber-defense education, training, and exercises;
- Improve sharing of best practices and expertise on preparedness and recovery (to include technology trends);
- Build on existing NATO initiatives for industry engagement, providing specific focus and coherence on the cyber aspects;
- Improve sharing of expertise, information, and experience of operating under the constant threat of cyber attack, including information on threats and vulnerabilities, for example, malware information sharing;
- Help NATO and Allies learn from industry;
- Facilitate access by Allies to a network of trusted industry/enterprises;

- Raise awareness and improve the understanding of cyber risks;
- Help build access and trust between NATO and the private sector;
- Leverage private-sector developments for capability development, and;
- Generate efficient and adequate support in case of cyber incidents.

THE GULF COOPERATION COUNCIL COUNTRIES

There is no doubt that the countries in the Gulf have suffered at least, if not more than, their fair share of cyber attacks. Reports in *Gulf News* in 2017 suggested that the United Arab Emirates (UAE) was the second most targeted country after the United States of America. Consequently, there has been a large increase in spending by companies in the Middle East, with predictions it will double over a five-year period, from $11.38 billion in 2017 to $22.14 billion by 2022. Qatar lists cyber security along with energy and water supply in their top-three challenges.

However, there are questions regarding how effectively the money is being spent because of an undue focus on technological solutions and a lack of spending on skills, education, governance, risk, and compliance. Consequently, the key criticism of laudable efforts in countries in the region is a lack of central accountability and strategy and diffuse, rather than coordinated efforts. Cyber interventions, therefore, give the appearance of being more tactical than strategic, despite geostrategic dynamics and the importance of the region to global economy and energy. Chatham House (2017) states:

As things stand, intra-GCC cooperation in combating cyber crime therefore relies on bilateral relationships and informal channels, such as police-to-police or agency-to-agency-cooperation.

In the aftermath of the Wannacry attacks of 2017, there were calls among cyber security experts in the GCC for greater collaboration, give, the threats critical infrastructure sectors were facing. Ibrahim Alshamranu, speaking in May 2017, was reported by *The National* to have recognized that cyber security fell squarely under national security, but that wasn't enough, given links across sectors and countries in the region. Despite the increase in security spending mentioned above, it was clear that most companies did not see security as a priority concern. Information sharing was once more picked out as an important function in collaboration. At the same event, there were also calls for better regulation. Kshetri points out that such initiatives also require, for example, the training of judges.

This is not to say that advances made at a national level should not be overlooked. For example, in 2017, the United Arab Emirates announced the development of a federal infrastructure to enhance cyber security and connectivity for local and federal agencies. The publication of Dubai's cyber security strategy signaled a clear economic driver, with an effort to link innovation with safety and security. Kshetri points out that GCC countries have also established a number of "free zones," citing Dubai International Financial Center and Dubai Healthcare City, which, in their efforts to attract and provide services for international investment and establish legal structures based on English Common Law and EU Regulations.

The critique of development of effective approaches in GCC and the Middle East highlight a number of cultural and structural issues. For example, the difficulty in applying Sharia principles to cyber crime and privacy has hindered the timely and effective development of legislation. Indeed, religious issues are present in GCC cyber security strategies, impacting approaches to censorship and online blackmail. This can demonstrate tensions between human rights and cyber security, where Internet use by the population is used, for example, for protest or is seen as contempt for religious ideas. Ibish reports that malware in the United Arab Emirates is used against criminals and terrorists and also for domestic espionage. Kshetri argues that Sharia principle give "sacred" protection to privacy in most GCC countries, but this has had the unexpected effect of making privacy regulations much more lax outside of the free zones.

Though Chatham House benchmarks digitalization at a lower level in the GCC countries than in western countries, cyber security and cyber crime problems are exacerbated by the rapid growth in the participation of citizens in a wider variety of online activities. The family ownership of many businesses is also claimed to have an impact on decision-making, with investment in capability considered to be a low-priority cost. A frequent critique is the difficulty in developing strategy that feeds through to implementation. On the other hand is the difficulty in trying to coordinate and cohere across a vast array of local and tactical initiates, in order to see how they build into a national strategy.

However, it has to be said that many of these difficulties are not particularly unique to the GCC; rather, they show themselves in local ways. For example, GCC countries are not alone in trying to follow through on implementation of strategy. Many other countries have difficulty trying to take long-established, predigital law and apply it in today's cyber space. The investment in technological solutions, and a reluctance to invest at all, are not peculiar to the GCC. What this points out is how the problems observed locally may, in some way, be the same as anywhere else but are experienced and tackled in ways which have a local expression and requirement for tailored solutions. This is something that will be explored further in the chapter's discussion.

Kshetri states that foreign businesses working in the region can face a number of compliance challenges due to a lack of Pan-GCC laws. Aboul-Enein, in discussing approaches to addressing the problem of cyber security in the Middle East, reviews the need to address social and economic challenges and low levels of knowledge and skills in cyber and to develop stronger regional legislation. In doing so, Aboul-Enein argues that four broad areas need to be tackled. These includes capacity building, diplomacy, legislation, and the establishment and implementation of norms. These strategic considerations presage the following discussion.

DISCUSSION

This chapter, so far, has briefly reviewed the positions of the United States, European Union, NATO, and GCC, with particular regard to international cyber-policy issues. This next section tries to draw together some of the key dynamics that might be represented as opportunities and pitfalls.

At a surface level, the four contexts described can be viewed as exercises in developing and implementing an approach that has vertical and horizontal dimensions. The vertical dimension attempts to draw a thread from the formulation of policy, through strategy and plans to activities and outcomes—and ideally back up the stack. A chain-of-command view could be overlaid on this vertical, with state, regional, and local levels. The horizontal dimension attempts to generate coordination and collaboration across and between public and private sectors and agencies, perhaps at differing levels. From the four contexts, we get a sense of who and what is to be coordinated and a sense, to some extent, of how well efforts are going and the difficulties that are faced in an international context. At a more fundamental level are indicators in our four contexts of how approaches are shaped by the values and perceived interests of the countries involved. Arguably, this, in turn, influences selection of national options, based on deep-seated assumptions about the way change is instigated and sustained.

For the United States, the cyber security requirement is articulated in strategy that may or may not result in the required action internationally, nationally, and at subnational level, given the skepticism associated with grand strategies. The current strategy is marked by a narrative of strength and interests, in which the United States expect others to do their parts, given the security guarantees that have existed in the past. It notes the need for a strong digital economy, where the United States consumes, as well as generates, content and technology. The GCC countries are dominated by energy, rather than tech sectors, and by the consumption of digital content rather than the production of digital content and services. They exhibit investment and activity at the tactical level, while strategy is still in development across the region. Cyber crime regulation is developed in the context of technology and theology. NATO seeks to address collective defense by building capacity in NATO countries, though they have explicitly left the lead for cyber at the national level, particularly when it comes to offensive operations. However, its effort is underscored by collective defense treaty obligations and the desire to educate and share knowledge, through, for example, the Cooperative Cyber Defence Centre of Excellence in Estonia. The European Union has, at its heart, the fundamental human rights of citizens and stability of a large single market. It is, therefore, no surprise that regulation in data protection and critical infrastructure is emerging strongly in this context. The implementation of strategy in an international context is, therefore, more than simply attending to a to-do list of actions. It is heavily influenced in its development by local contexts and the mixing of factors such as culture, perceived interests, economies, and aims.

There are however, plenty of task lists and guidance available online on what should constitute a national cyber security strategy or the factors that need to be considered for cyber security during digital transformation of economies. The Global Cyber Security Capacity Centre (GCSCC) at Oxford University in the United Kingdom is a good place to start and is an example of a structured approach to understanding the dimension of cyber security that should be addressed by nations. They have systematically developed a Cyber Security Capacity Maturity Model (CSCMM), which groups areas of maturity into five areas that can be assessed with increasing levels of maturity, described as "start-up, formative, established, strategic, and dynamic." The five areas in the 2017 revision of the maturity model are:

- Cyber security policy and strategy
- Cyber culture and society
- Cyber security education, training, and skills
- Legal and regulatory frameworks
- Standards, organizations, and technologies

Each of these are recognizable in some way in the examples described in our four contexts. Cyber security policy and strategy incorporates those areas to do with the accountability, organization, development, and monitoring of policy, strategy, and plans. It highlights areas of incident response, crisis management, critical infrastructure protection, and resilience. Cyber culture and society outline factors involving the cyber security mind-sets across government, business, and industry. It covers trust in the Internet, personal-information protection, and reporting mechanisms for cyber crime. It also reflects concerns about media and social-media usage and its relationship to public values, attitudes, and online behavior. Cyber security education, training, and skills cover the spectrum of awareness to training to education and professional-skills frameworks. Legal and regulatory frameworks capture the requirement for a comprehensive set of measures covering ICT security, privacy, freedom of speech, child protection, and IP protection. It highlights the need for well-developed and resourced justice systems and processes that are robust for investigation, through courts to prosecution. Formal and informal measures for crossborder cooperation is emphasized. Finally, standards, organizations, and technologies, are aimed at quality factors, assurance, cryptographic controls, and market dynamics involving technology and cyber security. Responsible disclosure is also highlighted for "receipt and dissemination of vulnerability information across sectors."

The maturity model addresses international issues in a number of ways. It was in the 2017 revision of the model that the specific issue of international cooperation in regulatory and legal frameworks became "its own factor" where it had previously been under the factor of "criminal justice system." Indeed, at the highest level of maturity in this area, "participation in the development of regional or international cyber security cooperation agreements and treaties, is seen as a priority."[8] Standards, organizations, and technologies, almost by definition, are an attempt to bring some sort of coherence within and across borders. More generally, the maturity model calls for consultation with international partners in the development of strategy at the "formative" level of maturity, and to take on a leadership role in strategy development internationally, at the most advanced level of maturity "dynamic." In terms of incident-response coordination, "international cooperation" is a requirement in the "established" level of maturity, while coordinating incident responses is highlighted in the more advanced level of "strategic" maturity. International elements are reflected in other areas of the model in increasing maturity regarding collaboration, coordination, leadership, international best-practice adoption, and the sharing of lessons.

One interesting dynamic at the early "formative" level of maturity is the idea that awareness campaigns could take account of international programs, but, even then, they may not be linked to national strategy. This highlights the ideas that actions and maturity are not linear unidirectional processes, exemplified by the fact that international initiatives might be adopted before national interventions. The area of "cyber defense" within the model specifically mentions international issues at the highest level of maturity in terms of discussion of rules of engagement in cyber space and "the debate in developing a common international understanding of the point at which a cyber-attack might trigger a cross-domain response."[9] This discursive element relating to rules and triggers exemplifies the process of norm creation, to which we now turn.

Cyber capacity is constructed on a brownfield site of existing initiatives, good ideas, and imperfect strategies and plans. When we examine our four contexts, there is a process of interaction that, in its most basic form, amounts to a series of questions: what should I be doing, what are others doing, how do I do it, and how much do I care? This process is the formation of norms from the perception of a social constructivist, where norms and meaning are created in a social context through interaction with others.

Martha Finnemore and Kathryn Sikkink define norms as "standards of appropriate behaviour." They argue that norms do not develop in a "normative vacuum" but emerge in competition with other actions and interests and are, in part, defined by pre-existing norms. Finnemore and Sikkink posit a "norm life cycle," of norm emergence, cascading through the norming actions of others until it is internalized and achieves "taken-for-granted" status. Paul Baines and Nigel Jones point out that the use of social media in cyber attacks to influence foreign elections is being subjected to scrutiny in terms of pre-existing and emerging norms. They argue that "cyber space is stress-testing norms of international behaviour, as politicians, diplomats, and spies compete for influence." They cite several examples including a perceived norm violation of state cyber espionage for commercial benefits rather than national security. This presents a blurred line, indicating the nuanced nature of many norms: it is not that espionage is wrong, but, rather, its intent is. There is also an emerging norm of cyber attack being acceptable under the law of armed conflict, but the distinction of civil and military targets still apply. Areas of cyber activity, where state actors use proxies and criminal communities, are challenging pre-existing laws and norms, utilizing the anonymity of cyber space.

So what does this mean in terms of opportunities and pitfalls?

There is no doubt that there has never been a better time to make the case for better cyber security and international collaboration. From the perspective of knowledge, guidance, and support, there are many sources and recommendations. International engagement is perhaps easier now because the topic is on the agenda, in part spread by fear and real-world threats, but also the need for us to do business in a connected and interdependent world. The nations of the world may think of themselves in different stages in the journey. For example, one representative from a Caribbean Island, speaking at a global summit on cyber space, argued that it was difficult for them to allocate resources to cyber crime when they had enough work to do investigating and reducing local violent crime. Indeed cyber crime was, in some ways seen, as being a crime affecting the rich, post-industrial economies, so why should they pay for that? On the other hand, increased digitalization of every economy will create victims there too. However, it does raise a good point about how collaboration is necessary in a world where victims and perpetrators are often separated geographically. So there is an opportunity for us all to feel the benefit of increasing collaboration on cyber security.

There are also opportunities related to the economics of cyber space—the ability for our business and citizens to trade, learn, and live with confidence in the security of gatherings systems and data. The World

Economic Forum report on cyber resilience highlights one policy issue relating to crossborder data flows. It discusses the trade-offs between free flow of data and its limitation. While limitations on data flow for the purposes of privacy and security are associated with greater costs, they also produce greater accountability in the private sector for their control of data. The WEF report is explicitly aimed at policies related to public—private collaboration in cyber security at an intra-state level. It cleverly sets out a wide selection of policy frameworks in 14 policy areas and raises a series of issues as trade-offs set against values. Those values are economic value, privacy, security, fairness, and accountability, as demonstrated in the crossborder data flow example above. The other policy areas have the appearance on the surface of being quite technical in nature and include:

- Research, data, and intelligence sharing
- Zero days
- Vulnerability liability
- Attribution
- Bonnet disruption
- Monitoring
- Assigning national information roles
- Encryption
- Notification requirements
- Duty of assistance
- Active defense
- Liability thresholds
- Cyber insurance

While many of these clearly have a technical foundation, as does cyber space, they encompass a set of policy questions that require a consideration of law, economy, society, and values. For example, zero-day vulnerabilities, when discovered, need some mechanism of trusted sharing and disclosure. To what extent should this be mandatory? To what extent should companies be held liable under the law for producing software with vulnerabilities? While not being privy to the discussion within the WEF regarding the creation of the list of policy areas, there is good reason for why they appear "more technical" in nature, rather than more obviously policy orientated. This list is prepared in the context of public–private collaboration. The factors in the cyber security capacity maturity model above are foremost aimed at governments. This list represents a practical set of issues on which governments and businesses need to work, and for which both sectors need each other. The list, therefore, helps us move from strategy to decisions around implementation, examining the trade-off with business. The result is a variety of frameworks that help parties explore notions of formal and informal control, collaboration versus coordination, accountability, cost and benefits.

One down side of the WEF approach is that it perhaps focuses too much on today's encryption and zero-day issues, for example, rather than the technology of tomorrow. How future proofed is this policy framework? So much of the discussion in today's policy forums, not just the WEF, is about getting people and nations up to speed, rather than future proofing. With the speed of technological development and innovation in services, this is arguably a policy pitfall. Moreover, with its focus on intra-state policy, the WEF report perhaps misses the opportunity that trans-national business presents for spreading good practice and acceptable norms more quickly than individual governments might. Of course, this same mechanism is also the one that can harm privacy on an international scale and create markets of winners and losers in cyber space. This is why the WEF is right to map trade-offs against the values of economic value, privacy, security, fairness, and accountability. It is not inconceivable that these values could scale to the international discussion. We have already recognized how perceived interest and values have shaped cyber security within and between the four contexts in this chapter.

If there are no value-free options in international cyber security, how do values translate into how we address the challenges of cyber space, and what pitfalls might they create? Perhaps at a technical level of interoperability of devices, this doesn't represent such a problem, though the provenance of devices does open up issues of trust and assurance. However, this question does create a range of issues when it comes to developing in the contexts of:

- Rights, freedoms, and responsibilities
- Markets and trade
- Trust and lawfare

As has been seen, Western economies in the United States and European Union declare a value-based approach to cyber space that incorporates notions of rights, freedoms, and responsibilities towards a rule-based international system. It immediately opens up a freedom of speech and privacy debate, both inside Western nations about where the boundaries of censorship and privacy lie, and between the West and, for example, the GCC. This has direct bearing on the choices that governments make for criminalization of online behaviours. On one hand, the West wishes to root out cyber exploitation, "hate speech," and terrorist propaganda. Others in the GCC wish to censor pornography in general, crimes relating to blasphemy, and activity that criticises ruling parties and people. The tools and techniques for such filtering operate in similar ways, yet their targeting is entirely value-based and focused on local priorities.

In some respects, this does not present a problem beyond that which has already existed in the pre-Internet era. The difficulty today is the provision of services by private-sector companies across multiple jurisdictions and the prosecution of investigation of cyber crime. However, how states protect their people in the way they see fit is perhaps not the concern of international law, the United Nations, and others, except in the case for duty to protect, as mentioned earlier in the chapter. Rather, international efforts must be directed toward the development of rules for the global commons of cyber space, and it's here that the action and omissions of states are important, say in ignoring spam servers and international cyber crime emanating from their territories. In part, this is about the stability of markets, information society, science and research, resilience and services, and infrastructure that increasingly makes our world work. In this, the power of the citizen as consumer is important in creating rules driven by companies. In turn, there are trade-offs to be made in the regulatory environment concerning companies and their stewardship of citizen data. Here is where the privacy law created by the European Union represents a cost to trading with EU citizen data, because it recognizes the value of data (even if the private citizen/consumer is ambivalent). This is value-driven as well as being a commercial imperative for influencing a market. It is worth noting that China has resisted attempts by U.S. technology companies to dominate its market at home. Some have seen this in control and censorship terms, and others have seen it as making space for Chinese alternatives to enter the market and grow. This represents a case where values and interests seem to be in tension, depending upon one's perspective.

We have also seen how the Trump administration has painted a picture in its policy documents, and rhetoric of a competitive international market where strength and power in all its forms is exercised. The extent to which this narrative drives collaborative working and positive outcomes for cyber space, shared by all, is yet to be seen. However readers may think about this will depend upon their own personal philosophies of what makes humans tick. Types are often portrayed as poles on a spectrum, comprising of carrots and sticks, zero-sum games and some win-wins. We wait to see if "America First" will be good for everyone.

Most diplomats will say that real negotiations can only occur when people come to the table in good faith. If trust is not present to start, a process of trust building will be essential before outcomes from a negotiation can be addressed. The Snowden revelations severely damaged the United States and United Kingdom's reputations while they were promoting Internet freedom. This cast intelligence, law enforcement, and freedom into tension. It also gave a stick to other offenders in the international community with which to beat the United States and United Kingdom. One problematic aspect of advocating a rules-based international system is setting a higher standard for one's own activities and having to negotiate the tactic of "lawfare." Lawfare is where the law is used by others to constrain another's actions, even when they ignore it themselves. This might be through wasting the opponents' time in lengthy litigation, narrowing their options, or causing reputational damage. This kind of asymmetric strategy is quite the opposite of coming to the table in good faith. Does an agreement made with another actor simply constrain those who care about upholding it? The recent international dynamics regarding the 2018 nerve agent attack in the United Kingdom show attempts at lawfare by Russia as a way of trying to delegitimize UK responses to the attack.

It is also through understanding our values and the effect we have on others that we can start to future proof policy for a changing world. When it is rooted in tackling today's technological challenges, it is likely to be out of date quickly. Attempts to bring some countries up-to-date risks always being behind. However, it is our values that we can make explicit, and by which one can judge and accommodate technological change and the policies and practices of others. There is no doubt that our values will also change as new services come and go, but understanding how they impact upon our choices requires critical capacity. The pitfalls and challenges of cyber space are, of course, technological to some extent. However, the greater challenges are often those created by the values and perceived interests of actors and the standards to which they are held accountable. On the other hand, it is the values of ethical companies, some with an economic value to rival countries; their consumers; governments; and citizens that can promote a safe, productive, and open but secure cyber space. In this, technology will most certainly have a role too in helping monitor, regulate, and facilitate a fair global commons.

NOTES

1. Peter Feaver, "Five Takeaways from Trump's National Security Strategy," *Foreign Policy*, December 18, 2017, https://foreignpolicy.com/2017/12/18/five-takeaways-from-trumps-national-security-strategy/. Accessed March 31, 2018.

2. U.S. Government, "National Security Strategy of the United States of America." December 2017. https://www.whitehouse.gov/wp-content/uploads/2017/12/NSS-Final-12-18-2017-0905.pdf. Accessed March 31, 2018. p. 13.

3. Ibid., p. 20.

4. Ibid., p. 26.

5. Salman Ahmed and Alexander Bick, "Trump's National Security Strategy: A New Brand of Mercantilism?" Carnegie Endowment for International Peace, August 2017, p. 6, http://carnegieendowment.org/files/CP_314_Salman_Mercantilism_Web.pdf. Accessed March 31, 2018.

6. Ibid.

7. NATO, "Wales Summit Declaration," issued by the Heads of State and Government Participating in the Meeting of the North Atlantic Council in Wales,

September 5, 2014. http://www.nato.int/cps/en/natohq/official_texts_112964
.htm. Accessed March 31, 2018.

    8. Global Cyber Security Capacity Centre, "Cybersecurity Capacity Maturity
Model for Nations." Revised edition. March 31, 2016. https://www.sbs.ox.ac.uk
/cybersecurity-capacity/system/files/CMM%20revised%20edition_09022017_1
.pdf. Accessed November 4, 2018. p. 41.

    9. Ibid., p. 23.

BIBLIOGRAPHY

Aboul-Enein, S. "Cybersecurity Challenges in the Middle East." GCSP Geneva
    Paper, Research Series. November 22, 2017. https://www.gcsp.ch/News
    -Knowledge/Publications/Cybersecurity-Challenges-in-the-Middle-East.
    Accessed March 31, 2018.

Ackerman, Bob. "The Trump Team Has Failed to Address the Nation's Mounting
    Cybersecurity Threats." *TechCrunch*, October 17, 2017. https://techcrunch
    .com/2017/10/17/the-trump-team-has-failed-to-address-the-nations
    -mounting-cybersecurity-threats/. Accessed March 31, 2018.

Ahmed, Salman, and Bick Alexander. "Trump's National Security Strategy: A New
    Brand of Mercantilism?" Carnegie Endowment for International Peace,
    August 2017. http://carnegieendowment.org/files/CP_314_Salman_Mer
    cantilism_Web.pdf. Accessed March 31, 2018.

Badam, Ramola Talwar. "GCC Urged to Coordinate Cybersecurity Following
    Wannacry Attack." *The National*, May 21, 2017. https://www.thenational
    .ae/business/technology/gcc-urged-to-coordinate-cyber-security-follow
    ing-wannacry-attack-1.90087. Accessed March 31, 2018.

Baines, Paul, and Nigel Jones. "Influence and Interference in Foreign Elections:
    The Evolution of Its Practice." *RUSI Journal*, March 16, 2018.

Cole, Leo. "Eight Cybersecurity Principles Needed to Protect the Public." *Gulf
    Business*, September 23, 2017. http://gulfbusiness.com/eight-cyber-secu
    rity-principles-needed-to-protect-the-public/. Accessed March 31, 2018.

Control Risks. "Cyber Security Landscape Report." 2017. https://cyberex
    change.uk.net/media/control-risks-group/resources/2017-05-30-cyber
    -report-2017.FINAL.APPROVED.pdf. Accessed March 31, 2018.

Cordesman, Anthony. "Gulf Security: Looking beyond the Gulf Cooperation
    Council." CSIS, December 12, 2017. https://www.csis.org/analysis/gulf
    -security-looking-beyond-gulf-cooperation-council. Accessed March 31,
    2018.

Diamond, Jeremy. "5 Things to Know about Trump's Security Strategy." CNN,
    December 18, 2017. http://www.cnn.com/2017/12/18/politics/5-things
    -to-know-about-trumps-national-security-strategy/index.html. Accessed
    March 31, 2018.

Eichensehr, Kristen. "The US Needs a New International Strategy for Cyberspace."
    Just Security, November 24, 2014. https://www.justsecurity.org/17729
    /time-u-s-international-strategy-cyberspace/. Accessed March 31, 2018.

ENISA. "Cybersecurity: EU Agency and Certification Framework." Factsheet,
    2017.

ENISA. "National Cyber Security Strategies: Practical Guide on Development and Execution." 2012.

EUGDPR.Org. "Key Changes with the General Data Protection Regulation." EU GDPR Portal. http://eugdpr.org/the-regulation.html. Accessed March 31, 2018.

EUR-LEX. "Directive (EU) 2016/1148 of the European Parliament and of the Council of 6 July 2016 Concerning Measures for a High Common Level of Security of Network and Information Systems across the Union." July 6, 2016. http://data.europa.eu/eli/dir/2016/1148/oj/eng. Accessed March 31, 2018.

European Commission. "Cybersecurity." Digital Single Market. https://ec.europa .eu/digital-single-market/en/cyber-security. Accessed March 31, 2018.

European Commission. "Cybersecurity Strategy of the European Union: An Open, Safe, and Secure Cyberspace." 2013. https://eeas.europa.eu /archives/docs/policies/eu-cyber-security/cybsec_comm_en.pdf. Accessed March 31, 2018.

European Commission. "Digital Single Market." https://ec.europa.eu/commis sion/priorities/digital-single-market_en. Accessed March 31, 2018.

European Commission. "The Directive on Security of Network and Information Systems." *NIS Directive, Digital Single Market*. https://ec.europa.eu/dig ital-single-market/en/network-and-information-security-nis-directive. Accessed March 31, 2018.

European Commission. "Making the Most of NIS—Towards the Effective Implementation of Directive (EU) 2016/1148 Concerning Measures for a High Common Level of Security of Network and Information Systems across the Union." October 4, 2017. http://eur-lex.europa.eu/legal-content/EN /TXT/?qid=1505297631636&uri=COM:2017:476:FIN. Accessed March 31, 2018.

European Commission. "Resilience, Deterrence and Defence: Building Strong Cybersecurity for the EU." September 13, 2017. http://eur-lex.europa .eu/legal-content/EN/TXT/?qid=1505294563214&uri=JOIN:2017:450: FIN. Accessed March 31, 2018.

European Union ISS. "The EU Cyber Diplomacy Toolbox: Towards a Cyber Sanctions Regime?" July 2017. https://www.iss.europa.eu/sites/default /files/EUISSFiles/Brief_24_Cyber_sanctions.pdf. Accessed March 31, 2018.

European Union Parliament. "Cybersecurity in the Common Security and Defence Policy." May 2017. https://www.sbs.ox.ac.uk/cybersecurity-capacity/sys tem/files/Cybersecurity%20in%20the%20CSDP.pdf. Accessed March 31, 2018.

Falkowitz, Oren J. "How US Cyber Policy Leaves Everyone Exposed." *Time*, January 10, 2017. http://time.com/4625798/donald-trump-cyber-policy/. Accessed March 31, 2018.

Feaver, Peter. "Five Takeaways from Trump's National Security Strategy." *Foreign Policy*, December 18, 2017. https://foreignpolicy.com/2017/12/18/five -takeaways-from-trumps-national-security-strategy/. Accessed March 31, 2018.

Global Cyber Security Capacity Centre. "Cybersecurity Capacity Maturity Model for Nations." Revised edition. March 31, 2016. https://www.sbs

.ox.ac.uk/cybersecurity-capacity/system/files/CMM%20revised%20edi
tion_09022017_1.pdf. Accessed November 4, 2018.

Hakmeh, Joyce. "Cybercrime and the Digital Economy in the GCC Countries."
Chatham House, June 2017. https://www.chathamhouse.org/sites/files
/chathamhouse/publications/research/2017-06-30-cybercrime-digital
-economy-gcc-hakmeh.pdf. Accessed March 31, 2018.

Hay Newman, Lilly. "Trump's Cybersecurity Executive Order Gets Off to a Slow
Start." *Wired*, September 3, 2017. https://www.wired.com/story/trump
-cybersecurity-executive-order/. Accessed March 31, 2018.

Ibish, Hussein. "The UAE's Evolving National Security Strategy. The Arab Gulf
States in Washington." AFSIW, April 2017. http://www.agsiw.org/wp
-content/uploads/2017/04/UAE-Security_ONLINE.pdf. Accessed October 16, 2018.

Klimburg, Alexander, ed. "National Cyber Security Strategy." Ministry of Transport and Communications. NATO CCDCOE, 2014. http://www.motc.gov
.qa/en/cyber-security/national-cyber-security-strategy. Accessed March 31,
2018.

Kshetri, Nir. "Cybersecurity Strategies of Gulf Cooperation Council Economies."
Georgetown Journal of International Affairs. March 15, 2016. https://www
.georgetownjournalofinternationalaffairs.org/online-edition/cybersecur
ity-strategies-of-gulf-cooperation-council-economies. Accessed March 31,
2018.

Marks, Joseph. "Trump Administration Plans a New Cybersecurity Strategy."
Defense One, October 25, 2017. http://www.defenseone.com/techno
logy/2017/10/trump-administration-plans-new-cybersecurity-strategy
/142042/. Accessed March 31, 2018.

Marks, Joseph. "Trump Releases Long-Delayed Cyber Order." Nextgov.com,
May 11, 2017. http://www.nextgov.com/cybersecurity/2017/05/trump
-releases-long-delayed-cyber-order/137787/. Accessed March 31, 2018.

National Cyber Security Framework Manual. http://www.ccdcoe.org/publications
/books/NationalCyberSecurityFrameworkManual.pdf. Accessed January 8, 2018.

NATO. "Cyber Defence." July 8, 2016. http://www.nato.int/cps/en/natohq/top
ics_78170.htm. Accessed March 31, 2018.

NATO. "Cyber Defence Pledge." July 8, 2016. http://www.nato.int/cps/en
/natohq/official_texts_133177.htm. Accessed January 8, 2018.

NATO. "Foreign Ministers Agree New Areas of NATO–EU Cooperation." December 6, 2017. http://www.nato.int/cps/en/natohq/news_149616.htm. Accessed March 31, 2018.

NATO. "NATO and the European Union Deepen Cooperation on Cyber Defence."
December 8, 2017. http://www.nato.int/cps/en/natohq/news_149848
.htm. Accessed March 31, 2018.

NATO. "NATO Communications and Information Agency." https://www.ncia
.nato.int/Pages/homepage.aspx. Accessed March 31, 2018.

NATO. "NATO Cyber Defence." Factsheet, December 2017. https://www.nato
.int/nato_static_fl2014/assets/pdf/pdf_2017_11/20171128_1711-factsheet
-cyber-defence-en.pdf. Accessed March 31, 2018.

NATO. "NATO's Flagship Cyber Exercise Begins in Estonia." November 28, 2017. https://www.nato.int/cps/ic/natohq/news_149233.htm. Accessed March 31, 2018.

NATO. "NATO Industry Cyber Partnership." http://www.nicp.nato.int/. Accessed March 31, 2018.

NATO. "Spending for Success on Cyber Defence." *NATO Review*, April 6, 2017. http://www.nato.int/docu/review/2017/Also-in-2017/nato-priority -spending-success-cyber-defence/EN/index.htm. Accessed March 31, 2018.

NATO. "Statement on the Implementation of the Joint Declaration Signed by the President of the European Council, the President of the European Commission, and the Secretary General of the North Atlantic Treaty Organization." December 6, 2016. http://www.nato.int/cps/en/natohq /official_texts_138829.htm. Accessed January 8, 2018.

NATO. "Wales Summit Declaration." Issued by the Heads of State and Government Participating in the Meeting of the North Atlantic Council in Wales. September 5, 2014. http://www.nato.int/cps/en/natohq/official _texts_112964.htm. Accessed March 31, 2018.

NATO. "Warsaw Summit Communiqué." Issued by the Heads of State and Government Participating in the Meeting of the North Atlantic Council in Warsaw, July 8–9, 2016. July 9, 2016. http://www.nato.int/cps/en /natohq/official_texts_133169.htm. Accessed March 31, 2018.

PWC. "A False Sense of Security? Cybersecurity in the Middle East." March 2016. https://www.pwc.com/m1/en/publications/documents/middle-east -cyber-security-survey.pdf. Accessed March 31, 2018.

Radcliffe, D. "Middle East Cybersecurity: Is Region's Big Spend Aimed at the Right Targets?" ZDNet, July 10, 2017. http://www.zdnet.com/article /middle-east-cybersecurity-is-regions-big-spend-aimed-at-the-right-targets/. Accessed October 16, 2018.

Strategy&. "Cybersecurity in the Middle East." 2015. https://www.strategyand .pwc.com/media/file/Cyber-security-in-the-Middle-East.pdf. Accessed March 31, 2018.

Unwala, Azhar. "Cybersecurity in Saudi Arabia Calls for Clear Strategies." *Global Risk Insights*, July 27, 2016. https://globalriskinsights.com/2016/07/cyber security-saudi-arabia-calls-clear-strategies/. Accessed March 31, 2018.

U.S. DoD. "The DoD Cyber Strategy." April 2015. https://www.hsdl.org /?view&did=764848. Accessed March 31, 2018.

U.S. DoD. "Taskforce on Cyber Deterrence." February 2017. https://www.acq.osd .mil/dsb/reports/2010s/DSB-CyberDeterrenceReport_02-28-17_Final .pdf. Accessed March 31, 2018.

U.S. Government. "Department of State International Cyberspace Policy Strategy." March 2016. https://www.state.gov/documents/organization/255732 .pdf. Accessed March 31, 2018.

U.S. Government. "Federal Cyber Security Research and Development Plan." February 2016. https://www.hsdl.org/?view&did=792104. Accessed March 31, 2018.

U.S. Government. "International Cybersecurity Strategy: Deterring Foreign Threats and Building Global Cyber Norms." Testimony of Christopher Painter, U.S.

Department of State, May 25, 2016. https://2009-2017.state.gov/s/cyberis
sues/releasesandremarks/257719.htm. Accessed March 31, 2018.

U.S. Government. "International Strategy for Cyberspace." May 2011. https://
www.hsdl.org/?view&did=5665. Accessed March 31, 2018.

U.S. Government. "National Security Strategy." February 2015. https://ccdcoe.org
/sites/default/files/strategy/USA_NSS2015.pdf. Accessed March 31, 2018.

U.S. Government. "National Security Strategy of the United States of America."
December   2017.   https://www.whitehouse.gov/wp-content/uploads
/2017/12/NSS-Final-12-18-2017-0905.pdf. Accessed March 31, 2018.

U.S. Government. "Presidential Executive Order on Strengthening the Cybersecurity of Federal Networks and Critical Infrastructure." The White House,
May 11, 2017. https://www.whitehouse.gov/presidential-actions/pres
idential-executive-order-strengthening-cybersecurity-federal-networks
-critical-infrastructure/. Accessed March 31, 2018.

CHAPTER 9

Global Strategies: The United Kingdom as a Case Study

Nigel Jones

The March 2008 National Security Strategy (NSS) was the first national security strategy published by the United Kingdom. It mentions the word "cyber" seven times in its 64 pages, twice as cyber crime, and five times as cyber attack. There are no specific mentions of "information security" or "information assurance." In fact, the word "information" is only mentioned 12 times, with one of those relating to dependency on "global electronic information and communication systems." Its publication was 11 months after the major cyber attacks on Estonia, and five months before Russia synchronized cyber operations with ground operations in its war with Georgia. In 2009, the UK government issued an update to the 2008 strategy. It mentions "cyber" 81 times in 116 pages. Note that "information assurance" is mentioned just once. "Information security" is not mentioned at all, so one cannot explain the relative absence of "cyber" in 2008 by terminological distinctions. On the same day as the publication of the 2009 update, the United Kingdom launched its first national cyber security strategy. Since then, the United Kingdom has published national security strategies in 2010 and 2015, each followed by a national cyber security strategy. For information (as you will want to know), the 201o strategy mentions "cyber" 29 times in 39 pages, and the 2015 strategy, 110 times in 96 pages. Cyber mentions per page have been steadily on the up. Of course, word count only gives a limited sense. When one starts to examine how the words are used, the 2010 strategy shows the emerging importance of cyber by assessing it as a "Tier One Risk," in terms of the impact and likelihood of "hostile attacks upon UK cyber space by other states and large scale cyber crime."

This chapter provides a comprehensive review of the United Kingdom's cyber security strategy and activities. It aims to chart the development of the UK approach and provide an understanding of key dynamics affecting its implementation. The chapter will first examine the chronology of the national strategies, tracking how their corresponding initiatives were implemented and changed over time, while trying to point toward the underlying drivers. The chapter will detail the current strategy, providing insight to public, private, and third sector perspectives. It examines the WannaCry attack and its impact upon the UK National Health Service as a way of assessing the strengths and weaknesses of UK approaches. This chapter draws upon official documents, including assessments by government and independent reviewers. In part, it is informed by the author through his work in the cyber security community, implementing a number of initiatives as a result of the strategy, and working in a number of cross-sectoral networks. The chapter doesn't so much focus on the particulars of the geostrategic challenges facing us, covered elsewhere in this book, as much as the perceived instrumentality in national responses and the barriers and enablers at work.

INFORMATION ASSURANCE: THE EARLY YEARS

Set up in 1999, the National Infrastructure Security Coordination Centre (NISCC) provided advice and coordination on the protection of critical infrastructure from electronic attack. It would later be absorbed into a newly formed Centre for the Protection of National Infrastructure (CPNI), an outward-facing part of the UK Security Services, MI5. The National Audit Office (NAO) credits the Communications-Electronics Security Group (CESG) as being the first to recognize the importance of data security, in 2001, and to recommend that a central sponsor be appointed for policy and management of the security of government data. At that time, CESG was part of the United Kingdom's strategic electronic intelligence organization GCHQ (Government Communications Headquarters) and was described as the UK technical authority for information assurance. This role has since been transferred to the National Cyber Security Centre, also part of GCHQ, and discussed in more depth below. A 2003 Web archive shows that CESG's recommendation led to the establishment of a unit in the Cabinet Office, with the role to provide "a central focus for information assurance in promoting the understanding that it is essential for government and business alike to maintain reliable, secure, and resilient national information systems." It defines information assurance as:

the confidence that information systems will protect the information they carry, and will function as they need to, when they need to, under the control of legitimate users.[1]

The Cabinet Office is akin to a government headquarters, in the sense that it is the focal point for policy that affects all government departments and supports the prime minister to ensure the effective running of government. It was the perfect location for a central sponsor, lying outside GCHQ, "providing strategic direction for Information Assurance (IA) across the whole of the UK," along with NISCC, with its focus on critical infrastructure.

The first National Information Assurance Strategy was published in 2004. According to the NAO, this strategy "established a network of Senior Information Risk Owners" in government, aiming "to lead and foster a culture that valued and protected information." However, four years later, with publications of the 2008 NSS, information assurance clearly had not yet made a significant impact on broader strategic thinking in government. There were, at this time, geostrategic changes in the way nonstate and state actors were acting and utilizing cyber space. The consumer landscape was also changing. The first iPhone was released on June 29, 2007, sparking a revolution in consumer interaction with business and government in ways that were not yet fully understood, in terms of legacy systems, consumerization, vulnerabilities, and attack surfaces. It would be another year, after the 2008 NSS, before the 2009 update to the National Security Strategy and the publication of the first National Cyber Security Strategy.

THE FIRST UK NATIONAL CYBER SECURITY STRATEGY

The strategy was published in June 2009, with 26 pages including annexes. It set out three strategic objectives:

1. Reduce risk from the United Kingdom's use of cyber space.
   - Reduce the threat of cyber operations by reducing an adversary's motivation and capability;
   - Reduce the vulnerability of UK interests to cyber operations; and
   - Reduce the impact of cyber operations on UK interests.
2. Exploit opportunities in cyber space.
   - Gather intelligence on threat actors;
   - Promote support for UK policies; and
   - Intervene against adversaries.
3. Improve knowledge, capabilities, and decision-making.
   - Improve knowledge and awareness;
   - Develop doctrine and policy;
   - Develop governance and decision-making; and
   - Enhance technical and human capabilities.

It announced organizational changes that would address these objectives and a series of work streams. It would establish a cross-government program that included growth of skills and funding for innovation in "technologies to protect UK networks." It would create a Cyber Security Operations Centre to be based in GCHQ. This would be the lead in protecting cyber space and the coordination of incident response, enabling an understanding of attacks, and generating advice on risks to business and the public.

The strategy announced the setting up of the Office of Cyber Security, which would replace the central sponsor title. It aimed to work closely with "public sector, industry, civil-liberty groups, the public and international partners." The civil-liberty dimension is interesting, as it picks up on tensions, described in the strategy, between security and liberty, founded on core values of "human rights, the rule of law, legitimate and accountable government, justice, freedom, tolerance, and opportunity for all." The office of cyber security would later have information assurance added (back in) in its title and become OCSIA.

Major themes of the 2009 cyber security strategy were dependencies and interdependence, hence the need for coordination across and between organizations. Indeed, interdependence was a key feature of the overarching NSS, a theme picked up in a number of recommendations in Chatham House's September 2011 research on cyber security and the UK's Critical National Infrastructure (CNI). It highlighted that interviewees in the private sector did not believe the government approach was joined up enough, giving the impression that the United Kingdom's approach was not centrally directed and organized. It was felt that many remained "generally unaware, uninformed, or unimpressed about the development and scope of the government's cyber security policy and strategy."[2]

Not only was there a problem in promoting collaboration between public and private sectors, but there was also the challenge of coordinating between agencies in the UK government. For example, how in practice did responsibilities between CPNI and GCHQ fall, when one has the lead for critical infrastructure and one is the United Kingdom's technical authority on information assurance? There wasn't always an easy relationship in terms of culture or the distinction, for example, between information assurance and industrial-control systems.

The 2009 strategy had been developed under a Labour government. A new government was elected in May 2010, bringing in a Conservative Party and Liberal Democrat Coalition. Consequently, 2010 saw the publication of a new National Security Strategy entitled, "A strong Britain in an age of uncertainty." It was this strategy that assessed the tier-one risks by impact and likelihood, as:

- International terrorism affecting the United Kingdom or its interests, including a chemical, biological, radiological, or nuclear attack by terrorists and/or a significant increase in the levels of terrorism relating to Northern Ireland.

- Hostile attacks upon UK cyber space by other states and large scale cyber crime.
- A major accident or natural hazard that requires a national response, such as severe coastal flooding affecting three or more regions of the United Kingdom or an influenza pandemic.
- An international military crisis between states, drawing in the United Kingdom and its allies, as well as other states and nonstate actors.

A National Cyber Security Strategy was published in November 2011.

THE SECOND UK NATIONAL CYBER SECURITY STRATEGY

The 2011 national strategy presented a vision for the United Kingdom in 2015:

To derive huge economic and social value from a vibrant, resilient, and secure cyber space, where our actions, guided by our core values of liberty, fairness, transparency and the rule of law, enhance prosperity, national security and a strong society.[3]

This was a change in tone, in that it made security the servant of economic well-being, rather than an end in itself. The NAO notes differences for the previous strategy that included an emphasis "on the role and responsibilities of public and industry in helping secure the UK," recognizing that "legislation and education at all levels should incorporate cyber security within mainstream activities."[4] This also recognized that more needed to be done in coordinating and collaborating throughout industry and at all levels of education.

The strategy laid out four key objectives in pursuit of its vision, as represented in Figure 9.1.

A series of measures were introduced through the creation of a National Cyber Security Programme, funded initially with £650 million. This would increase to £860 million during the period of the strategy to March 2016. The program would coordinate activity across six government departments and nine other government organizations, including intelligence and security agencies. For example, as part of objective one, the home Office would lead on tackling cyber crime with the Serious Organised Crime Agency (now NCA), Child Exploitation and Online Protection, Police Central E-Crime Unit, police forces, and National Fraud Authority. The Department of Business, Innovation, and Skills, together with a range of organizations, would promote confidence in cyber space. The Cabinet

Objective 1:	Objective 2:	Objective 3:
The UK to tackle cyber crimes and be one of the most secure places in the world to do business in cyberspace.	The UK to be more resilient to cyber attacks and better able to protect our interests in cyberspace.	The UK to have helped shape an open, stable and vibrant cyberspace which the UK public can use safely and that supports open societies.

Objective 4:
The UK to have the cross-cutting knowledge, skills, and capability it needs to underpin all our cyber security objectives.

Figure 9.1

Office and the intelligence and security agencies would lead on objective two, along with the Ministry of Defence. "Better able to protect our interests in cyber space" was taken by many to be a euphemism for developing offensive cyber capability. This was confirmed by the UK Defence Secretary in 2013, when he announced the development of offensive cyber capability ahead of the Conservative party conference, much to the surprise of many officials who were more used to talking in hushed tones regarding this aspect of cyber. However, it seems to have emerged in today's environment as an unsurprising development, and one that is discussed at times of geopolitical tension.

The disclosure of budgets and the allocation of responsibility across departments was a major step in making this strategy a business document aspiring to outcomes. It heralded a range of initiatives and activities, and it is only possible to name some of them here. It included awareness activities for business and the public, such as "10 steps to cyber security," "cyber security advice for small business, and "be cyber streetwise." In law enforcement, a National Cyber Crime Unit was established in the National Crime Agency, with subunits established in each of the nine Regional Organised Crime Units.

Another £3 billion (separate from the £850m) was identified to spend over a nine-year period[5] in developing national cyber capabilities, working with small business, and development of cyber specialists. In addition, a Cyber Growth Partnership with TechUK, a major UK tech industry association, was established to bring tech companies together with government and academics on trade. Today the Cyber Growth Partnership aims to increase export market understanding and access of the United Kingdom's cyber offer and brand for overseas markets and development of skills, research, and innovation. In terms of incident response and crisis management, the United Kingdom established CERT-UK in March 2014 to:

work closely with industry, government and academia to enhance UK cyber resilience. This includes exercising with government departments and industry partners, sharing information with UK industry and academic computer emergency response teams and collaborating with national CERTs around the globe to enhance our understanding of the cyber threat. (CERT-UK Launch press release)

CPNI was also charged with an extended role in protecting the United Kingdom's critical infrastructure and intellectual property, through, for example, counterespionage efforts. Regarding international norms in cyber space, a series of global conferences in cyber space was supported, known in UK policy terms as the "London Process." To date, conferences have been held in London, Budapest, Seoul, the Hague, and New Delhi.

A major educational initiative was the development of academic centers of excellence for cyber security research. This was an effort to increase the quality of UK research and the number of PhDs conducted in the field. Universities had to apply for the program and demonstrate that they had:

- commitment from the university's leadership team to support and invest in the university's cyber security research capacity and capability
- a critical mass of academic staff engaged in leading-edge cyber security research
- a proven track record of publishing high-impact cyber security research in leading journals and conferences
- sustained funding from a variety of sources to ensure the continuing financial viability of the research team's activities.[6]

To date, there are 14 universities that have received Center of Excellence status from GCHQ and the Physical Science Research Council. GCHQ also implemented a scheme to certify the quality of masters programs in cyber security and digital forensics. The government funded the development of a massive open online course with the Open University.

A series of independent research institutes, sponsored by GCHQ, were established, with a view to "transforming our collective understanding" about cyber security. Each of the institutes is comprised of several universities, with a remit to engage other universities and stakeholders from the private and public sectors. Today, the research institutes are:

The **Research Institute in Science of Cyber Security** (RISCS). This is hosted by University College London. It is engaged in projects with a "strong behavioural element, addressing the measurement, modelling, visualisation, and influence of human security behaviours."

The **Research Institute in Automated Program Analysis and Verification** (RIAPAV) is hosted by Imperial College London. Its projects "investigate new ways of automatically analysing computer software to reduce its vulnerability to cyber threats."

The **Research Institute in Trustworthy Industrial Control Systems** (RITICS) "focuses on understanding the industrial control systems which oversee the correct functioning of parts of the UK's critical national infrastructure." It is also hosted at Imperial College.

The Cyber Essentials scheme was created and specifically aimed at small businesses in order to encourage them to adopt the most basic of controls and security practices, working on the principle that good cyber hygiene would tackle 80 percent of the threats faced by business. In October 2014, it became mandatory for government suppliers of personal and sensitive-information contracts to use Cyber Essentials controls. From January 2016, the Ministry of Defence required suppliers handling identifiable MoD information to have Cyber Essentials certification. This is a good example of contractual approaches, short of legislation, that can influence behavior, at least in the government and defense supply bases.

With the increase in activity through the period of the 2011 strategy to 2016, the government reported on progress in 2012 and 2013. Outputs from these reports, together with associate forward plans, are available online. They largely read as lists of completed activities and forthcoming activities, with numbers added to show levels of performance and effort. For example, this is an extract from the December 2013 progress report:

- "Over the last year the Government has held 10 exercises, working with 30 industrial partners and 25 government departments and agencies, to test cyber resilience and response in key sectors including finance, law enforcement, transport, food and water. There has also been liaison with both EU and U.S. exercise discussion and planning groups."
- "The Joint Forces Cyber Group (JFCyG) was stood up in May 2013 to deliver Defence's cyber capability. The group includes the Joint Cyber Units (JCUs) at Cheltenham and Corsham, with the new Joint Cyber Unit (Reserve) which is using innovative approaches to attract skilled cyber security professionals into a 'Cyber Reserve.' JFCyG continues to develop new tactics, techniques and plans to deliver military capabilities to confront high-end threats."

Of course, though necessary for showing that objectives are being addressed, lists of activities are not measures of outcomes. The NAO, in its reviews in 2013 and 2014, point out the difficulty in showing value for money for activities. Their reviews report on how money has been spent and summarize activity. In 2013, it acknowledged that "demonstrating the optimal use of resources on cyber security may not be easy in terms of measuring outcomes when the desired result is for nothing to happen."[7] To help the government, the NAO set out an approach to measuring outcomes in an annex to the 2013 report. This involved a process that included at a high level:

- Define what good looks like.
- Identify and collect the data and evidence required, including on resources.
- Decide comparators and evaluate performance.

The 2014 NAO update stated:

From those interviewed, it is clear that there is a belief across all sectors—government, academia and industry—that there is a good understanding of the threat by central government, with an average rating of 3.7 out of 5 in our survey of stakeholders. But this understanding diminishes the further away organisations are from the centre. Stakeholders believe that central government departments unused to dealing with national security or fraud-related threats and NHS and local government organisations have a more varied, but limited understanding of the threat and they do not yet understand what would represent an appropriate level of threat protection.[8]

While this comment does, in effect, show one form of assessment, the update document goes on to argue that the Cabinet Office is "managing the Programme effectively, but can't yet demonstrate a clear link between the large number of individual outputs being delivered and an overall picture of benefits achieved."[9] Moreover, there is a difficulty in publicly discussing benefits in classified programs (which actually may represent the bulk of spending). Nevertheless, the NAO sees clear delivery of benefits under all four objectives, receiving considerable international acclaim for UK leadership in cyber security. Interestingly, it urges the Cabinet Office to set out which activities should become mainstream across government (for example, making security planning part of routine project management) and those that are "transformational" and led by successor programs. All stakeholders agreed that a successor program was vital.

To its credit, the UK government subjected itself to assessment by the Global Cyber Security Capacity Centre (GCSCC), through its Cyber Security Capacity Maturity Model. This model was introduced briefly in the chapter eight. The report was published in 2016 and is publically available. Data was gathered during a series of workshops in September and October 2015 and through a stakeholder survey. Participation in the workshops involved government departments and ministries, universities, criminal justice and law enforcement, legislators, CERT, private sectors, and telecommunications and financial sectors. It was assessed that, for most factors in the maturity model, the United Kingdom lies between the "established" and "strategic" stages of maturity—that is, between the third and fourth levels of maturity out of five. The dimensions of strategy and policy and legal and regulatory frameworks seemed to indicate that they could be at the highest "dynamic" level of maturity. However, evidence needed to be collected that would show all factors at a given level as having been completed, before it could be assessed at that level of maturity.

Eighty-one recommendations emerged for the report. Some of the observed deficits in maturity included the lack of a central responsibility for incident response, despite the establishment of CERT-UK. There was no clear regulation to ensure that all incidents would be reported. The Cyber Information Sharing Partnership was seen as evolving, with information sharing and operational benefits assessed as variable. In terms of CNI, priorities and processes for cyber security had not been well-enough synchronized between national and local levels. This national–local spilt was also observed in terms of funding in crisis-management exercises and in investigative capacities of law enforcement. An absence of a cyber defense strategy was picked up as something to be addressed. As pointed out in the 2014 NAO review, organizations closest to the cyber security problem were seen as the most adept at developing a cyber security mind-set. Perhaps related to this, the assessment argues that the case for harm resulting from a lack of national cyber security had not yet been made to the general public. A difference between large companies and small- and medium-sized enterprises was noted, as was a perceived skill shortage.

Taken together, these factors seem to suggest that it is easier to develop maturity in strategizing, but it is harder to implement and spread along a number of axes. First is the axis that runs between national, regional, and local approaches to cyber security. Second is an axis that runs between those closest to the cyber security problem, and those that are distant (say the difference in perceptions between the intelligence services and the health service). Third, there is an axis between large and small companies. These can, in some ways, be summarized as differences in interests and differences in size and recourses. The implications of this are visible to some extent in the 2016 National Cyber Security Strategy.

THE THIRD UNITED KINGDOM NATIONAL CYBER SECURITY STRATEGY

The United Kingdom published a new National Security Strategy (NSS) in 2015. "Cyber" remained a tier-one risk. It notes that cyber underpins many of the other risks faced by the United Kingdom, denoting its rise to be more than a discreet series of threats relating to the cyber attacks and cyber crime mentioned in the first strategy of 2009. Once again, this strategy continued to link security and prosperity, something that would be reinforced in the Cyber Security Strategy. The NSS announced a further £1.9 billion budget for cyber and another five-year National Cyber Security Programme from 2016. The TalkTalk attack occurred in 2015, which may come to be seen as the UK case that raised the issue of cyber security to the board room, more than any other to date. Indeed, it is given a "box" in the following 2016 national cyber strategy. This telecoms and ISP company suffered a data breach relating to 157,000 customers, costing the company £60 million and a loss of 95,000 customers. Two other cases are described along with TalkTalk in boxes in the Strategy. The SWIFT payment system of Bangladesh Bank was attacked in early 2016 with the theft of USD 101 million. Attacks on the Ukrainian Power Grid in 2015 caused a blackout for 222,000 customers and was confirmed as the first use of "a disruptive cyber attack on an electricity network."[10]

The 2021 vision for the 2016 strategy was reframed as:

The UK is secure and resilient to cyber threats, prosperous and confident in the digital world.

The strategy objectives were also reframed with a more memorable set of active verbs. The description of each is quoted in full below:

DEFEND We have the means to defend the UK against evolving cyber threats, to respond effectively to incidents, to ensure UK networks, data and systems are protected and resilient. Citizens, businesses and the public sector have the knowledge and ability to defend themselves.

DETER The UK will be a hard target for all forms of aggression in cyber space. We detect, understand, investigate and disrupt hostile action taken against us, pursuing and prosecuting offenders. We have the means to take offensive action in cyber space, should we choose to do so.

DEVELOP We have an innovative, growing cyber security industry, underpinned by world-leading scientific research and development. We have a self-sustaining pipeline of talent providing the skills to meet our national needs across the public and private sectors. Our cutting-edge analysis and expertise will enable the UK to meet and overcome future threats and challenges.

A "fourth" objective is the need for "international action," underpinning each of the above objectives. The action-orientated language is also bolstered by a new confidence in talking about offensive cyber operations as part of a deterrent posture. Also detectable is a more coherent set of terms and concepts, as the United Kingdom develops its thinking about the challenges it faces and the means by which they might be addressed.

The strategy lists a number of principles that will guide actions in pursuing the objectives. While these include the traditional values statements, they also carry forward the action-orientated language such as:

- "Our actions and policies will be driven by the need to both protect our people and enhance our prosperity;
- We will treat a cyber attack on the UK as seriously as we would an equivalent conventional attack, and we will defend ourselves as necessary;
- We will act in accordance with national and international law and expect others to do the same."
- "We will not accept significant risk being posed to the public and the country as a whole as a result of businesses and organizations failing to take the steps needed to manage cyber threats."

The "driven" nature of the strategy is emphasized in the government's role in "driving change," both in the role of the market and its own "expanded role." In terms of the market, the strategy claims that, while the 2011 strategy achieved much, the market had not responded as expected. "The market is not valuing, and therefore not managing, cyber risk correctly."[11] The market was not seen as moving quickly enough, and, therefore, this needed short-term government action. This would entail four broad areas of work in an "ambitious and transformational programme."[12]

First, levers and incentives through investment in skills and innovation are highlighted along with the identification of talent. These actions are clearly not new, though the leveraging of forthcoming European Union law, the General Data Protection Regulation and potential, other regulation is signaled. The insurance sector is specifically mentioned as one that can shape the behavior of businesses. Second, intelligence is also expanded to facilitate early warning and pre-emptive notice of adversary intent and capabilities.

Third, the strategy also discusses the 2016 launch of the National Cyber Security Centre as a "single, central body for cyber security at a national level."[13] This would be part of GCHQ but would be a public-facing body that would continue to draw on its expertise. As previously noted, the NCSC would replace CESG. It also absorbed CERT-UK and cyber elements from CPNI. Around the same time, OCSIA was combined with another part of the Cabinet Office to form the Cyber and Government Security Directorate in the Cabinet Office. This would lead on the crosscutting aspects of the government's cyber security agenda, including delivery of the cyber security strategy and management of the National Cyber Security Programme. The Cabinet Office would, therefore, push implementation out to appropriate departments and agencies. For example, the cyber skills and cyber-economy portfolios would be led by the Department for Culture Media and Sport (DCMS, since renamed to the Department of

Digital, Culture, Media, and Sport). In the United Kingdom, popular culture has sometimes named this the Ministry of Fun. It's not very obvious relationship to cyber is through the department's relatively long-standing responsibility for electronic-spectrum management in relation to media and telecommunications.

Perhaps the one aspect of the strategy that has received the most attention is "development and deployment of technology in partnership with industry, including Active Cyber Defence measures."

ACTIVE CYBER DEFENCE (ACD)

In the commercial world, active defense involves a number of strategies, including the use of honeypots or honeynets, which attract attackers into areas of a system where they can be observed but can do no harm. They are a form of deception used to influence attackers' behavior. GCHQ and NCSC mean something different and more strategic. Rather than operating at the company or individual level or end-point device, active defense is more strategic in nature, deployed at a higher level to prevent attacks from flowing down through the system. *Computer Weekly* reported that tens of millions of cyber attacks are being blocked every week by industry partners implementing NCSC's Active Cyber Defence program.[14] GCHQ and NCSC have disclosed four "initial measures" described in the strategy and discussed in their first annual review for the year 2017.

The first is "blocking fake e-mails" through implementing the domain-based message authentication reporting and conformance protocol, DMARC. *Computer Weekly* also reports that in 2016, a pilot program at Her Majesty's Revenue and Customs reportedly blocked 300 million malicious or fraudulent e-mails.[15] NCSC provides an example of an occasion when 120,000 e-mails were blocked from one @gov.uk address. The knock-on effect is that there are fewer e-mails that are exploiting the credibility of a spoofed government address to commit theft or fraud, a major problem in the United Kingdom. Details of the DMARC protocol are available online, and list a range of high-level features arising from its use:

- Minimize false positives.
- Provide robust authentication reporting.
- Assert sender policy at receivers.
- Reduce successful phishing delivery.
- Work at Internet scale.
- Minimize complexity.

A second approach is described as "stopping government systems veering onto malicious websites." This service was reportedly built by Nominet, the official registry for .UK domain names.[16] The system identifies malicious addresses automatically or from data gathered by GCHQ and its industry partners. The system then blocks users from visiting those domains—"automatic protection for staff visiting infected sites whilst using work systems." This is known in the cyber security strategy as domain names system (DNS) blocking/filtering. Fifty-one organizations are adopting this service, and, in August 2017, it blocked 20,410 unique domains.[17]

The third is "Web check." This is a "free-to-use website configuration and vulnerability scanning service" aimed at guarding the United Kingdom's "digital estate." It helps users identify vulnerabilities that need to be fixed in their Internet-facing services, particularly when Web sites may be left without updates over a period of time.

The fourth measure is "removing bad things from the Internet, [phishing and malware mitigation]." Working with a commercial partner Netcraft, the NCSC has issued takedown notices to the hosts of e-mail and phishing sites. According to reports, the NCSC technical director, Ian Levy, has said that "Web injection hosted in the UK—which used to last about a month—is now being taken down in a couple of days, while UK government phishing hosted anywhere in the world used to last two days, but is now being taken down within six hours."[18]

Taking the NAO's advice on planning to measure the effectiveness of initiatives, ACD will be measured against a number of factors outlined in the strategy, including that a larger proportion of "malware and technical artifacts associated with cyber attacks" are blocked, and that the United Kingdom's Internet and telecommunications are less vulnerable to rerouting.

According to one UK official, there has been significant international interest in the United Kingdom's more active stance in protecting cyber space, with it being seen as a novel and innovative approach. In particular, it is seen as a way of mitigating the failure of cyber security awareness and the market in shaping the behaviors of individuals and businesses. Early filtering of threats shifts the burden for the discrimination in a phishing attack from the individual users to something that the government can do on their behalf. NCSC has responded to some media reports that argue that this approach is like China's "great firewall," by distinguishing content filtering and intelligence gathering from "catching cyber attacks."[19] It is in policy approaches such as these that the core values that are always stated in UK cyber strategies earn their money.

DEVELOPING SKILLS

In the develop track of the strategy, a number of interesting proposals attempt to shape the development of cyber security skills through improving supply and standards. The scope ranges widely from identification of talent at schools, improving the content of courses and degree programs, to ensuring the best qualification for professionals. There are also initiatives relating to diversity, including attracting more girls to Science, Technology, Engineering, and Mathematics (STEM) subjects. There are initiatives that target career changers and returners and initiatives aimed at teachers to improve their ability to teach cyber security. One targeted are in the National Cyber Security Strategy, with a view to impacting on the practitioner community, is:

Developing the cyber security profession, including through achieving Royal Chartered status by 2020, reinforcing the recognised body of cyber security excellence within the industry and providing a focal point which can advise, shape, and inform national policy.[20]

This is an example of an intervention that caused a ripple across existing professional bodies and associations, giving them a substantive reason to get around the table with government to discuss ways forward. Some of these already had chartered status, such as the BCS, the Chartered Institute of Information Technology, and the Institute of Engineering and Technology (IET). One, the Institute of Information Security Professionals, was in the process of making an application for chartered status. Many others are working on aspects of cyber security, such as Crest, with penetration testing. A consultation was conducted in 2018 as to the shape and scope of any new body with results yet to be published at the time of writing. Currently, there is an emerging willingness to create a body that allows the existing organizations to work more effectively together, for instance, to map qualifications and cohere on professionalization of cyber security. This approach, subjected to consultation, is consistent with a paper published in 2017 by the Information Assurance Advisory Council on the profession of cyber security. It has a number of recommendations, including the view that cyber security as a profession is more like a "profession of professions," as it requires engineers, architects, operators, defenders, testers, lawyers, psychologists, and others to play a role. Each could belong to other professional bodies, but a focal point for championing cyber security is nevertheless critical for leadership and development of security in the digital world. A key measurement for this initiative is that "cyber security is acknowledged as an established profession with clear pathways, and has achieved Royal Charter Status."

STRATEGY IN PRACTICE—THE NATIONAL HEALTH SERVICE

Success measures for the strategy as a whole are in annex three to the National Cyber Security Strategy, laid out in a table with indicative success measures, such as those for active defense and the Royal Charter discussed above. As previously mentioned, measuring success when things are going right is difficult. It can, however, be instructive to look at matters when they go wrong. The May 2017 WannaCry attack affecting the UK National Health Service (NHS) and others is an example that we shall use here as a case study. The attack received wide press coverage and resulted in a number of government publications, including its review by the NAO and NHS and, as an example, in the NCSC Annual Review.

Symantec describes WannaCry in May 2017 as more dangerous than any other common ransomware. Ransomware is a malicious software that encrypts data on the computer it infects, and then the attacker demands payment to have it decrypted. The WannaCry variant was virulent because of the way it exploited unpatched vulnerabilities in Windows to spread across an organization's network. It exploited a vulnerability known as "Eternal Blue," for which Microsoft had released a software patch in March 2017. A system that had been updated was, therefore, unaffected by the ransomware. After a successful infection, WannaCry searched for 176 kinds of files, and then appended .wcry to the end of the filename and demanded a Bitcoin ransom of USD 300. It first appeared on Friday May 12th, 2017.

According to the NCSC annual review, WannaCry was the "biggest test of the year." They report that it "affected more than 100 countries, including Spanish telecoms and German rail networks." The UK government is right to present the WannaCry attack as severe and not targeted specifically at the NHS. Indeed, the way it spread through the world, it targeted unpatched machines, regardless of location or purpose.

The National Health Service in the United Kingdom is administered through a network of trusts. The Department of Health and Social Care reported in February 2018 that most health care organizations were unaffected. However, it affected at least "80 out of 236 NHS trusts." It states that 603 primary care organizations were infected, involving 595 out of 7,454 local general practitioner (GP) practices. Interestingly, at the time of the NCSC annual review report, they state that 47 NHS trust were affected. An October 2017, NAO report provides details on why there is a difference. Thirty-seven trusts were infected and locked out, of which 27 were hospitals, known as acute trusts. A further 44 trusts were not infected but reported disruption. One reason why is that some trusts, not having received central advice early enough, took a precautionary measure of shutting down e-mail and other systems and resorting to "pen and paper." The NAO reports:

Without clear guidelines on responding to a national cyber attack, organisations reported the attack to different sources including the local police, NHS England and NHS Digital.[21]

Later, 21 other trusts were found to have attempted to communicate with the WannaCry domain but were unaffected. Two theories are proposed for this. One is that this communication happened after security research had found a "kill switch" for the ransomware. The second is that their own cyber security activity might have been responsible.

The Department of Health and Social Care believes that the NHS responded well to the attack, "with no reports of harm to patients or patient data being lost."[22] Nevertheless, the impact was felt locally, and, while no one was physically harmed and no data was lost, thousands of appointments and operations were cancelled. Patients in five areas had to travel further for accident and emergency care. It is unclear how much the attack cost the NHS and, therefore, the UK taxpayer.

According to an infographic in the NCSC annual review, the NCSC, having been notified of the attack on the afternoon of May 12, deployed staff to "victim sites" and worked beside hospitals and law enforcement officials. Within 90 minutes of notification, they issued a statement to the media. NCSC state that a record number of professionals collaborated in a "secure space" to try to defeat the attack. Over Saturday and Sunday, guidance was produced and updated. Members of the Cyber-Security Information Sharing Partnership (CiSP) shared information about the attack. Within 24 hours, a Cabinet Office crisis meeting was held, run by the Home Secretary. NCSC provided an overview of hugely increased levels of traffic on information-sharing sites, Web sites, and tweets regarding the incident. The NCSC CEO was interviewed on the evening news to reassure the public. Eventually, the NHS was back online.

There is no doubt that measures taken through rounds of strategic planning had led to an infrastructure that could react to an incident and provide platforms and organizations for information sharing and expertise to the victims of the attack. However, it is important to not simply provide statistics about what happened, such as levels of communications. Lessons need to be learned from the crisis. NCSC led the Government's review of lessons learned. The October 2017 report on the NAO's investigation found that the Department of Health "was warned about the risk of cyber attacks on the NHS a year before WannaCry and, although it had work underway, it did not formally respond with a written report until July 2017." It also found that "the department and its arm's-length bodies did not know whether local NHS organizations were prepared for a cyber attack." In terms of the response to the attack, the following headline points were made:

- "The Department had developed a plan, which included roles and responsibilities of national and local organisations for responding to an attack, but had not tested the plan at a local level."

- "As the NHS had not rehearsed for a national cyber attack, it was not immediately clear who should lead the response and there were problems with communications."
- "In line with its existing procedures for managing a major incident, NHS England initially focused on maintaining emergency care."

In terms of lessons learned, it was found that "relatively simple actions" could have been taken to avoid the attack, including patching and firewall management. It was found that there was no clear relationship between vulnerability to WannaCry and the quality of trust leadership. The Department and NHS had learned that they needed to develop response plans and establish roles and responsibilities. They needed to implement critical alerts from their CERT, "CareCert." They also needed to ensure that critical communications would continue to get through during attacks and when systems are down. Finally, they needed to ensure that organizations, boards, and staff would take the cyber threat seriously, understand the risks, and work to reduce the impact on patients.

Standing back from this case study and reviewing it in the light of the strategic narrative developed in this chapter, a number of issue come to the fore. The most fundamental point is that this episode might have been a lot worse but for the planning and implementation that had been done to this point. While preparation for a crisis will help diminish its effects, it will not necessarily do away with the crisis all together. The fact that the crisis emerges quickly in the context of an already busy working environment and, in the case of an organizationally fragmented NHS, means that such an attack will always be difficult to manage. Also note, that "busy working environment" doesn't do justice to the reality of what it is like to be a doctor or nurse working in a tightly resourced UK hospital. Taking time to think about cyber security, when time is in short supply for caring for patients, may seem like a big ask.

In this context, it is clear why the establishment of the NCSC was necessary in the form described in this objective from the same strategy:

- "The Government will provide a single, joined-up approach to incident management, based on an improved understanding and awareness of the threat and actions being taken against us. The NCSC will be a key enabler, as will partnership with the private sector, law enforcement and other government departments, authorities and agencies;
- The NCSC defines clear processes for reporting incidents, tailored to the profile of the victim; and
- We will prevent the most common cyber incidents, and we will have effective information-sharing structures in place to inform 'pre-incident' planning."[23]

We can see this in evidence in the management of the WannaCry crisis, but we can also see how a lack of central advice and fragmented reporting to multiple organizations, show how the reality is more difficult in practice. Having said that, the NCSC was only officially launched in the February before the May attack.

However, this case is instructive because we can also see evidence that apparently confirms the 2016 assessment of Cyber Security Capacity Maturity Model. In this, we detected three axes, which were described as: the axis that runs between national, regional, and local approaches to cyber security; the axis that runs between those closest to the cyber security problem and those that are distant (say the difference in perceptions between the intelligence services and the health service); and the axis between large and small companies. When this is mapped against the case study, one can see this dynamic in action. One NHS official told the author that one should not think of the NHS as a single amorphous organization but as thousands of small businesses and larger industries. Some are very local in terms of primary care to small communities. Having common standards and approaches to security in such circumstances is not impossible, but the difficulty in establishing and sustaining them should not be underestimated. Indeed, this is acknowledged in the 2016 National Cyber Security Strategy:

Health and care systems pose unique challenges in the context of cyber security. The sector employs around 1.6 million people in over 40,000 organisations, each with vastly differing information security resources and capability. The National Data Guardian for Health and Care has set new data security standards for the health and social care systems in England, alongside a new data consent/opt-out model for patients. The Government will work with health and social care organisations to implement these standards.[24]

DISCUSSION

Making the strategy count at a local level and across all sizes of organizations, even when people don't immediately see the threat to them, is *the* challenge of cyber security strategy. Having a strategy is essential, but it is only the start. It is about rallying the nation across all sectors. The 2016 strategy recognized that there were market failures and that cyber security awareness campaigns were not changing behaviors quickly enough. Consequently, we saw the emergence of active-defense measures that are designed to remove threats to the United Kingdom as early as possible to mitigate some of these problems. Much more needs to be done in terms of engineering and design; the production of better software; and, of course, changes in behaviors at a local level. This is not simply about teaching people to not click on dubious links. Attackers are sophisticated, and users should be considered victims. This is as much about mobilizing leaders to make cyber security a priority that is managed and reported on and for which there is some form of accountability. We can see all of this in the wide variety of measures included in the 2016 UK National Cyber Security Strategy, which has, on the whole, been received positively by the UK cyber security community. Implementation remains a problem and, perhaps, where there is most debate in the community.

It is difficult to characterize this debate without it seeming like criticism of the efforts of groups of dedicated people who have managed to make a difference to the cyber safety and security of the nation and communities. No criticism is intended; it is, rather, an analysis of the problem of implementation. At its heart is the tension between central direction and devolved responsibility and action. Of course, one can view this as a spectrum. So the debate is really about where the best approaches to implementation lie along the spectrum and the trade-offs that one approach entails compared to another. Arguably, this is also at the heart of why distance from the center is observed as an important dynamic. Undoubtedly, better software, technologies, and defensive systems, designed at the center and by industry, will help the overall security of the country and communities: it simply makes security easier for citizens and consumers and their use of the Internet safer. Legislation and regulation also have their parts to play. As we have seen, a small technology company in the north-east of England has to adopt Cyber Essentials to contract with the Ministry of Defence in central government. However, there are limits to which the scale of the problem and need for action can be driven, controlled, and implemented from the center.

Community criticism of intelligence-agency led initiatives are sometimes framed as one of adopting a command-and-control relationship with cyber security, rather than as an enabler for pre-existing initiatives. Perhaps it is an easy target for assessment by stereotypes. One has to remember that it is still early days for, for example, the NCSC approach. Some cultures are hard to adapt when they have been established for very sound operational reasons. Arguably, one can sometimes observe a tendency to purchase cooperation through contracts, rather than to enable others. This can result in government appearing to own initiatives rather than support them, though, in this way, they can feel some assurance about the outcomes being delivered. There are good reasons for seeing the world in this way, as culture change is required within industry and communities too—desperate for money, but not always desperate to be measured against outcomes. It is easy to spend money on initiatives without seeing benefits.

To illustrate the dynamic, here is a small example. At one point, there was a little tension between a voluntary development of a cyber security body of knowledge by professional bodies and others, and the government's contracted approach to a consortium of universities to develop a cyber body of knowledge. The upside to the contracted approach was that it released money into the development of the body of knowledge, and the government believes it will get a product that is seen to be systematically rigorous in its development. This will support NCSC's aim to have international impact with this work. On the downside, there is a risk in creating barriers to community ownership of the resulting body of knowledge—something critical to its success. One can see the trade-offs at work in this and, in fact, the approach to developing a cyber security professional body, as discussed earlier. Other mechanisms also exist. For example, the government recently issued a call to fund ideas with immediate impact on skills and diversity in cyber security. This will bring some existing projects into the fold; the money will enhance their efforts; and, of course, a degree of accountability will also be structured into the project.

There is also the issue of how national security is defined in practice. It can be seen in a narrower sense, for example, driven by intelligence agencies and security forces as a fight against other intelligence agencies and militaries. Or it can be seen in a broader sense of the security of business and community in the United Kingdom. The strategies emphasize the economy; however, the financial sector continues to operate without the need for continual reference to national security strategies. The apparent scale of demand for skills cannot be drummed up by any one part of government but requires leadership from within all sectors. Consequently, there are many cyber security groups in industry and communities that are not formally affiliated with the national strategy or government, yet are working on the matters that affect all our security.

There are some local community examples. In the northwest of England, Martin Howlett, working with the Youth Federation, has been actively involved in a cyber safety initiative that is engaging young people in a "magic triangle" of schools, youth organizations, and the home. The key to this has been getting parents involved too. The excellent team at the University of Chester, working with the local Philip Barker Charity, joined Martin in initiatives that bring the creative arts to cyber education. Young people perform for parents, and everyone learns. Their work extends to improving cyber education in schools through teacher training, including direct links with universities and schools in Estonia. The Information Assurance Advisory Council (IAAC), solely funded by industry sponsorship, and the Digital Policy Alliance are working to bring national-level attention to regional initiatives, such as Martin's and the work by Michael Dieroff in Plymouth in the southwest of England. Their innovative efforts aim to create secure operations centers, run by local business and young people, for local businesses. This provides work experience for young people without the perceptions of risk to business from interns in cyber security.

At a national level, there is work by the Trustworthy Software Foundation to maintain the agenda of having industry provide better software. Undoubtedly, some of this work will be carried forward into the government's digital charter work on security by design. This is currently in development. Of particular note is work done by the Cyber Security Challenge UK in its highly successful efforts to promote cyber skills through competitions and talent spotting. Many of these initiatives have links with government, NCSC, and DCMS, with enabling relationships. Very little would be possible without the direct and indirect support of industry, which also brings a level of international knowledge transfer that lies beyond many government initiatives.

There are too many other initiatives to mention here. However, what this chapter has highlighted is that it is getting the balance right between directing and enabling, strategizing and implementing, and security design and education, that forms the basis of the story of development of UK strategy in cyber security. It is hoped that this might help in the deliberations and actions of those doing the same.

NOTES

1. UK Government Web Archive, "The National Archives. Central Sponsor for Information Assurance." 2003. http://webarchive.nationalarchives.gov.uk /20031220222908/http://www.cabinet-office.gov.uk/csia/. Accessed March 31, 2018.

2. P. Cornish and D. Clemente, *Cybersecurity and the UK's Critical National Infrastructure: A Chatham House Report*. London: Royal Institute of International Affairs, 2012, p. 11.

3. UK Government, "The UK Cyber Security Strategy." 2011. https://www.gov .uk/government/uploads/system/uploads/attachment_data/file/60961/uk -cyber-security-strategy-final.pdf. Accessed March 31, 2018, p. 21.

4. UK NAO, "The UK Cyber Security Strategy: Landscape Review." February 2013. https://www.nao.org.uk/wp-content/uploads/2013/03/Cyber-security-Full -report.pdf. Accessed March 31, 2018, p. 11.

5. UK Government, "2010 to 2015 Government Policy: Cybersecurity—GOV. UK." https://www.gov.uk/government/publications/2010-to-2015-government -policy-cyber-security/2010-to-2015-government-policy-cyber-security. Accessed March 31, 2018.

6. NCSC, "Academic Centres of Excellence in Cyber Security Research." https://www.ncsc.gov.uk/articles/academic-centres-excellence-cyber-security- research. Accessed March 31, 2018.

7. UK NAO, "The UK Cyber Security Strategy: Landscape Review." February 2013. https://www.nao.org.uk/wp-content/uploads/2013/03/Cyber-secu rity-Full-report.pdf. Accessed March 31, 2018, p. 30.

8. UK NAO, "Update on the National Cyber Security Programme." 2014. https://www.nao.org.uk/report/update-on-the-national-cyber-security-programme/. Accessed March 31, 2018, p. 10.

9. Ibid., p. 22.

10. UK Government, "National Cyber Security Strategy 2016–2021." https://www.gov.uk/government/uploads/system/uploads/attachment_data/file/567242/national_cyber_security_strategy_2016.pdf. Accessed March 31, 2018, pp. 20–21.

11. Ibid., p. 27.

12. Ibid.

13. Ibid., p. 28.

14. Warwick Ashford, "UK National Cyber Security Centre Looks to Future in Annual Review." ComputerWeekly.com, October 3, 2017. http://www.computerweekly.com/news/450427340/UK-National-Cyber-Security-Centre-looks-to-future-in-annual-review. Accessed March 31, 2018.

15. Warwick Ashford, "NCSC Rolls Out Four Measures to Boost Public Sector Cyber Security." ComputerWeekly.com, June 30, 2017. http://www.computerweekly.com/news/450421761/NCSC-rolls-out-four-measures-to-boost-public-sector-cyber-security. Accessed March 31, 2018.

16. Warwick Ashford, "UK National Cyber Security Centre Looks to Future in Annual Review." ComputerWeekly.com, October 3, 2017. http://www.computerweekly.com/news/450427340/UK-National-Cyber-Security-Centre-looks-to-future-in-annual-review. Accessed March 31, 2018.

17. NCSC, "The 2017 Annual Review." October 3, 2017. https://www.ncsc.gov.uk/news/2017-annual-review. Accessed March 31, 2017.

18. Warwick Ashford, "Cyber Security Should Be Data-Based, Says NCSC." ComputerWeekly.com, September 29, 2017. http://www.computerweekly.com/news/450427211/Cyber-security-should-be-data-based-says-NCSC. Accessed March 31, 2018.

19. Shaun Nichols, "Great British Block-Off: GCHQ Floats Plan to Share Its DNS Filters." *The Register*, September 14, 2016. https://www.theregister.co.uk/2016/09/14/great_british_blockoff/. Accessed March 31, 2018.

20. UK Government, "National Cyber Security Strategy 2016–2021." https://www.gov.uk/government/uploads/system/uploads/attachment_data/file/567242/national_cyber_security_strategy_2016.pdf. Accessed March 31, 2018, p. 56.

21. UK NAO, "Investigation: WannaCry Cyber Attack and the NHS." October 2017. https://www.nao.org.uk/wp-content/uploads/2017/10/Investigation-WannaCry-cyber-attack-and-the-NHS.pdf. Accessed March 31, 2018, p. 24.

22. UK Government, "Securing Cyber Resilience in Health and Care." 2018. https://www.gov.uk/government/uploads/system/uploads/attachment_data/file/678484/Securing_cyber_resillience_in_health_and_care.pdf. Accessed March 31, 2018, p. 3.

23. UK Government, "National Cyber Security Strategy 2016–2021." https://www.gov.uk/government/uploads/system/uploads/attachment_data/file/567242/national_cyber_security_strategy_2016.pdf. Accessed March 31, 2018, p. 44.

24. Ibid., p. 38.

BIBLIOGRAPHY

Ashford, Warwick. "Cyber Security Should Be Data-Based, Says NCSC." ComputerWeekly.com, September 29, 2017. http://www.computerweekly .com/news/450427211/Cyber-security-should-be-data-based-says-NCSC. Accessed March 31, 2018.

Ashford, Warwick. "NCSC Rolls Out Four Measures to Boost Public Sector Cyber Security." ComputerWeekly.com, June 30, 2017. http://www.computer weekly.com/news/450421761/NCSC-rolls-out-four-measures-to-boost -public-sector-cyber-security. Accessed March 31, 2018.

Ashford, Warwick. "UK National Cyber Security Centre Looks to Future in Annual Review." ComputerWeekly.com, October 3, 2017. http://www.computer weekly.com/news/450427340/UK-National-Cyber-Security-Centre -looks-to-future-in-annual-review. Accessed March 31, 2018.

Bada, Maria, Ivan Arrehuín-Toft, Ian Brown, Paul Cornish, Sadie Creese, William Dutton, Michael Goldsmith, et al. "Cyber Security Capacity Review of the United Kingdom." GCSCC, November 2016. https://www.sbs.ox.ac .uk/cybersecurity-capacity/system/files/Cybersecurity%20Capacity%20 Review%20of%20the%20United%20Kingdom.pdf. Accessed March 31, 2018.

Cornish, P., and D. Clemente. *Cybersecurity and the UK's Critical National Infrastructure: A Chatham House Report*. London: Royal Institute of International Affairs, 2012. https://www.chathamhouse.org/sites/default/files /public/Research/International%20Security/r0911cyber.pdf. Accessed November 4, 2018.

Defence Contracts Online. "MoD Implementation of Cyber Essentials Scheme." MOD-DCO, 2017. https://www.contracts.mod.uk/announcements/mod -implementation-of-cyber-essentials-scheme/. Accessed March 31, 2018.

DMARC.org. "Domain Message Authentication Reporting & Conformance." https://dmarc.org/. Accessed March 31, 2018.

House of Lords Library Note. "To Call Attention to the United Kingdom's National Security Strategy." January 29, 2010. http://researchbriefings.parliament .uk/ResearchBriefing/Summary/LLN-2010-004. Accessed March 31, 2018.

Jones, Nigel, and Louisa-Jayne O'Neill. "The Profession: Understanding Careers and Professionalism in Cyber Security." IAAC Publication, 2017. https:// www.iaac.org.uk/wp-content/uploads/2018/02/2017-03-06-IAAC -cyber-profession-FINAL-Feb18-amend-1.pdf. Accessed March 31, 2018.

NCSC. "The 2017 Annual Review." October 3, 2017. https://www.ncsc.gov.uk /news/2017-annual-review. Accessed March 31, 2017.

NCSC. "Academic Centres of Excellence in Cyber Security Research." https:// www.ncsc.gov.uk/articles/academic-centres-excellence-cyber-security -research. Accessed March 31, 2018.

NCSC. "Research Institutes." February 11, 2016. https://www.ncsc.gov.uk/infor mation/research-institutes. Accessed March 31, 2018.

Nichols, Shaun. "Great British Block-Off: GCHQ Floats Plan to Share Its DNS Filters." *The Register*, September 14, 2016. https://www.theregister .co.uk/2016/09/14/great_british_blockoff/. Accessed March 31, 2018.

Norton-Taylor, Richard. "Britain Plans Cyber Strike Force—With Help from GCHQ." *UK News. The Guardian*, September 30, 2016. https://www.the guardian.com/uk-news/defence-and-security-blog/2013/sep/30/cyber -gchq-defence. Accessed March 31, 2018.

Symantec. "What You Need to Know about the WannaCry Ransomware." https:// www.symantec.com/blogs/threat-intelligence/wannacry-ransomware -attack. Accessed March 31, 2018.

UK Government. "2010 to 2015 Government Policy: Cybersecurity—GOV.UK." https://www.gov.uk/government/publications/2010-to-2015-govern ment-policy-cyber-security/2010-to-2015-government-policy-cyber-secu rity. Accessed March 31, 2018.

UK Government. "Cyber and Government Security Directorate—GOV.UK." https://www.gov.uk/government/groups/office-of-cyber-security-and -information-assurance#policies. Accessed March 31, 2018.

UK Government. "The Cyber Security Strategy of the United Kingdom." 2009. https://www.gov.uk/government/uploads/system/uploads/attach ment_data/file/228841/7642.pdf. Accessed March 31, 2018.

UK Government. "The Cyber Security Strategy Report on Progress—December 2012 Forward Plans." https://www.gov.uk/government/uploads/sys tem/uploads/attachment_data/file/265402/Cyber_Security_Strategy _Forward_Plans_3-Dec-12_1.pdf. Accessed March 31, 2018.

UK Government. "The National Cyber Security Strategy: Our Forward Plans— December 2013." https://www.gov.uk/government/uploads/system /uploads/attachment_data/file/265386/The_National_Cyber_Security _Strategy_Our_Forward_Plans_December_2013.pdf. Accessed March 31, 2018.

UK Government. "National Cyber Security Strategy 2016–2021." https://www .gov.uk/government/uploads/system/uploads/attachment_data /file/567242/national_cyber_security_strategy_2016.pdf. Accessed March 31, 2018.

UK Government. "National Security Strategy and Strategic Defence and Security Review 2015: A Secure and Prosperous United Kingdom." 2015. https:// www.gov.uk/government/uploads/system/uploads/attachment_data /file/555607/2015_Strategic_Defence_and_Security_Review.pdf. Accessed March 31, 2018.

UK Government. "The National Security Strategy of the United Kingdom." 2008. https://www.gov.uk/government/uploads/system/uploads/attach ment_data/file/228539/7291.pdf. Accessed March 31, 2018.

UK Government. "National Security Strategy: Update 2009." London: Stationery Office, 2009. https://www.gov.uk/government/uploads/system /uploads/attachment_data/file/229001/7590.pdf. Accessed March 31, 2018.

UK Government. "Progress against the Objectives of the National Cyber Security Strategy." December 2012. https://www.gov.uk/government/uploads /system/uploads/attachment_data/file/265401/Cyber_Security_Strat egy_one_year_on_achievements.pdf. Accessed March 31, 2018.

UK Government. "Progress against the Objectives of the National Cyber Security
    Strategy—December 2013." https://www.gov.uk/government/uploads
    /system/uploads/attachment_data/file/265384/Progress_Against_the
    _Objectives_of_the_National_Cyber_Security_Strategy_December_2013.
    pdf. Accessed March 31, 2018.
UK Government. "Securing Cyber Resilience in Health and Care." 2018. https://
    www.gov.uk/government/uploads/system/uploads/attachment_data
    /file/678484/Securing_cyber_resillience_in_health_and_care.pdf.
    Accessed March 31, 2018.
UK Government. "A Strong Britain in an Age of Uncertainty: The National Secu-
    rity Strategy." Norwich: Stationery Office, 2010. http://www.cabinetof
    fice.gov.uk/sites/default/files/resources/national-security-strategy.pdf.
    Accessed March 31, 2018.
UK Government. "The UK Cyber Security Strategy." 2011. https://www.gov.uk
    /government/uploads/system/uploads/attachment_data/file/60961
    /uk-cyber-security-strategy-final.pdf. Accessed March 31, 2018.
UK Government. "UK Launches First National CERT." March 31, 2014. https://
    www.gov.uk/government/news/uk-launches-first-national-cert. Accessed
    October 16, 2018.
UK Government Web Archive. "The National Archives. Central Sponsor for
    Information Assurance." 2003. http://webarchive.nationalarchives.gov
    .uk/20031220222908/http://www.cabinet-office.gov.uk/csia/. Accessed
    March 31, 2018.
UK NAO. "Investigation: WannaCry Cyber Attack and the NHS." October 2017.
    https://www.nao.org.uk/wp-content/uploads/2017/10/Investigation
    -WannaCry-cyber-attack-and-the-NHS.pdf. Accessed March 31, 2018.
UK NAO. "The UK Cyber Security Strategy: Landscape Review." February 2013.
    https://www.nao.org.uk/wp-content/uploads/2013/03/Cyber-security
    -Full-report.pdf. Accessed March 31, 2018.
UK NAO. "Update on the National Cyber Security Programme." 2014. https://
    www.nao.org.uk/report/update-on-the-national-cyber-security-pro
    gramme/. Accessed March 31, 2018.

Index

Page numbers followed by *t* indicate tables and *f* indicate figures.

Active Cyber Defence (ACD), 225–226
Acton, Brian, 146
Adams, Anne, 136–138
Advanced persistent threat (APT), 63, 119; APT1, 163; APT28, 63, 64; APT29, 61; Best Advanced Persistent Threat Protection award, 162*t*, 162; Dragonfly, 13–14; and nation states, 13–14
Ahmadinejad, Mahmoud, 16
Ahmed, Salman, 190
AirBnB, 115, 159, 168*t*, 169
Al-Qaeda, 2–6
Al-Qaeda on the Arabian Peninsula (AQAP), 5
Alexander, Keith, 24
Alibaba Group, 37, 38
Amazon, 18, 115, 116
Anthem Healthcare attack (2015), 25–26, 29, 31
Arab Spring, 53, 62–63
Aral, Sinan, 147
Arbuthnot, James, 77
Archuleta, Katherine, 28

Artificial intelligence and machine learning, 10, 36, 117–120; autonomous vehicles, 83–84, 117–118, 122; and data analytics, 117, 118–120; definitions of, 117; and innovation, 162–167, 174; and social media, 9–10; trust and ethics, 118, 122–127
Aruba Introspect, 164
Asimov, Isaac, 80–81, 81*t*; 98
Assad, Bashar, 66–67
Assange, Julian, 57
Assassins (Shia Islamic sect), 1–2
Autonomous vehicles, 83–84, 117–118, 12
Awlaki, Anwar, al-, 5

Baines, Paul, 203
Barcelona attacks (2017), 7
Bauman, Melissa, 117–118
Benghazi attack (2012), 55
Bezos, Jeff, 18, 116
Bick, Alexander, 190
Big data and data analytics, 110–116, 127, 167, 169, 174; in consumer

Big data and data analytics (*continued*)
market, 114; definition of, 110–111;
emergent properties, 123; in health
care industry, 112–114; in sports,
111–112; and tech companies,
115–116; trust and ethics in, 122–
127; value of, 111; Xebec (realty
company) example, 114–115. *See also*
Cambridge Analytica
Bin Laden, Osama, 2–3
Black Lives Matter movement, 69
Bolton, John, 15, 150
Bossert, Tim, 30
Brazile, Donna, 56–57
Breedlove, Philip, 67
Brennan, John, 54
Brexit, 65–66
British Computer Society (BCS), 76–77,
101, 227
Brostoff, Sacha, 93–94
Buckshot Yankee (cyber breach), 134
Budanov, Viktor, 61
Bush, George W.: and Iran's nuclear
program, 15–16; State of the Union
address (2002), 15; and threat of
ISIS, 3

"Call for a Global Islamic Resistance,
The" (al-Suri), 4
Cambridge Analytica, 70, 116, 144, 145,
146, 151
Carter, Ash, 8, 19, 151
Centre for the Protection of National
Infrastructure (CPNI), 214, 216,
219, 224
CERT-UK, 219, 222, 224, 230
Christensen, Howard, 159
Churchill, Winston, 142
Cisco, 17
Clark, Dan, 146
Clark, Wesley, 67
Clausewitz, Carl von, 43
Clinton, Bill, 15, 51, 54–55
Clinton, Hillary, 51, 54–60, 63, 69
Coats, Dan, 68–69
Cold War, 2, 68, 195
Color Revolutions, 53
Comey, James, 58

Committee on Foreign Investment
(Cifus), 149
Communications-Electronics Security
Group (CESG), 214, 224
Cool, Alison, 152
Corbyn, Jeremy, 66
Crowdstrike, 17, 38, 168*t*, 169, 176;
Falcon, 165–166
Cyber crime: academic education
against, 32–33; Anthem Healthcare
attack (2015), 25–26, 29, 31; CIA
standard (confidence, integrity,
and availability of data), 25–31;
computer and network intrusion,
24–25; corporate commitment
against, 31–32; costs of, 24–31;
Cyber Command, 33; and data
protection and security measures,
31–41; definition of, 23; emerging
properties, 40–41; Equifax attack
(2017), 30–31; EsteeMaudit cyber
weapon, 30; FBI's jurisdiction over,
23; and Global Center for Cyber
Security (Geneva), 39–40; HBO
attack (2017), 27–28; international
standards and cooperation against,
34, 39–40; and modernization of law
enforcement, 41; Office of Personnel
Management attack (2014/2015),
28–29, 31; and Olympic Games
(2018), 40; ransomware, 25–26;
scope of, 24–31; social cyber crimes,
23; Sony Pictures attack (2014),
26–27, 29, 31; targets of, 24–31; and
technology, 35–36; types of, 23;
Uber cyber attack (2016), 32; and
vulnerabilities equities process
(VEP), 36; WannaCry attacks (2017),
29–30
Cyber Essentials, 220, 232
Cyber Security Capacity Maturity
Model (CSCMM), 201–202,
221–222, 231
Cyber security skills and education,
226–227
Cyber Security Ventures, 139, 169
Cyber terrorism, 11–21; definition of,
3; historical precursors to, 1–2; and

ISIS's use of the Internet, 4–9; and social media, 9–10
CyberBerkut (hacktivist group), 51

Dark Web, 4, 5
Darktrace, 168*t*, 169
Data analytics. *See* Big data and data analytics
Deep Web, 4
Defense Innovation Unit (DIUx), 19
Democratic National Committee (DNC) hack, 55–57, 60
Disruptive innovation, 159–160, 166–167, 169, 175–17. *See also* Innovation
Dragonfly, 13–1
Dresner, Daniel, 80–81, 81*t*, 98
Dual-authentication security, 13, 18

Eichensehr, Kristen, 192
Elite Security Holdings, 61
Energetic Bear, 17
Equifax attack (2017), 30–31, 142
Estonia, 34; Cooperative Cyber Defence Centre of Excellence, 12, 197, 201; cyber attacks of 2007 against, 11–13, 51, 213; cyber education in, 233

Facebook, 35, 46, 144–146, 151–153; agreement to curb the spread of terrorist propaganda, 9; and big data, 115–116; and Cambridge Analytica, 116, 144, 146, 151; fined by British Information Commission, 145; identifying terrorist clusters, 10; image matching, 10; recidivism of fake accounts, 10; and U.S. 2016 presidential campaign, 62, 65, 144–145
Fake e-mails, 26, 225
Fake news, 51, 68, 145, 146, 147
Fake social media accounts, 10, 62, 65
Fake social media posts, 9
Fancy Bear (hacking group), 60, 67
Finnemore, Martha, 203
Fireeye, 163
Foreign Intelligence Surveillance Act, 48

Frago, 17
Free speech, 9, 62, 126, 141

Game theory, 88–92
Gates, Bill, 133, 154
General Data Protection Regulation (GDPR), 124–125, 152, 169, 195
Gerasimov, Valery, 52
Gerasimov Doctrine, 52
Gertz, Bill, 37–38
Global Agreement on Tariffs and Trade, 18
Global Center for Cyber Security, 39–40
Globalization, 45, 181, 182–183
Google, 113–116, 122, 151–153, 176
Government Communications Headquarters (GCHQ), 214–216, 219, 224–226
Grasty, T., 158
Greenwald, Glenn, 46, 47
"Grizzly Steppe: Russian Malware Cyber Activity," 52
Guccifer 2.0 (hacker group), 57
Gulf Cooperation Council Countries, 198–200, 205

HackerRank, 167
Hadlington, Lee, 138
Hamas, 1
Hasan, Rikky, 115
Hawkins, Adrian, 55–56
HBO attack (2017), 27–28
Health and Safety Executive (HSE), 92–94
Hess, Markus, 51
Hoffman, Robert, 123–126
Hollande, François, 7
Huawei Technologies, 36–38

Illusive Network, 165
Information Assurance Advisory Council (IAAC), 73. *See also* Internet of things (IoT), smart living
Innovation: and artificial intelligence and machine learning, 162–167, 174; basic research, 157–158, 160, 175–176; breakthrough research, 159–160, 166, 171, 175–176; Cyber

Innovation (*continued*)
Security Division, 171–173; cyber
security innovation policy, 169–175;
definition of, 158; disruptive
innovation, 159–160, 166–167,
169, 175–176; examples of cyber
security innovation, 160–169; and
funding, 160, 169, 171, 174–176;
and IoT, 160; in Israel, 170–171, 173,
174, 176–177; playbook, 159–160,
176–177; and quantum technologies,
174; sustaining innovation, 159–160,
175; technology awards and prizes,
161–169, 175–176; time horizons
for, 158–160, 175; TRUST Award
categories (*SC Magazine*), 161–162*t*;
types of, 157–158; in the UK, 169,
173–177; in the U.S., 169–173, 176;
UK Cyber Security Science and
Technology (S&T) Strategy, 173–174;
United States–Israel Cyber Security
Cooperation Enhancement Act, 171
Inspire Magazine, 5
International policy and organizations:
and Cyber Security Capacity
Maturity Model (CSCMM), 201–202,
221–222, 213; and duty to protect,
182, 206; and European Union,
192–195, 201; G8, 183; G20, 183;
Global Agreement on Tariffs and
Trade, 183; and globalization, 181,
182–183; Gulf Cooperation Council
Countries, 198–200, 205; ICANN,
183, 189; International Monetary
Fund, 183; North Atlantic Treaty
Organization (NATO), 195–198, 200–
201; Treaty of Osnabruck, 182; Treaty
of Westphalia, 182; United Nations
Charter, 182; United States national
security strategy, 183–192, 200;
World Bank, 183; World Economic
Forum, 39, 116, 203–205, 183
Internet addiction, 138
Internet of things (IoT), smart living,
20, 73–74, 101–104, 153, 159–160,
172, 174, 194–195; analogy of
engineering ethics, 97–98; analogy

of Health and Safety Executive,
92–94; and British Computer Society
(BCS), 76–77, 101, 227; and data
exchange and generation, 83–84;
and Cities2050 roundtable, 77–78;
and consumer-protection regulation,
94–97; and degree of control,
82–83; design and development
principle, 102–103*t*; and design
thinking, 88–92; development
of principles, 98–101; emergent
properties, 82; and game theory,
88–92; good practice principle, 104*t*;
governance principle, 103*t*; IoT
Security Foundation, 78, 80; liability
principle, 104*t*; multi-stakeholder
perspectives, 84–85; and Open
Web Application Security Project
(OWASP), 78–82, 104*t*; overlap
of confidentiality, integrity, and
availability of information, 75, 76*f*;
and Oxford Internet Institute, 76;
policy and governance challenges
of, 76–82; preservation, 102*t*; and
privacy versus confidentiality,
75; regulation and legislation
principle, 104*t*; security, safety,
trustworthiness, and harm, 74–76,
84; smart living defined, 74; societal
impact by frameworks, 85–87;
"Table of Eleven" dimension, 100,
100*t*; transparency principle, 103*t*;
Trustworthy Software Foundation
(TSFdn), 75, 89–90
Internet Research Agency, 62, 69
IoT. *See* Internet of things (IoT), smart
living
IoT Security Foundation, 78, 80
Iran: 2017–2018 protests, 4, 53; cyber
capabilities and hackers, 27–28, 34,
37, 39, 44, 189; Natanz uranium
enrichment facility, 14–17, 135; and
Stuxnet, 14–17, 43, 135, 150
Islamic State in Iraq and Syria (ISIS),
19, 63, 151; Amaq News Agency,
5; Assassins (Shia Islamic sect)
as precursor to, 1–2; and global

recruitment, 5; al-Hayat Media Center, 6; "human faces" of, 5–8; and the Internet, 4–9; *Rumiyah* (online magazine), 8; U.S. gun laws video, 6; *zakat* (charity activities), 5

Jobs, Steve, 158
Johnson, Boris, 65–66
Joint Task Force Ares, 8–9
Jones, Neira, 80–81, 81*t*, 98
Jones, Nigel, 203
Joyce, Rob, 33, 36, 150
Jumio, 166

Kaspersky, Eugene, 50
Kaspersky Lab, 49–50, 138
Kepel, Gilles, 4
Kerry, John, 67
Khan, A. Q., 15
Kim Jong-un, 26, 44, 49
Kiselev, Dmitry, 67
Kleeman, Alexandra, 146
Klein, Naomi, 181
Kompromat, 64
Kogan, Aleksandr, 116
Koyen, Jeff, 122

Lahouaiej-Bouhlel, Mohamed, 6–7
Langevin, Jim, 154
Lawfare, 205, 207
Le Pen, Marine, 64
Lee Cheol-hee, 49
Lockheed Martin, 67, 141

Machine learning. *See* Artificial intelligence and machine learning
Macron, Emmanuel, 64, 66
Madnick, Stuart, 94
Malaysian Airlines MH17, downing of, 66
Manfra, Jeanette, 58
Martin, Harold T., III, 48
Mateos-Garcia, Jose, 124
Mattis, James, 151
May, Theresa, 65–66
McAfee, 28
McCain, John, 155

McCormack, Philip, 126–127
McFaul, Michael, 51
Medvedev, Dmitry, 54
Merkel, Angela, 45, 64–65
Mesri, Behzad, 27–28
Milgram, Stanley, 127
Mills, Lindsay, 46
MoneyGram, 37, 149
Morgan, Steve, 139
Mubarak, Hosni, 53, 54, 62
Mueller, Robert, 60

National Cyber Security Centre, 214, 224–226, 228–234
National Cyber Security Crime Unit, 218
National Cyber Security Programme, 217–218
National Cyber Security Strategies (UK): 2009 National Cyber Security Strategy, 213, 215–216; 2010 National Cyber Security Strategy, 216–217; 2011 National Cyber Security Strategy, 217–218; 2015 National Cyber Security Strategy, 222–225; 2016 National Cyber Security Strategy, 227–228, 231; 2017 National Cyber Science and Technology (S&T) Strategy, 173–175
National Cyber Security Workforce Alliance (U.S.), 140
National Health Service, 214, 221, 227–231
National Infrastructure Security Coordination Centre (NISCC), 214–215
National Security Agency (NSA), 20, 29–30, 33, 36, 148; and Snowden, Edward, 36, 45–49, 138, 163, 192, 206; Tailored Access Operations Division, 50
Navalny, Alexei, 45, 68
Nerve agent attacks, 66, 207
Net neutrality, 183
Netverify, 166
New York City truck attack (October 31, 2017), 7–8

Nice, France, truck attack (July 14, 2016), 6–7
Nielsen, Kirstjen, 154
Nonproliferation Treaty (NPT), 14
North Atlantic Treaty Organization (NATO), 195–198, 200–20
Nuclear Posture Review, 151
Nuclear weapons and programs: and Cold War, 2; advanced persistent threat actors and, 13–14; and Iran, 14–17; North Korean missile tests, 49; nuclear path, 15; uranium enrichment path, 15

Obama, Barack: and Chinese hacking, 37–38; and Iran's nuclear program, 15; NSC under, 150; national security strategy, 184, 190; and OPM attack (2014/2015), 28–29; and Putin, 47; and Russia's annexation of Crimea, 12; and Russia's role in the 2016 election, 54–55, 59–63; and Russian sanctions, 61, 153; and Silicon Valley, 151; on Sony hack, 27; and Stuxnet, 17; and threat of ISIS, 3; and U.S.–Iraq Status of Forces Agreement, 4–5
Office of Personnel Management attack (2014/215), 28–29, 31, 138, 142
Olympic athletes, Russian doping infractions, 40, 60
Olympic Games (2018), hacking of, 40
"Olympic Games" cyber attacks (Stuxnet), 14–17, 43, 135, 150
Open Web Application Security Project (OWASP), 78–82, 104t
Operation Moonlight Maze, 50

Painter, Christopher, 192
Pakistan, 3, 14, 15
Palantir Technologies, 167, 168t, 169, 176
Palmetto Fusion, 17
Pascal, Amy, 27
Password security, 35, 74, 78, 79, 136–138, 142
Patriot Act, 147–148
Paul, Rand, 48, 148

Perry, Richard, 146
Petraeus, David, 67
Pinterest, 168t, 169
PlugX (malware), 29
Podesta, John, 56–57
Poitras, Laura, 46, 47
Pompeo, Mike, 154
Popkin, Gabriel, 121
Powell, Colin, 67
Press, Gil, 170–171
Prigozhuin, Yevgeny, 69
Putin, Vladimir, 11, 44–45, 47, 52–54, 59–70, 134, 140

Qaddafi, Muammar, 16, 53
Quantum computing, 120–122, 127, 149, 153, 174; definition of, 120; entanglement, 120–121, 149; field applications for, 121t; quantum key distribution, 122; superposition, 120–121, 149

Research Institute in Automated Program Analysis and Verification (RIAPAV), 220
Research Institute in Science of Cyber Security (RISCS), 89, 101, 219
Research Institute in Trustworthy Industrial Control Systems (RITICS), 220
Rice, Susan, 55
Robertson, Dave, 113
Robots, three laws of (Asimov), 80–81, 81t
Rogen, Seth, 26
Rogers, Mike, 70
Roman Empire, 1
Rosenstein, Justin, 146
Rosenstein, Rod, 69
Rouhani, Hassan, 53

Saipov, Sayfullo, 8
Salim, Hamid, 94
Sanders, Bernie, 56, 69
Sasse, Angela, 93–94
Satell, Greg, 158–161, 166–167, 171, 173, 175–177

Saulsbury, Brendan, 28
Schneider, B., 125–126
Schumer, Chuck, 144
Securonix, 163–165
September 11, 2001, 1–2, 7, 147
Shadow Brokers (hacker group), 29
Shmeleva, Elena, 140
Sikkink, Kathryn, 203
Silicon Valley, 19, 32, 35, 115, 146, 151, 170
Skripal, Sergei, 66–67
Smart living, definition of, 74. *See also* Internet of things (IoT), smart living
Smith, Richard, 23, 31
Snowden, Edward, 36, 45–49, 138, 163, 192, 206
Sofacy, 12
Sommerville, I., 87
Sony Pictures attack (2014), 26–27, 29, 31, 59, 142
Soros, George, 116
SpaceX, 168*t*, 169
Stamos, Alex, 62–63
Stevens, Chris, 55
Strasse, Angela, 136–138
Stuxnet, 14–17, 43, 135, 150
Sullivan, Joe, 32
Suri, Abu Musab al-, 4
Symantec, 17, 228

Tamene, Yared, 56
Technology awards and prizes, 161–169, 175–17
Thomas, Raymond, III, 8–9
Thugi (Indian Hindu criminal ring), 2
Translator Project (codename for Russian information warfare operation), 69
Trump, Donald, 6, 30, 49, 63, 66; and creation of Cyber Command, 33; and media, 18; national security strategy, 143–144, 149–150, 153–154, 183, 184–190, 206; and presidential election of 2016, 54–60, 67–70; and ZTE, 143–144

Trustworthy Software Foundation (TSFdn), 75, 89–9

Uber: 115, 118, 159, 168*t*, 169; cyberattack (2016), 32, 115
Ukraine, 66; cyber attacks against, 11–14, 18, 51–52, 69; election commission cyber attack against (2014), 18, 51; NotPetya ransomware attack (2017), 13; power grid cyber attack against (2015), 12–13, 52; Russia's annexation of Crimea, 12, 53, 66, 69; and Soviet Union's collapse, 11–12, 53
U.S. Cyber Command, 8, 33, 48, 70
U.S. Special Forces Command, 8–9

Vehicle attacks, 6–8
Viner, Jacob, 190

WannaCry (malware), 29–30, 33, 34, 214, 228–231
War crimes, 10
Warner, Mark, 30
Wasserman Schultz, Debbie, 56
WCRY. *See* WannaCry
WikiLeaks, 56–60
Woods, Chris, 10
World Economic Forum, 39–40, 116, 183
Wu, Tim, 152–153
Wyden, Ron, 48, 144

Xebec (realty company), 114–11
Xi Jinping, 38, 44, 134, 144

Yeltsin, Boris, 53
Yemen, 5

Zarqawi, Abu Musab al-, 4
Zealots, 1
Zhengfei, Ren, 36
ZTE, 143–144, 150
Zuckerberg, Mark, 116, 139, 145–146, 151
Zwinggi, Alois, 39

About the Authors

JACK CARAVELLI's senior assignments in the U.S. government included serving as director for nonproliferation on the White House National Security Council Staff (1996–2000) as President Bill Clinton's adviser on Russia and Middle East nonproliferation issues. Dr. Caravelli joined the Department of Energy in 2000 as deputy assistant secretary with oversight of the department's international nuclear and radiological threat reduction programs. Those programs secured more than 400 metric tons of fissile material.

Dr. Caravelli began his career at the Central Intelligence Agency. He is a visiting professor at the UK Defence Academy and served for seven years on the advisory board of Oxford University's (St. Antony's College) Pluscarden Program for the Study of Terrorism and Intelligence. Dr. Caravelli is the author of books on national security issues. He is a frequent guest speaker and has appeared on the BBC and Fox News. He was co-chair in 2015 of a cyber security conference in Lugano, Switzerland, and 2017 and 2018 cyber conferences in Oxford. He currently serves as partner in Cymatus, an international cyber security group.

NIGEL JONES specializes in the information and human dimensions of security and the interplay of technology and behavior. He is an interdependent consultant and researcher and the part-time CEO of the Information Assurance Advisory Council (IAAC), a not-for-profit network and strategic-research organization bringing industry, government, and academic sectors together to work on information society challenges—and opportunities. He is a visiting fellow at King's College London, Department of Defence Studies. Previously he was at Cranfield University at the UK Defence Academy, where he developed the cyber postgraduate program for defense. He has also directed the Technology Strategy Board's (now Innovate UK) Cyber Security Knowledge Transfer Network. He did this while at QinetiQ, where he ran a cyber security and information operations consultancy team, working across sectors in the critical infrastructure. His interests in education and communications in security and conflict stem from his time in the British Army.

Printed in the USA
CPSIA information can be obtained
at www.ICGtesting.com
LVHW080406280124
770072LV00002B/139